It's not the END...

It's not the END...

Breast cancer at 50 – Faith & Courage

Wendy Gracey Walker

To order additional copies of this book, contact:
Xlibris
800-056-3182
www.Xlibrispublishing.co.uk
Orders@Xlibrispublishing.co.uk
805996

Wendy is not a medical professional and all health opinions within the book are her own views.

It's real, raw, and honest.
I do sincerely hope it gives a much greater understanding
of tackling cancer head on. I am gonna share with
you my diagnosis and the journey that follows.
I have come face to face with a life changing illness.
I hope it gives courage if it happens to you or someone you
love dearly, the strength to walk the path and what to expect.
It's not easy but you can do this.
Cancer is the toughest fight most of us will ever face.

To.

My dearest old friend Maggie
special lady...
with much love
from

Wendy
x .

I dedicate this book to my wonderful husband Nigel and my beautiful boys Matthew & Alexander. You make my life complete. I love you all so very much. X

PROLOGUE

I had just turned fifty. Life was good - very good. I felt great, healthy and very happy.

My two beautiful boys had gone to University in the September. It was a new time for us all. Matthew was in Edinburgh and Alexander in Southampton. Both settled, happy and pursuing their education.

Nigel & I home alone. We joked about now being *Darby & Jone* (proverbial phrase for a married couple content to share a quiet life of mutual devotion) rattling around in our big house but excited too, as it was now time for us to do some things, we had planned together now we had more time. As up to now our lives were for our boys, a close family unit of four. We did so much together, shared everything, rarely apart.

I was three years away from retiring. I have been a police officer for twenty-seven years, a career I love so very much. I celebrated my fiftieth birthday on the twenty-eighth September with a delightful twelve night Mediterranean cruise. It was an amazing holiday. We had great fun. We laughed so much. Just the most wonderful time with amazing memories made.

I had been to England in early November with my family to celebrate my beautiful sister-in-law Mandy's fiftieth birthday. A huge party held as a black-tie event. A very special weekend made even more special, as Mandy is *terminally* ill with cancer and has been fighting hard for some years, but a fine example of a brave lady and an inspiration to us all.

In one moment, life changed for me - life changed for my family.

I always like to write things down. I like to make notes always have. Nigel suggested I should consider a *diary* as a way of capturing all my thoughts. Just writing what's going on, what's happening to me. I know he believes this will help me as I take this journey and walk the path. He knows me so well *practical Wendy.*

He's right. I need to do this.

So here goes my *dear journal* you will be with me every step of the way.

I can only imagine at this time this won't be easy in fact might be brutal - a tough road ahead.

You're going to get it all *lock, stock and three smoking barrels.*

It's real, raw, and honest.

I do sincerely hope it gives a much greater understanding of tackling cancer head on. I am gonna share with you my diagnosis and the journey that follows.

I have come face to face with a life changing illness.

I hope it gives *courage* if it happens to you or someone you love dearly, the strength to walk the path and what to expect.

It's not easy but you can do this.

Cancer is the toughest fight most of us will ever face.

THURSDAY, 15 DECEMBER

Christmas is nearly upon us. Preparations are well underway, and the boys are home from university. We just all love the holidays—there is such excitement. It doesn't matter what age they are; the feelings are always the same. We love our time together. In the evening Nigel and I were relaxing in the family room, watching a movie together. I had a strange feeling in my right chest shoulder area. I rubbed the area, moving down onto my right breast, and almost immediately found a lump! A *lump* that I knew was just not normal!

I told Nigel that I'd found a lump in my breast. Of course, never missing an opportunity to fondle my breasts, he said, "Let me feel it." He couldn't feel anything.

A short time later I felt the area and again felt a lump. "I definitely have found a lump," I said out loud. I got Nigel to examine my breast, and this time he felt it. But very calmly, without fear or panic (as he always approaches matters), he said, "Maybe you should see the doctor in the morning."

FRIDAY, 16 DECEMBER

This morning I went to the see the GP. I asked to see a lady doctor and got to see a GP I hadn't seen before. I told her my concerns, and after an examination she confirmed she could feel a lump. She felt it was nothing to be overly concerned about, but she wanted me to have a mammogram to make sure all was okay. Because the holidays were approaching, she advised there might be a delay through NHS. Private health insurance to the rescue! So glad I had it. A few phone calls later, and I had an appointment at the Ulster Independent Clinic in Belfast to see a Mr Mallon on Monday the nineteenth at 7.55 p.m. That was quick!

I am concerned, as I don't have a good feeling about what I have found. But hopeful all will be okay.

Tonight I must go to work. I am a Sergeant in the Police Service of Northern Ireland and have been for many years. I have a weekend of working night shifts, two of which are twelve hours long.

It will be a distraction - I hope!

MONDAY, 19 DECEMBER

Weekend went okay. The night shift is always tough. I tried not to think about the lump, although I did feel it lots and kept thinking each time it would be gone.

Nigel and I headed off early evening to Belfast for the appointment at the Ulster Independent Clinic. We told the boys we were off doing some Christmas shopping. I didn't want to say anything to concern them, and I thought I would be coming home with no worries and nothing to tell. We arrived a few minutes early at the clinic. I was a little nervous as we settled into the waiting room. Fifty minutes later, I was still waiting and had to check with reception what the delay was. One hour after my appointment time a nurse came to get me, and when I walked into a consultation room to see this stranger, a consultant named Mr Mallon, I was so angry and annoyed at being kept waiting for so long that I could hardly speak. Apparently, they missed my name on the appointment list. He did apologise several times, asking if I was still happy to see him. Like, why was I there? Of course I was! A little tearful, I tried to explain what I had found in my right breast.

An examination followed. He drew on my breast, indicating where I had highlighted. He felt the lump but didn't appear too concerned and sent me off for a mammogram and ultrasound. Nigel and I went to the other side of clinic. I underwent a mammogram and meet a Doctor Crothers—a very nice man. He showed us both the mammogram X-rays, saying he was not concerned at all and didn't see anything. *Fantastic!* I thought, jumping inside. *This is great news.* He said that just to be sure he'd run an Ultra Scan of my breast.

Off to another room for this procedure. Nigel stayed outside the room, sitting on a chair as I went in and prepared. Dr Crothers started the Ultra Scan and asked me to show him the location of where I think I have found something. Almost immediately, he says, "This didn't show up on your mammogram." OMG!

A biopsy followed—a needle was inserted into my breast and into centre of lump, where they took a sample of the tissue. It was uncomfortable for sure. He measured the lump at 8 mm. I didn't realise I hadn't breathed until he had finished and the nurse who was holding my hand at this stage said, 'and breathe'. The sample left swiftly to go to the pathology department within the clinic for testing. He then checked my armpit. He said he was checking lymph nodes—that one appeared prominent and he wanted to take another sample. It wasn't as painful as the last, although he had the needle in for some time.

Once the sample was obtained, he sent it also out to pathology. He measured the lump again, saying it was now 1.2 cm bigger, maybe because he was working at it and it may be bleeding. Dr Crothers was very honest and upfront in a nice way, which I liked. "I am concerned," he said to me.

That's all I heard. I just knew it wasn't good. I knew the lump in my breast was abnormal. I got dressed, and we went back to wait for Mr Mallon to get the results. Within minutes a nurse came to get us. Nigel and I walked to the consultation room. I walked in first, with Nigel close behind. I looked at the consultant. I just knew I saw something there in his face. I think he told me to sit down in the chair—the same chair I had sat on a short time earlier, angry at him for keeping me waiting. I stared straight at him, eye to eye, and said, "It's cancer, isn't it?"

He replied, "I'm sorry; yes, it is cancer."

I felt such a rush of emotions. My world just stopped. I turned to Nigel, and we looked at each other. He looked so pale—I could see how shocked he was. He held me tightly, and I cried and cried and cried. Mr Mallon continued to explain what would happen next. I did listen, but everything was swirling around in my head.

I asked again: "Are you sure its cancer?"

He looked down at papers on his desk, looked back at me, and said, "Yes, it's cancer."

I cried with Nigel holding me tightly.

The consultation was over. I agreed to move forward with Mr Mallon at Belfast City Hospital, where he was a breast surgeon. The nurse in the room—an older lady—looked at me, and her face said it all. We walked out into the corridor with the nurse, and she said she was so sorry and hugged me. Nigel hugged me again, saying, "We'll get through this."

I met Dr Crothers in the corridor. He looked at me and said something—I have no idea what it was. I told him I had gotten my results and walked on. Nigel and I left the hospital and got into the car, where he just held me.

The conversation immediately turned to my boys. What was I going to tell my boys, my beautiful wonderful babies (eighteen and twenty years old, but always my babies)? When would I tell them? What was I going to say? Should I leave it to after Christmas holidays? What about the rest of my family? When should I tell them? "Maybe after Christmas," I said. "My mum will be really upset."

Nigel said, "We will tell the boys now. We are a tight foursome, a strong, bonded family who stick together." So, decision made, we planned to tell them when we get home. No secrets.

We got home, and I let the boys have their supper. They said they were off to bed, and Nigel told them we needed to talk to them.

So we all went into the lounge, which had a big, cosy, warm fire burning.

The Christmas tree was shining brightly. I could feel my tummy turning over with nerves. I thought I wasn't going to be able to breathe. I then just said straight out that I had something to tell them. I told the two most beautiful special people in my life that I had cancer. I had breast cancer.

Well, there was total disbelief in the room. Matthew kept saying, "What? What? No–what you are saying, Mummy?" There were floods of tears. Alex was almost hysterical. Tears and more tears; they kept coming.

We were all crying. They hugged me so tightly I almost couldn't breathe. Matthew sat with his head on my lap, and Alex hugged me so tightly as I sat on the sofa, numb. I couldn't believe this was happening. There, I had said it—I had told my precious boys. We spent the next hour or so just hugging and holding on to each other. Nigel just cried and sobbed. That was difficult to watch; he was always so together, the strong one. Nineteenth December 2016 - a day I'll never forget.

TUESDAY, 20 DECEMBER

The morning after the night before. Was it a dream? No, it's real. I didn't sleep well and got up with butterflies in my tummy. I knew it was going to be a tough day ahead. We had decided as a family that I would tell all those whom I loved and wanted to know today. A difficult decision. I still considered leaving it to after the holidays, as I didn't want to spoil Xmas for any of them. This was my problem, not theirs. Okay, first I had to deal with the day's plans, keep calm and carry on. I was taking Nigel's mummy, Myrtle, to a funeral at one o'clock. My sister-in-law was burying her mother. It was already a sad day for them as a family, so I needed to keep quiet, say nothing, and go to the funeral as arranged. I would do all this before I visited my mummy to tell her. That was the order I wanted to do it in: first Mummy, then my siblings.

I took a phone call from my doctor told her my diagnosis. She was a little shocked. She honestly thought it would all be ok. Need to come off my HRT (oh my days!) can't wait for the hot flushes. She advised me that I need to come out of work, have enough to deal with in the days ahead. This will be difficult. A prescription written for some medication to help with flushes.

Got through the funeral with my mum-in-law. I felt bad being with her and not saying anything as we are very close, always have had an amazing close personal relationship with her, but I just couldn't, and the timing wasn't right. It was strange sitting in church. I couldn't concentrate was a bit distracted. I was talking to God asking for help to stay strong and for him to walk with me in the days ahead asking for strength and courage.

I planned to leave home later to go see mummy. I messaged my sister and asked her if she was around and free that I was going to mummy's as chance goes my sister was already at mums. I arrived, and my beautiful niece Zoe was also there. Everyone appeared to be in good spirits and mummy was showing me some new clothing she had bought, and everyone was chatting away happy and cheerful and I was thinking, ok Wendy you need to say something. Yes, I needed to say something but just didn't know when to burst their bubble.

I then just said it,

"I've got some news for you" they all looked at me and I said, "I've got cancer."

Mummy stared at me and immediately said "where?" I said, "breast cancer".

Well for the next I don't know how many minutes those in the kitchen were in meltdown. Mummy, Shirley, Zoe everyone cried and hugged me it was just awful.

Lots of questions asking why? Lots of tears. I honestly thought Mummy and Shirley were going to faint. The butterflies in my tummy that had been there since I woke this morning had eased slightly. I had said out loud I had breast cancer.

I then had to make *three* difficult phone calls Geoffrey, Eddie & Cecil my brothers. Each one clearly shocked and devastated at the news, and I knew they didn't know what to say to me.

Nigel arrived into mums and oh boy he looked a broken man, so pale, cried lots and just sat close to me.

I had to make another difficult visit to see my mother in law knowing it would be a difficult conversation. Well, she was so emotional and cried and hugged me very tightly, total disbelief. I knew Nigel was wanting to tell his brothers so all would know, so he was making phone calls. So now all the family knew.

I spoke to Lena from church our pastoral assistant. She was so lovely as always. I took a call from my beautiful sister in law Mandy a tough chat as I felt so much for her battling the disease herself, what a special girl.

I cried some more.

Two final calls I wanted to make. Jill and Judy my dear friends.

Judy was clearly in shock when I told her, not her usual practical bubbly self, then how could she be. She said very little was supportive with her words, but they were few tonight!

Jill was so upset on the telephone asked where I was and said, "I'm on my way". Within half an hour Jill and Alan her husband turned up on my doorstep. Lots and lots of tears, such a wonderful couple and dear friends. We chatted and chatted, and I cried lots all the while they were trying to reassure me. They left a little while later everyone in shock. It's the end of day one and I am totally exhausted both mentally and physically.

WEDNESDAY, 21 DECEMBER

Woke up this morning having had a restless night to a kiss from Nigel. What a wonderful man I have.

Still in shock and the same feeling is it real?

I picked up the sick line the doctor wanted me to have and I made a trip to work. I am a Police officer with twenty-seven years' service. I was going into work to tell my supervisor that I have *cancer* and was going to be out of work for a little while.

Though I didn't want to go sick at work thought about working through the holidays as I didn't want any of my colleagues to have to do my work over Christmas as I was scheduled to cover for others in my department.

Judy rang as I was making my way to work. She was emotional. She was almost hysterical with me when I suggested working through the holiday period. She told me I needed to be off work and preparing myself for what lay ahead. Still a bit undecided by the time I arrived at work. I know the correct decision would be to go out of work as my doctor has suggested. I have breast cancer, and this is now about me. No other stress I just concentrate on me and the journey ahead.

As I walked through the doors, I had made my decision and so before going to see my boss, I logged onto the IT system turned the *out of office* on, completed a few pieces of administration and logged off. Telling the new boss was ok not a great conversation to have but he was nice albeit a little awkward but supportive. I then told one of my dear colleagues that the boss had brought up to his office. I don't think she knew what to say! I left work today knowing I wouldn't be back for a while.

Some other calls I needed to make. I wanted to tell some people they needed to hear it from me. Kelly Anne my dear work colleague who had become a great friend in work, such a sweet girl, She was so tearful totally shocked (just like me!)

Then I phoned another dear colleague Mandy whom I wanted to know. She was shocked but wonderful with me and wanted to drive over to my house clearly concerned. I told her I was ok no need and that my sister in law Marian had arrived and I would be okay.

The rest of Wednesday was filled with phone calls, texts, WhatsApp messages from friends and colleagues who had just heard passing on their messages of concern and support.

I made more calls and sent messages as I really didn't want my diagnosis told to some by others. Everyone very kind and asking what they could do.

Nothing anyone can do - this is my fight.

I'm exhausted. It is becoming more real now. I think the more times I say I have *breast cancer* the more its sinking in.

I look at my boys. I'm so sorry for upsetting them. I know they are hurting.

Alex and I had a little late lunch just the two of us some normality and a little retail therapy!

THURSDAY, 22 DECEMBER

Today I have my appointment at Belfast City Hospital at the breast clinic. Not sure what to expect but hope I will know a little more about this cancer. Nigel came with me and as we arrived and parked the car and made out way into the hospital, I looked up at the building to my right and the sign said *Cancer Centre* oh my days!

The building is new as it used to be the Jubilee Maternity hospital. That's where I gave birth to my beautiful boys. I looked back at the building as I went inside the Tower block again saw the words *Cancer Centre* and I said out loud "I have cancer". It's the little things that stops you in your tracks!

The little lady at the reception desk was so friendly and pleasant. She told me that Mr Mallon had been asking if I had arrived and she got my file and showed me that written on the front of it was the words *Mr Mallon only.* Oh, my I'm special - no I'm sure not, but this was the man who had to give me the shocking results on Monday night.

The consultation with Mr Mallon went ok. He asked how I had been since Monday evening, *Crap* thank you very much. He explained that today would involve a core biopsy to allow further investigations into the type of cancer and what we are dealing with.

Off I went for the biopsy. So many women in the department. I'm sure not all getting the news I did on Monday night. The consultant radiographer was Dr Pearce such a lovely lady. They are so good at what they do so talented. She explained everything that was going to happen. I think when she first spoke with me, she didn't realise I already knew I had cancer. She left the room came back in having read my notes and explained my latest mammogram, the fact it hadn't picked up the tumour cos of dense breast tissue in the breast. She confirmed she would request a copy of my last mammogram which had taken place in February 2016 at Action Cancer (they offer a screening service up to age of forty-nine and then over the age of seventy) and it was normal.

Biopsy was completed under local anaesthetic, wasn't painful just weird and strange. She confirmed the tumour at 1 cm.

A long afternoon at the hospital. I had another mammogram and back to see Mr Mallon. He called me into the consultation room and this time he had a breast cancer care nurse with him a lovely nurse called Cathy McDaid. Mr Mallon explained it would be a week before biopsy results would be known. Unable to tell me anything else further about surgery or treatment at this time he advised he would ring me on thirtieth December and a further appointment for eleventh January was arranged to discuss all results and the way forward.

Cathy the breast nurse then took over, completed some notes gave me some advice explained some things and answered my questions.

She was so lovely.

This is what she said to me at the end of our chat; "Wendy if you remember nothing else from today remember this that I have written down for you - THIS IS VERY TREATABLE."

I did cry a little.

Nigel took my hand and squeezed it tightly. There's a bit of me that doesn't want to know any more just yet. I am still trying to digest and process the news it's so big to comprehend you have cancer. My goodness I never thought it would happen to me not at fifty, breast cancer at fifty.

I love life, I love my life, I love my Nigel, I love my boys. I don't want this.

Mr Mallon commented today that it was good that I found the lump myself. Thank goodness I did!

Tonight, I'm exhausted mentally and physically tired. I have just updated those in my life close to me. There's nothing more I can do for now. I have a week to wait on results.

FRIDAY, 23 DECEMBER

Today I tried to have some normality whatever that is now) went to do some final Christmas shopping, didn't enjoy it too distracted.

I walked around the supermarket looking at everyone rushing around, fussing and pushing and shoving to get that last bag of *brussel sprouts* and I was saying to myself, "I have cancer I have cancer". It just didn't feel normal and a bit surreal.

In the afternoon I went to have a shower. As I took off my clothes and looked at my right breast, I removed the plaster from the previous day's procedure and slightly moved the paper stitches that had been placed over the incision. I felt a little weak and a little sick. I saw the incision on my beautiful breast it looked battered and bruised. I got upset as I was frightened to shower in case the paper stitches came off. I got dressed came up to the kitchen and just wanted to cry.

By the time Nigel got in I was so emotional broke down in tears and was so upset. I am always normally very together not today just couldn't process everything. Of course, calming Nigel brought me back down saying its ok let's look at your breast. He removed the paper stitches saying the wound was fine didn't need them. Back in the shower all was ok. I let the water run over my breast.

I had calmed down.

I looked at my poor breast. I loved my breast always loved my breasts and had a fine set (if I do say so myself!) today its throbbing cos anaesthetic worn off so a little tender.

We went out this evening to my brother in law John's house. Some friends round and a great distraction for a short time at least.

SATURDAY, 24 DECEMBER - CHRISTMAS EVE

Doorbell rang and there on the doorstep was my friend Jill and her son Adam. A tight hug and kiss from Jill along with some flowers. Then the biggest shock of all. Adam was so visibly upset, he held me tight so tight I could hardly breathe, and he sobbed and sobbed. He never said a word.

I told him not to be upset it would be ok.

There were more tears, and more hugs. I told him I loved him. He is such a good boy. This was such a shock for me, a pleasant shock nonetheless as he was so *overt* with his feelings. I just didn't know he cared so much about me - I'm humbled.

I'm exhausted.

Messages of support are pouring in. Such lovely messages from so many people clearly shocked.

The news is spreading about my diagnosis!

SUNDAY, 25 DECEMBER

Christmas morning. Just my beautiful wonderful husband and my two boys here.

Everything as normal.

All our wee traditions nothing changed but just felt a bit more poignant this year. Pressies, tea, coffee, oh but no *bucks fizz* this year nobody wanted any.

I'm having strange thoughts about drinking and alcohol. I know I don't drink a lot occasional glass of *sauvignon blanc* or a *gin* but already I'm thinking of lifestyle changes, all going around in my mind. Mandy my sister in law has sent me an email about some foodstuffs I could try but I'm not rushing at doing anything just yet still getting my head around the diagnosis.

I had a shower and my beautiful breast is so very bruised. It makes me sad when I look at it. It's throbbing. It's had a tough week with all the procedures no wonder it's painful.

I've had another little cry with Nigel, just a little one and as usual he hugged me, told me he loved me, loved everything about me, fancies me like mad (his words not mine!) He wants to put his hands all over me *steady* but doesn't want to push it or upset me.

I'm very lucky but then I've always known that.

I told him I wanted him to kiss my breast just do it before it's not there anymore or if I'm lucky I will keep it but for sure it will most likely look different after surgery which is a given. He said, "I will kiss it anytime."

All things considered we had a lovely Christmas day just the four of us. Quiet and peaceful. I feel very relaxed today the first since last Monday evening. Everything feels more normal like it's always been.

Then it *rockets* into my head, a reality check and I realise *shit* I've got cancer.

As part of the whole process I must come off my HRT brilliant eh! This is going to be fun NOT. I've been off it before last time when I went in for some spinal surgery. Gosh it wasn't easy HOT flushes in abundance, but more so very emotional.

Ladies I know often say *tempers* and *tantrums* when needing a boost of *hormones* but for me I was *emotional* and I would have it expressed through *tears*. So that will be another challenge ahead.

You know I have asked the question; "had my HRT caused my cancer?" as they say HRT increases the risk. My breast care nurse says it's impossible to say and that a high percentage of women getting breast cancer is NOT on HRT. Reports suggest that you should consider coming off HRT between forty-eight and fifty-two years. I'm fifty so it was my plan to consider it over next couple of years, but cos I felt so healthy on it there was no rush. I had just felt great. Well decision taken from me now. I have started trying to wean myself off it slowly so that the effects are not too horrific.

THURSDAY, 29 DECEMBER

It's been ten days since my diagnosis a whole ten days. What a rollercoaster of emotions yesterday and today. I have felt in a low mood can't really describe it. I'm not sure if it's the diagnosis of cancer or my reduction of HRT now taking it every third day in my efforts to wean of it asap. No flushes coming through yet although very *headachy* and *emotional*.

I visited a work colleague this morning dearest Mandy. It was refreshing to go to different surroundings. That was a nice visit and lifted my mood.

I came back and went for a walk to clear my head.

My breast is still throbbing not sure why must be all the *hoking* and *poking* they did since nineteenth

I'm not sure what my mummy truly understands about it all and she keeps coming off with weird comments. The latest today is "maybe you won't need surgery" like come on what does she thinks is going to happen. It frustrates me. I understand she's older and it's difficult to take in, but oh my days! I know she is shocked and upset.

Tomorrow is an important day as Mr Mallon is due to ring with some results. I'm nervous but equally want to know what I'm dealing with. The type of cancer, the stage of cancer and what the professional's plans are for me.

Hopefully I get some answers.

FRIDAY, 30 DECEMBER

Ten past two when I got the call from a *private number* I knew it would my consultant. It's early the call came sooner than I was expecting. Nigel was planning to be at home at four so he could be here with me. Mr Mallon was very pleasant and very matter of fact. He said the team had had their meeting (multi-disciplinary team that discusses all new patients, their results and the way ahead). My results had shown the cancer was *Invasive Ductal Breast Cancer* oh that sounds serious. He then said it was the *most common* type of breast cancer that sounded better, and the plan would be surgery no surprise there.

A wide local excision (new more modern name for Lumpectomy!) I then asked if the mammogram results were back from Action Cancer with the comparisons checks to be done. NO was the answer, but he agreed they would be important in how treatment would progress. Don't know the stage of the cancer and don't know what treatment will follow.

That was it telephone call over.

He would see me again on eleventh January where the pathway would be discussed. Surgery would most likely be the sixteenth January unless further tests needed.

Oh, how do I feel? emotional and scared - that all came so fast at me and when I heard words invasive ductal breast cancer shit that rocked me sounds bad doesn't it.

I spoke to Alex when he came in to the room. He appeared to understand what I had said, so resilient. I immediately messaged Nigel to say no need to come home early call, already happened.

I have been online to the Cancer Research UK website just reading a little trying to be informed and understand all the information that it coming to me. I always like that. That's why I am writing everything down you become informed and empowered. I've just read up on invasive ductal breast cancer. Some of it scares me other stuff I understand.

I have a pain just above my beautiful breast it's a strange feeling it's like the feeling on that Thursday night when I found the lump. It feels more like a pain now. I will mention it to Mr Mallon on eleventh January.

Nigel arrived home and I cried.

As always, he's supportive and keeps me calm always logical as well.

I know he's scared too.

He keeps saying he can't live without me, but truth be known I can't live without him. He's my rock my best friend!

Calls and messages keep coming, everyone wonderful and so concerned about me, so kind of them taking time to think of me.

The list of callers gets longer.

SATURDAY, 31 DECEMBER

It's the last day of 2016.

What a year, such emotions from the beginning.

My cruise had been planned, booked and enjoyed - my fiftieth birthday treat. I had such a wonderful time with my amazing man we had a ball! Many memories made. I also was a mummy who had to let her beautiful boys go off to University oh that was tough. I cried lots and lots. I was so proud of them wished them so much happiness but for me such a void. That's what I get for creating such a strong family unit a family where being close was so the norm. It was difficult them leaving but you know I coped, got used to them not in the house and I survived the very best and with modern technology I got to chat to them each day (in our wee family WhatsApp group) which helped lots. Overall my health was good. A good year a few little niggles in the neck but certainly I felt well. Got to celebrate my super extraordinary fantastic sister in-laws fiftieth birthday what a weekend and more special as she is battling terminal cancer and remains so positive. Breast cancer that has travelled to her bones but four years later she's still fighting her disease.

Now it's me, I have *CANCER* yes cancer in my breast its true.

I'm glad Christmas is over can't say it was great. I would be lying if I did. I just felt exhausted, tired and as a woman who is always strong it's knocked me.

You know you never think it will happen to you. It's always someone else, it's the person next door, down the road, up the street but this time it's me.

So as the year ends, I know 2017 is going to be tough and is going to be bumpy. I have no idea what to expect.

I am SCARED.

Mandy recommended a book for me to read - The Cancer Whisperer by Sophie Sabbage. I've just bought it and quickly flicked through the pages and I found this line;

"There's an old Norse saying that the Gods give the heaviest burden to those who are best able to the take the load" so yes there you go.

I'll take it as a positive and turn this death threat into a big challenge.

MONDAY, 2 JANUARY 2017

Now it's 2017. Today is the second.

Spent a lovely morning with Nigel, my boys and Granny Walker (Nigel's mum) we took a walk down the farm fields at Magherabeg (where Nigel grew up).

It will soon no longer be a *Walker* residence as its being sold to allow mum to move into town.

We wanted to have a last dander and see *Horsepark* the old house where Nigel's dad was born.

A beautiful fresh January morning, sun shining and really cold. It was just lovely with my family. The boys will be going back to Uni at the weekend.

I looked at the boys and Nigel today - my world my life. I've nothing without them. The boys are not saying much just getting on with things, but I know they are in pieces inside. I do hope they don't bottle things up and talk to me or their daddy.

This afternoon I picked up the Sophie Sabbage book and read a few chapters. It nearly took my breath away the things she had written. I'm saying them too. That's how I feel. Those are my thoughts, my worries. I'm scared too. She talks about the *Compass* and I'm certainly just at the first point then I push to second point as I need to be informed, it's like empowerment needing to know, to understand the disease, what's happening and what's coming down the track.

My beautiful breast is still showing signs of interference it's still got bruising and the scab has come off the incision.

I've touched the lump again it's still there! Sometimes I hope when I feel it will be gone.

I still have the strange feeling above my breast in my chest area. This is all very serious, cancer is very serious. I got news today of a colleague at work who has died of possible *alcohol abuse* resulting in organ failure. I'm both sad and angry at the news. Is this self-inflicted behaviour, with no concern for family or loved ones or, for the gift of *life*?

Angry – that's a word Nigel has used lots. On New Year's Eve we went to bed and made love. The first since my diagnosis. Such a wave of emotions and closeness knowing I had cancer, my breast bruised and with a disease inside it, but it was lovely. Nigel was so gentle with me, he's amazing.

Anyway, it was then that he said, "he was so angry with my cancer and he was going to fight it and he needed me to fight too, he has nothing without me, and he couldn't survive without me". Gosh that's serious stuff!

I'm NOT angry not yet anyway. I haven't yet said *Why me*? Cos why not me it has to be someone and it's my turn.

I'm still receiving messages of support and kindness. Phone calls, texts, WhatsApp messages that's so lovely. I'm happy for people to know. It's not a secret it makes it all feel real.

It's now two weeks since diagnosis and it's much more real.

WEDNESDAY, 4 JANUARY

Yesterday I met with my dear friend Judy and another lovely friend Chris for lunch. A lovely distraction. I was able to chat with Chris who had had breast cancer four years ago. She has done so well, changed her life and is very happy and healthy right now.

Got to spend some time after with Judy alone. She was very emotional cried a little and opened her heart. Oh, I love her so much.

I went to do my shopping and as I walked around the store looking for some ingredients for our new *Nutri Ninja* device! I was amazed at how much health foods obvious on the shelves - Is it cos it's the New Year and new start. Everyone kick starting health regimes or am I just super sensitive about all these health food products berries, seeds, fruits, nuts, honey, yoghurt. For me a choice of foods to aid my body, help fight this cancer and give myself the best chance of survival there I said it *survival.'*

As I made my way down an aisle in the supermarket, I met a lovely girl I know Hilary who just burst into tears, pulled me close, hugged me tightly and cried some more. Such a lovely girl who wears her heart on her sleeve. She was so supportive.

Today I got a visit from Jill and Katie her lovely daughter. Jill has been so kind supportive and a great listener and just there for me always. I'm lucky to have them in my life. Someone who is just there when you need them and gets you, I love her dearly.

Alex and I chatted at breakfast time about how he were feeling. He wanted to know how I was feeling. I asked him if he had any questions. He didn't. He just said that he didn't want me keeping anything from him when he goes back to Uni. I told him I will tell him everything and I have been honest.

I don't want my illness affecting the boys. I want them to keep going stay strong. I am so proud of them both and I want them to continue their studies get their education which will shape their futures.

I will fight the disease. It's my battle not theirs and just knowing they are pushing forward will be good enough for me.

Messages keep coming along with beautiful flowers arriving. The list is getting longer of those getting in touch. It's so lovely and you just don't realise what people feel and think about you.

FRIDAY, 6 JANUARY

A strange day feeling emotional can't really explain it. A bit deflated. This is huge everyone speaks of me as a *strong woman* who will get through this, but you know a strong woman can struggle too.

The waiting is difficult.

A mixture of feelings in one hand getting the news like this allows me to digest it all but waiting on results is difficult and wondering how the medical team are going to proceed.

I'm not sleeping very well although I do feel tired.

My mind is racing - last thing I think of and first thing when I awake. It's funny how the mind operates. I'm running one-way change direction run back.

I'm thinking I need to exercise more, eat foods that are more healthy stop foods that are bad for me. I need to stop my HRT and so on … head spinning stuff and yet the strong woman within tells me SLOW DOWN WENDY one step at a time. Deal with your shock and diagnosis and everything else will fall into place.

I know Nigel is not sleeping well either he's concerned, he's worried.

I'm getting lots of hugs he's so good to me so calming.

SUNDAY, 8 JANUARY

I'm not looking forward to today.

Matthew & Alex leave for Uni this afternoon. Goodness, I'm going to miss them both. They have been in the house since I got my diagnosis and just been nice having their company and presence and it has surely helped. They have kept me busy and we have had some laughs.

I am so glad I have this *cancer* and not them my beautiful boys. I don't want them to be ill, happy it's me and I'm glad they are going back to their lives at University as it will be a distraction for them, I *HOPE!*

It wasn't the best Christmas and new year for them that I do know.

I've had a little cry as Jill sent me a lovely little message telling me today would be tough and she was thinking about me. She knows me so well. I love her.

The trip to the airport was tough. Matthew was very brave didn't cry said he wasn't going to which was good. I did cry of course. He said, "don't mummy I'm not doing this." Well as for Alex he was so emotional so upset he hated leaving me. We had some time between their flights taking off. He cried, he talked, he held my hand. He again asked me not to keep anything from him. He told me he felt bad leaving me at home to deal with cancer without him. He was so mature, such a good boy. They both are super sons. I need them to be strong.

I survived the airport, drove home alone and cried the whole journey felt so lonely and knew the next time I saw the boys I would have had surgery to remove the cancer.

WEDNESDAY, 11 JANUARY

I thought this day would never come!

Nigel and I went to the hospital for my ten o'clock meeting with Mr Mallon. Nervous, yes, I was, its results day of sorts. I just hope all results would be available. It's been going on now for three weeks seems like an eternity.

The waiting in the waiting room is always tough.

So many people there, so many women all worried no doubt and each not knowing their fate. I did though I knew I had cancer as I sat there.

I would know *the plan* for me, what was going to happen.

Nigel & I sat in the little consultation room three. A tiny little room, very cold and unwelcoming not even a seat for Nigel, he had to sit on the examination bed. I was so nervous. Nigel asked if I was ok.

Thirty minutes passed then Mr Mallon appeared through a door apologised for keeping me waiting but that he was waiting on a breast nurse and they were busy this morning. He continued to say radiographer team had looked at my mammograms from 2014 & 2016 and all good they were happy that no change *Phew!* A first positive since nineteenth December.

He then left the room and Nigel and I looked at each other. Is that good? what does that mean? Well most likely changes type of surgery. A short time later he returned with breast care nurse Siobhan. I mentioned to Mr Mallon my concern about my chest area something not just right. He said he would examine me and asked if its ok, of course its ok. Mr Mallon started to speak about surgery type and the plans! *Wide local excision* and removal of *lymph nodes.* I got up onto the bed boobies exposed and another examination. He wasn't concerned about the area I was referring to its muscle and not breast tissue however, he did say when he would be completing surgery, he would check area I was referring to and remove tissue shavings if necessary, for examination. Mr Mallon then delivered another bombshell he would need to remove my *nipple* WHAT? Yes, my nipple as the tumour was so close to the area and that he would not be able to save it.

Oh no not my nipple.

He confirmed to get the tumour and enough tissue around it the nipple would have to be taken off as the *nodule* was so close to it. Oh, my not what I was expecting to hear. I thought they would go in the side of my breast to get tumour. I know if I had been told I was having a Mastectomy then maybe my whole breast would be gone including nipple, but this was such a shock - remember I have always loved my breast. I loved my areola and nipples all perfectly proportioned amazing boobies if I do say so myself.

I know I know I need this cancer taken away and to be gone so whatever needs to be done that's fine but still a shock will I be that same woman?

What will Nigel think? How will he look at me?

Mr Mallon advised that he had considered surgery on the sixteenth but due to theatre allocation and other ladies ahead of me surgery would be week of twenty- third January.

I had eight questions written down needing answered

1. Chest Area concerns
2. Mammograms comparisons
3. Grade/stage of cancer
4. MRI is this something that is considered
5. ER+ is it a hormone driven cancer?
6. Surgery type?
7. Treatment after surgery radiotherapy or Chemotherapy?
8. Type of Cancer

All answered for me -

1. Chest AREA NO CONCERNS
2. Mammogram result ok no concerns
3. Grade 2 - 1 cm Nodule
4. No MRI at this stage
5. Invasive ductal breast cancer
6. Wide local excision with Sentinel Lymph node biopsy
7. ER+ Oestrogen markers positive
8. Post op radiotherapy and Hormone therapy

Wow that's a lot of information.

Nigel said to me, "I am more than a breast to him. I am his life, he can't do life without me. I am his world and we can get through this. We have so much more living to do more places to visit and see."

I left Mr Mallon and went with the breast care nurse. I had a cry, composed myself although you don't need to with breast nurses, they so get you, they are wonderful. They just know what to say, when to say it, speak at the right time, they keep quiet at the right times and they explain everything with precision.

I was given so much information, a folder of literature which is great for me. It's good as I need it. I like to be informed it empowers me. It allows you to understand all that's coming at you at hundred miles an hour. This info is all about way ahead, my surgery admission to hospital, pre-op exercises, physio classes and then other scary stuff like Lymphoedema.

What the heck is that? Something that can happen after surgery or years down the line cos the lymphatic system will have been interfered with and leaves a vulnerability oh, and not giving blood in right arm, washing up, using moisturisers, too much info. I can't deal with it that's for later.

I'm in the here and now. I'm about to have cancer removed from my breast and I'm going to lose part of my breast my nipple, the nipples that Nigel loved.

I got my pre-op assessment, ECG and bloods and lots of questions. My nurse for pre-op was Patricia McPolin empathetic and understanding. So important for me as it is scary. Three and a half hours later Nigel and I left Belfast City Hospital armed with the *PLAN*.

Family friends and colleagues have continued to message or call offering words of comfort, support, coffee dates (I don't drink coffee but love TEA).

Jill continues to be wonderful just little messages with special words.

Mummy is doing well I think but is always upset around me.

Shirley my dear sister ever-present and offering support. She took me to Asda today, and we had a nice lunch together after. She's emotional. I know it has had a profound effect on her. I'm always the strong one she's my wee sister.

After Wednesday's consultation I messaged all those I wanted to.

Updated and thanked everyone but telling them that I now needed to prepare for surgery. I was courteous, but it was my way of saying I was withdrawing. I needed space and time to get my head around what was coming now. I want quiet time and peace just for me. I'm getting everything in order. I need everything to be in place.

THURSDAY, 19 JANUARY

One calendar month from diagnosis so much has happened in that month.

My surgery is now four days away not long now.

My tough road starts on the twenty-third.

Yesterday I went to the physio department at the Cancer Centre. The CANCER CENTRE oh those words make it very real. When I entered the centre, it was strange going in there. People everywhere, coming, going, sitting, staring, reading. People with no hair, people with some hair, people drinking coffee and tea.

I scanned reception trying to get my bearings looking for the physio department. I saw lots of signs. I saw people who were clearly unwell. I didn't know anyone and had come alone felt very vulnerable look I could have brought mummy or Jill or Shirley or some other dear person but I didn't think I needed any support to attend a physio exercise talk but when you are reading words like chemotherapy and radiotherapy it makes it very real and company might have been a good idea!

I found the area I was looking for. I recognised a mother and daughter whom I had seen last week clearly attending same class as me. It was a male physio and I just didn't get the connection with him, didn't like his delivery. Only four ladies present including me, and I was clearly the *baby* in the group. He asked each one of us what type of surgery we were having, brilliant share with everyone in the room! The whole thing was a PowerPoint detailing everything I had already read in leaflets provided. A bit of a waste of time but heh-ho. A lot of information thrown at me digested as much as I could and just wanted to leave.

Though I totally understand the reason for such a class as not everyone will read everything provided like me and the guy was doing his best. We were asked if we had any questions and one lady proceeded to ask when she could walk her dog again and then proceeded to tell the group that thirty nine years ago when she had surgery she had woken up before it finished. What the heck! Brilliant just what I need to here. I honestly wanted to slap her and shout out loud *shut your mouth*. Look I know, important to her, but I didn't want to hear such detail.

I was glad to leave and walked around the corner to the Macmillan Support Centre. Again, walking in to this building another first and so strange, but this was all about me now. Met a lovely lady, very quietly spoken and very calm asking would I like a tea, oh yes please I'd like a tea. She provided me with some more information leaflets. It's such a great service and somewhere nice to go to and just be yourself, sit quietly people will understand you and let you be.

I'm sure I will back at the Macmillan centre.

I have continued to cry some things make me very sad. I'm not sleeping well. Nigel and I have talked about so much he's such a good friend. I know this is tough for him. He loves me so much I see that. This has rocked his world.

Today he sent me a WhatsApp message with a link to a piece of music a song by Dennis Locorriere (Dr Hook) called Years from Now. Wow! I've always loved Dr Hook grew up listening to it. I opened the link and listened to the song. I remembered it so well. Tears poured from my eyes so beautiful and so sad. I sent a link back with my piece of music to him. Again, Dr Hook 'If not you' it says it all from me to Nigel and Nigel to me. I love you so much Nigel x

More messages of support are flooding in.

SUNDAY, 22 JANUARY

This morning was very emotional. Nigel and I had a little extra sleep in.

I did sleep a little better. Nigel didn't he said he had so many thoughts and he couldn't. Bless him he's been so strong for me and taking the rough tough days. We chatted in bed about my cancer he said "you know you will never be cured" like what are you saying to me Nigel - he was just trying to get me to understand the enormity of it all and that he needed to me to dig deep and fight hard and to use my mind to get better. The doctors will deal with the medical stuff and I need to be positive. I know what he was saying but it is tough to hear. He again said he needs me, life is nothing without me and of course the boys. He said this morning he would rather just have my one breast and have me. I asked him to kiss my breast for the last time in its current format. It would never be the same again. He kissed it, kissed my nipple ever so gently as I cried and cried.

You see it's a massive thing to be facing losing your breast or part of it although I need the professionals to do what they must get this cancer from my body.

I had a hysterectomy at thirty-eight that was mentally tough as you worry about no longer being a woman or less of a woman but those were *nonsense* thoughts. I never looked back, became so healthy and felt *sexy* and all *woman*!

This bombshell is on a whole new level. This is outward surgery. I'm going to see the effects of surgery every single day and it will be a reminder, but you know what *glass half full* it will remind me I'm here and survived.

Took a walk with Nigel to prepare my head. I've always liked to walk and try to always have one but now it seems so much more important thinking of being fit and healthy hopefully stick to me in my recovery. Nigel says I need to fight I need to look forward. I'm just not there yet with those sentiments. I'm still processing.

Took a relaxing bath washed my beautiful breasts and prayed to God to be with me tomorrow as I go for surgery. I gave thanks.

My phone rang, and it was my beautiful boy Matthew what a lovely distraction. He sounded so full of life was buzzing as he chatted. He was walking back from the swimming pool and gym. How lovely to have the chat and here him being normal. Of course, *cars* came up in the conversation. He loves all things cars a new M4 BMW being released. His third exam is on Wednesday. I told him to keep going. It was difficult chatting as when I heard his voice, I wanted to cry but I didn't important not to upset him or his brother. He wanted to know what's happening tomorrow, so I told him all the details.

In at seven and hopefully home tomorrow night. He was surprised I would get out same day, so was I! He appeared ok with all the info and said he would ring later.

Oh, I love him so very much, both my boys all three of my boys! They are my life and they are worth fighting for.

Had a lovely visit from my two nephews Scott and Luke. They wanted to see me before I went for surgery - how kind of them.

MONDAY, 23 JANUARY - SURGERY DAY

Off we went to the hospital at six thirty for short journey to the City Hospital. Crap the traffic on the M1 was horrendous. Monday morning so expected. I got a bit anxious cos I was to be in for seven and didn't want to be late, hate being late for anything. There wasn't much conversation between Nigel and I in the car both lost in our own thoughts.

No need to panic got there in time and upon arrival at day procedure unit there were lots of women waiting to be booked in. Taken to B WARD and as I walked in there, I saw on a white board above a bed

Wendy Walker Mr Mallon 3rd all day.

Flip that's me! My emotions were all over the place nervous, sad, worried, tearful. This lovely nurse called Julie-Ann came introduced herself and explained what would be happening and then said to Nigel "not my rules but relatives have to leave." I looked at Nigel he looked at me and I could feel my heart beating faster. He was going to be leaving me. We said our goodbyes. I told him I would see him the other side. We hugged very tightly and kissed each other and then Nigel was gone.

I was alone very alone.

All the booking in procedures started shortly after. Mr Mallon my surgeon arrived lovely guy. We exchanged pleasantries. I signed the consent and I asked him a couple of questions

1. Will he check area where I am complaining about feeling pain/strange sensation?
2. Do they test lymph nodes he removes in surgery while surgery ongoing?

Yes, to first question and no to second as the tissue/lymph nodes will go to pathology for full testing. He left, more procedures followed and that was me ready to go. Oh no, I had to go to Breast clinic to have a wire inserted into my breast. It was being positioned right at the tumour to aid the surgeons when removing tumour. Local analgesic to have procedure completed. A lovely doctor Dr Davies completed procedure. I decided not to look felt a little queasy been fasting so probably why. Then as she finished, I turned to look at my beautiful breast with a wire protruding from it, a good four inch long. I was bleeding a little got patched up then another mammogram required. A little more anxious as I thought machine would be squashing my boobie causing more pain. It was ok not so painful at all. The lady was lovely who completed it. You know everyone I have met thus far have been wonderful so kind and caring and supportive. Back to the ward waiting to go to theatre. Nope not just yet another procedure required. I needed to go to *Nuclear Medicine* What on earth? Nuclear Medicine located in the Cancer Centre so off I go again. I must have an injection into my breast. This is a radioactive procedure will aid and highlight the lymph nodes in the armpit. Another lovely doctor Martin Lynch completed procedure. Just a little pinch injection into breast all over in a minute. Was back to the ward at eleven. Time to get undressed and put my 'sexy op socks' on and my operating gown. Into bed and a warm blanket turned on this is to keep you warm in prep for surgery. There were five ladies in my ward waiting on surgery. Each one left and I remained. The hours passed by. I was still waiting hours later, been fasting, taking a headache and the pain relief was wearing off in my breast where the wire was protruding. I had no phone with me nothing to read as I thought I would be in and out in no time not to be! At three twenty-five I got some pain relief and at four thirty-five Mr Mallon appeared at my bedside apologising for the delay. Just some earlier complications with other ladies. What could I say to him, it couldn't be helped, these things happen. It was so nice of him to leave theatre and come speak with me.

I did joke with him saying "am I like a fine wine, best kept to the last" he laughed *(sense of humour tick).* I said "I'm glad you and I are not dating cos that's twice now you've kept me waiting wouldn't bode well" he laughed again *(sense of humour tick)* He said surgery would happen today. That was my concern it wouldn't go ahead. I had managed to ring Nigel a couple of times by using Julie-Ann the nurse's mobile phone, so he was kept updated. Four fifty- five they came for me it was time. This was it I was off to surgery. At last it was happening. What a wait *ten hours.* I was wheeled in my bed to theatre Julie-Ann was with me. Now having had unrelated surgery years before I know the journey for me to theatre is always a lonely one. Arrived in prep room so many strangers around me. It's always cold in theatre or I feel cold, strange feelings, strange smells. As I lay there while the team prepped me a strange lady appeared at my beside. She introduced herself as Jennifer Ard she was a nursing sister, a friend of Gemma's and that Gemma had told her I was going for surgery today and to look after me. She squeezed my hand said I would be ok wow! what a lovely lady and so kind to think of me and come speak to me. It made me very emotional and I cried. A kind male nurse got me a hanky and I dried the tears.

I woke up in recovery well I wouldn't say I woke up just about conscious! Problems with the cannula in my hand needed relocating. Pain relief not fully going in maybe just as well the morphine not getting through as my pulse was down as low as six. Six should I be dead, heart nearly stopped WOW SHIT! I recall slipping in and out of a sleepy stupor for the next while. Then my beautiful husband arrived at my beside. He drove the whole way to the hospital just to see me knowing I would be in another planet post-surgery, post anaesthetic it was around ten in the evening I was told. I remember them continuously checking my breast or whatever was left there I just couldn't look at all. At eleven thirty-five I was taken to the ward certainly not going home now!

A rough night with pain and constant obs. A concoction of codeine on an empty stomach bearing in mind I had been fasting since eleven o'clock on Sunday night. It caused total havoc! Oh boy was I sick so not well. Got a slice of toast and tea *(bliss)* at six but too late codeine had the damage done.

A trip to the toilet and a serious lie down.

Such a noisy ward way too much noise so busy and I felt so unwell just wanted to be home. Got some lunch and sickness lifted slightly. Mr Mallon came to see me said surgery had went well. Tumour along with margin around it had been removed along with tissue from chest area and one Sentinel Lymph node *(master)* removed. Anti-sickness advised, and he was gone. Results in twelve to fourteen days. My little ground angel the breast care nurse (as I call them) arrived at bedside. This time it was Brenda so lovely, so nice to see her such a fabulous way with her but all the breast nurses I'd seen were amazing. I had a cry with her. She told me I needed to take one day at a time *(a mantra I've been using a lot)* We needed to wait on results. She said results would determine treatment plan. I said to Brenda I thought I would be having radiotherapy. She said need to wait on results of op. She said need to wait on grading etc. I said I know grading it's a two but Brenda says yes that's on a small biopsy. It may change and it may change what treatment will be whether radio or chemo or tablet it's not HER2 so no Herceptin drug will be required. As I lie waiting for four hours on pharmacy department getting my release drugs, I'm so frustrated and annoyed on the delay it's taking so long.

I'm off home with Nigel to my beautiful home where I can rest in peace and quiet, Nigel will take care of me.

Wow I've just had a crazy five weeks.

I got told I had cancer and now I have had surgery it's moving fast.

I have been peeking down my pyjamas at my breast area feeling anxious about seeing my breast for the first time. It's now time to remove the bandages there are two. One on my breast and one under my arm. How am I going to do this? I'm not sure I want to see this. Nigel is going to help me shower and assist in the removal of the bandages and whilst I want and need him in the en-suite with me I'm not sure about him seeing my breast not sure how he will react - I'm not sure how I will react!

In the bathroom the shower is turned on the water heated I strip off, exposed, naked step into the shower and I stand for a few minutes trying to get the courage to remove the bandages. It's becoming tougher and tougher to do so. I'm wetting the bandages as Brenda the breast nurse said to do. I'm getting weaker and weaker as they come away and I can see the awful mess, the slice in my beautiful breast the blood-stained bandage is sticking to my wound. I'm going to faint it's getting so hot. I can hear Nigel standing outside the shower asking if I am ok how's it going? Are you ok? I need his help I open the door having sat down on the shower seat. I'm feeling really faint he helps. I keep trying he helps and off they come oh my it's a mess. An incision on my breast it looks around three inches and it was across where my nipple was, it's gone alright! Both wounds a bit messy and paper sutures all the stitching was internal.

You know Nigel never flinched at the sight he saw. He remained so calm got me out of the shower and dried me like a little baby patted me down, dried my broken body and was just wonderful. I was shattered felt so unwell and looked at my breast that was unrecognisable.

Nigel continues to be with me when I'm taking my showers, he's so protective and caring.

I'm off-line in respect of messaging and getting in touch with everyone since surgery. Just not up to chatting but the messages are coming in so many of them fast and steady. Everyone is just so wonderful.

I had fifty-seven new messages waiting to be read. I will get back to those lovely people just not yet. I've had visitors. It's been tough having them, but I know they need to see me. My mummy and Shirley. My sister started off the *carers rota* just being with me at home. It is nice they are here if I need a cry or cup of tea (de-caf now of course!)

My dearest friend Jill has just been wonderful. She just knows what to say or not to say. She came to see me after surgery just held me tightly. My diagnosis has had a profound effect on so many people. They like me cannot believe I have cancer. My quiet thoughts range from still a bit of disbelief to fear what does this all really mean? To sometimes forgetting I have cancer although it's very real this week cos of new pain. The breast is now stinging a little but manageable pain. I have a high threshold it's getting itchy is that a good sign? I'm scared as I don't know what this all means what the future holds. I feel like sometimes this will not beat me and other times I think I'm gonna die much sooner than I had imagined in my life. I had so many plans as I moved towards retirement. Things Nigel & I had talked about travel, the garden not huge things but very important things for us both as we grew old together.

My minister Reverend Trueman came to visit today. That was nice and very comforting. Gary is a very down to earth guy an easy person to be around with of course heavenly being! The day he called I had lots of visitors in the house, but it was a such a nice visit and good to chat with him. Of course, there was cups of tea being made.

I am close with God and gave my life to him some years ago in fact it was January 2005. I asked Jesus into my life and started my walk with him. You know I fail him every day. I fall short, but I keep going and talk to him in prayer daily. These last five weeks I have read the bible finding peace in the scriptures. I also have so many people praying for me right now, please God they continue to do so. Back to the visit from Rev Gary. One of my visitors today was my brother Cecil. He was in the sunroom while my minister chatted. I asked Gary if he would say a prayer which of course he had planned to and when we bowed our heads my brother sat forward on the sofa bowed his head and prayed with us and as it ended my brother said out loud "Amen." I'm crying as I write this as it was so good to see and hear that from my brother. It's funny sometimes how difficult situations can bring about such happenings.

Nigel keeps telling me I must fight this, and he continues to be angry with my cancer I'm not. I don't have any feelings like that it has happened and its fine. I will deal with it. What it has done is made me look at life what's around me, what's really important and the future will be different, but I can do different. My cancer is a positive. Anyone who knows me will say I'm organised, structured, so together, strong (most of the time) everything has its place, things get planned, tasks achieved daily. Well that is still the way but just not able to function the same right now.

I have tried to look at everything now practically on the basis what if I'm not going to be here - Is everything in order? Just created a little book of all our family passwords and account details. I know them all, have them all in my head, but they now need writing down, so Nigel has them just in case I *die*. Nothing will be left complicated for him.

Look it's not *negativity* it's being practical and organised.

I have thought about my *funeral*. Wow! that was a difficult word to write. Yes, I have, and arrangements have been considered. What I want on that very last day. Flowers, candles, music, time of the day, order of service, hymns, photo of me in the church. Yes, I have thought of this. I should write this all down. I think I might. I can't talk about this anymore not right now.

I have had flowers, magazines, candles, more flowers, books, biscuits, cakes, more flowers. Wonderful kind gestures from such kind people. You know I am truly humbled overwhelmed at the response from some incredible people.

SUNDAY, 29 JANUARY

Boys are back and spending time with me post-surgery lovely having them at home. Some normal family stuff which is great. Oh, since my surgery the old bowel department isn't working disaster! Severe abdominal pain and many trips to the toilet. No joking the pain was excruciating worse than child birth! I tell you, this so you know you can get constipated post-surgery. It's the drugs that cause it so always worth getting onto laxatives as early as possible. My breast is now a new shade of black, blue and yellow. It's a sorry state and its throbbing and itchy. The underside of the breast has severe heavy bruising. The breast wound very raw. Six weeks into this nightmare, no it's not a nightmare it's a life changing experience. Stupidly hurt my breast as I turned over in bed caught it on edge of mattress ouch! Convinced myself it was bleeding, but it wasn't. Disastrous night didn't sleep got into shower and cried and cried.

Breast looks like a *bad car crash* taking plenty of pain relief. GP has had to be contacted for bowel department!

WEDNESDAY, 1 FEBRUARY

Got my letter from the hospital today.

Follow up appointment with Mr Mallon eighth February at eleven fifteen. Just one more week to get results. I will know then full scale of my cancer and the way forward! Alex has gone back to Uni now. I had a lovely time with him, and he was so useful and helpful around the house. More importantly lots of hugs and kisses. A little sad he's gone, but I'm just feeling a bit of *empty nest* as I feel vulnerable. Matthew still at home which is great. I know he's upset about me and worried.

Anyway, what beautiful flowers I have got. The latest is the most amazing display of tulips. I don't normally get to have tulips inside my house as I grow them in my garden. Doreen my friend was so kind and thoughtful. You know I am amazed how she has kept in touch so attentively since my diagnosis. An old school friend who I didn't have much direct contact with. We are part of the *High School* group who meet a couple of times a year but nothing more and yet she has been amazing. It's funny how life changing situations can introduce new openings.

I have said that the last almost seven weeks has created life changing circumstances. My life will be different now, but I'm positive about that.

My cancer will allow me to move forward living life differently. Gosh I'm starting to feel more positive that's the first time I've felt like that. While my breast is still very tender the wounds are healing still a little pain and all that sticky residue from the bandages have left stuff behind and that's annoying, but it will come off, still too tender to scrub just yet.

I'm now showering without any company progress!

SATURDAY, 4 FEBRUARY

This week has been strange, yes strange. Pain eased slightly (more me trying to move on).

I've not wanted visitors and that's not me being ungrateful just not up to chatting face to face with everyone. Messages keep coming on my phone and I am answering them.

Mummy has come and went respecting my privacy. She has been wonderful very helpful in her own practical way around the house which has been good for me as I need everything in the house to be in order.

I got out of my pyjamas this week first since surgery that allows you to feel a little more human. The *bowel* departments remain a stumbling block. I'm working on it, laxatives in abundance.

I have looked out at my garden so wanting to be out there doing my winter clean-up and preparing for Spring, but I can't it is so frustrating cos I just would not be fit. Nigel continues to be my rock just gets on with things makes sure I'm ok. Funny how you feel and think when weak. He got up Tuesday morning left me in bed, had a shower and went to work leaving me there. I was so emotional. He hadn't spoke to me before he left nor kissed me. I just lay there crying. He was to be with me this morning while I tried to wash my hair for the first time. I thought he's had enough of me can't be bothered anymore he's fed up, he's pissed off. I disgust him, my body disgusts him, he can't do this anymore. I text him saying I had managed to shower and wash my hair. He immediately rang me saying he knew I had had a horrendous night in bed, (I did) so he left the bedroom so as not to wake me and let me get some sleep. Oh, how I had got that wrong! He says my reasoning is crap it was not his thoughts. I think your mind can play havoc with you when you are little vulnerable - no a lot vulnerable. Oh I love him.

The messages of support and prayers keep coming.

MONDAY, 6 FEBRUARY

A tough day today not as such for me, but for my beautiful boy. Matthew's three-year relationship with his girlfriend has ended. It's been a tough week for him so sad, so many tears, my *shoulder* used a lot this week and today I needed to support him as he was hurting so much. He also is returning to Edinburgh to continue his studies. I always feel sad when they are preparing to leave home again. He broke my heart today when he sobbed and said "I've had the two worst things happen to me in the last month, my mummy has cancer and my relationship with my girlfriend is over I can't take any more bad news" that was tough to hear. As a mummy I do not have enough *cotton wool* to wrap him in.

I know this will be difficult, but he will survive the heartbreak and I'll get better.

TUESDAY, 7 FEBRUARY

Kelly Anne my dear work colleague - my team mate came to see me. It was so nice spending time with her. I was emotional around her think it was cos it's the first time I've seen her since my diagnosis. She was great and very practical. She brought a bean stew for Nigel and me. Some scones for a wee cuppa which we enjoyed together She also brought me a little gift pouch called a 'bag of happiness'. Inside was special little items. When I get visitors, they want to ask me questions. They want to know what's going on and so I end up going over and over the details and I relive everything from fifteenth December that *night* I found the lump. When you say it out loud its sounds so serious and I always end up exhausted. KA said I had lost weight. That's the first person to say that although she worked with me every day so saw me all the time and clearly now sees the change. Family and other friends haven't said it, not sure if they have noticed but are not saying. It's true I have lost weight having stepped on the scales I can see I have lost one stone in seven weeks that's a lot. When I look in the mirror the person looking back doesn't look well!

Tomorrow is an important day eighth February *results* day. This will be it or should be. I should get all post op results. Did they get the tumour? Did they get a clear margin around the tumour? Is any further surgery required? Grade of the cancer? Stage of the cancer? Lymph node results? Chest Tissue removal results? Treatment? What is required now, what do I need to do to give myself the best chance. I'm not sure how I'm feeling a range of emotions. I think the most prevalent one is I'm *scared*. This is a massive juncture in the road, which direction will I be going?

Oh gosh so many messages coming in. Everyone has remembered that tomorrow is results day. Such lovely messages hoping all goes ok.

I keep going from, this is not real to, yes, it is real. *Shit* I've got cancer this is tough. I've got a lot to go through to aid my survival *(I'm using that word again!)*

Nigel & I have not spoken about what's happening tomorrow. We just both know tomorrow is going to be huge for us. Nigel will be with me and that's all that matters, every step of the way and that gives me the comfort I need. My breast is still painful but not nearly as much and the scars are not as scary looking healing well and not as severe to the eye. I've always had fast healing skin and any scars I have in the past heal quickly and well (I thank my parents for this positive great skin).

I've felt so restricted wearing bras 24/7 as I always loved to get the boobies free from their holder! Loved to have them released but the last fortnight would have been unbearable not to have them supported. I thought tight fitting tops would have looked strange after surgery, but it doesn't. All looks just fine. My breast is still very swollen so looking bizarrely bigger than the left one but I'm sure it will settle with time and it's not too abnormal looking.

WEDNESDAY, 8 FEBRUARY

The journey to the hospital was a quiet one not much said between Nigel & me.

A straightforward journey into the city with no traffic problems until we get to hospital and then no parking available for patients who have appointments. Another issue with our hospitals. I end up out of the car walking into the hospital alone as Nigel tries to find a space to park.

Got booked in took a seat and Nigel joined me a short time later with time to spare. A busy waiting area. It never changes. Women coming and going all the time with their own issues and worries. Nigel took my hand squeezed it and asked if I was ok. He always just knows what to say. Forty-five minutes later I got called to the consultation room and one hour after my due appointment time! A nurse had explained the delay, a lady before me had some issues with her bandages, poor woman.

In comes Mr Mallon such a lovely man so nice, courteous and mannerly. He always does make you feel ok and comfortable. He says hello to us both and asks how I've been and then begins explaining the surgery he had carried out. He started drawing diagrams on paper of what he did and found on surgery day. He was explaining everything by words and pen. Really strange but I was calm, my heart was beating a little faster, but I held it together as he talked. I did ask him questions as he progressed. The *cop* in me was saying inwardly just hurry up, get on with it, give me the facts, no messing about I wanna know.

This is what I got told, surgery removed the cancer tumour 1.5 cm, invasive ductal breast cancer with removal of wide margin around tumour showing clear. Other shavings of tissue taken away in upper area of breast/chest and it has confirmed more CANCER. Yes, cancer in other areas in my breast. He called it DCIS (Ductal Carcinoma in Situ). Cancer in the ducts not yet spreading out but in different areas. I asked about the lymph node that he had removed cos he hadn't mentioned it. He confirmed cancer was found in the lymph node. So, it's spreading SHIT CRAP BLOODY HELL. The cancer is moved to a Grade three that's because its travelled to my nodes *SHIT.* The OPTIONS now - I didn't need telling, in my head there was only really one way forward - they need to remove my breast. My beautiful breast. I will need to have a MASTECTOMY. I had heard everything. I really did hold it together. I had more questions I asked about stage of cancer, he couldn't answer that, this result would come later. Further lymph nodes would be removed to see how far it has travelled. I asked him what he believed needed to happen and he said breast removal. He was very honest and sincere, direct but pleasantly so. This is about best chance of SURVIVAL, there's that word again! Conversation then moved quickly to RECONSTRUCTION of breast did I want one? What type? and again he explained pros and cons nothing left unsaid.

I certainly could make no decisions at this precise moment.

I needed time to think. Oh, and yes, my treatment post-surgery would now most likely be CHEMOTHERAPY. Shit this is crap it's getting worse. This is NOT what I was expecting, worst possible results today. *Nightmare!*

This is getting way more difficult.

Nigel did take over and ask some questions practical and sensible important questions which Mr Mallon answered for him. Several times in the room Nigel and I just kept looking at each other. He moved closer to me and held and squeezed my hand. I think I heard him telling Mr Mallon he needed me and couldn't live without me! Glenda the breast nurse was in the room throughout she was quiet, silent and spoke when totally appropriate to do so. I broke down once when the conversation was around having a breast or not. I was handed a hanky. Those nurses are my ground angels. I've now met four of them and each one a God send. Such wonderful and important people in this journey of mine.

Mr Mallon then asked to examine my breast. He was happy with it after two weeks from surgery. Glenda the nurse was impressed and said you obviously have great skin for healing as its going well. (What have I told you before I always have had great skin don't even have one stretch mark from birth of my boys).

Mr Mallon confirmed surgery already planned and pencilled in for week commencing Monday twentieth Feb that's quick!

Thank goodness. He agreed to see me on thirteenth to discuss final decision on breast reconstruction. That was it forty-five minutes later I had been told I had more cancer in my breast, in my lymph nodes and I needed to have a MASTECTOMY and most likely CHEMOTHERAPY. *Oh, my days!*

Nigel & I got the worst results and possible news ever, well the worst since the nineteenth December!

We left the room and went with the breast nurse where she gave me another hanky along with lots of literature on breast reconstruction.

You know it's impossible for me to write down how I felt at that very moment. In shock, numb, moving through this nightmare and it doesn't feel real.

I now must tell my loved ones, my two beautiful boys that all is not well.

I made the calls to the boys even before I left the multi-storey car park at the hospital. Alex appeared to process it and asked questions.

Matthew went quiet, not good! I had to tell them the truth as they had asked for honesty. Then first calls to my sister, mummy, my dearest friends Jill and Judy, my mother in-law, and my sister in law Mandy and each one of them took the news in their own way and all very differently, but it was clear I could detect their shock and concern.

I was exhausted but practically the show must go on so got Nigel to stop at Sainsburys, so I could do some shopping. You can't just stop you must keep going and that's what I am doing.

I updated those who were waiting to hear results. The toughest thing for me is to see Nigel a broken man. I'm not saying he's not coping or on his knees. He has such strength and I know it's a cliché but he's my ROCK. Today he cried that's tough to watch and he keeps using his mantra "we will beat this we can get through this. I can't do this on my own Wendy".

You know I've never said why me as why not me? And I still say that God has a plan. My faith says leave it to God. I'm reading the word of God and some verses just jump out of the page to me, but I cannot remember a word I've read. I cannot right now repeat the scriptures my mind is retaining nothing. I read and think WOW and yet I remember nothing and so all I can do is keep reading, keep praying and allow God to be ever-present.

The only words going over and over in my head right now from my bible is

BE STILL AND KNOW THAT I AM GOD.

As the saying goes the morning after the night before or in my case the day after the previous day. I awoke thinking was it a dream. Those first few moments when you refocus you open your eyes it's not real then reality kicks in. It is real, my feelings are shock. This is the worst case ever for me. Shit I've just had surgery, and I must undergo more in ten days or so and the next op is even bigger.

The messages are flooding in, incredible support so many kind people saying hope yesterday went well and others are sending best wishes and offers of support already knowing the outcome of yesterday. They have had time to digest it.

One dear friend Judith Blemmings sent this to me

"You are without doubt my role model and if I can be half the sergeant, woman, lady, wife and mother that you are I'll be happy. Your family unit is so solid, and you have enough friends around you to start a small ARMY so use them to help you gather strength for the tough road ahead".

How amazing for someone to say such a lovely thing to me. Yes, I do indeed have amazing people around me, and I am very humbled truly I am.

SATURDAY, 11 FEBRUARY

Today I had my dear friend Judy come to visit. Much awaited visit from her as I hadn't seen her since my diagnosis. We had constantly chatted on the phone and messaged. She arrived and as I opened the door I could see she was already visibly upset armed with a box of amazing flowers and a little message within saying; "Chin up get well soon all my love Judy" and of course armed with one of her special curries for Nigel and I all in her granny's little basket along with strawberries and cream. How thoughtful how practical just Judy. We hugged and hugged and cried and cried. I have never seen her so upset in the twenty-seven years I know her. I think she's devastated, it has really affected her. She asked lots of questions and listened attentively. I'm so lucky to have her as my friend - what a lovely day we had.

From last Wednesday's consultation I am still reading all the material provided on breast reconstruction. I have a huge decision to make. I have read the literature several times and even had a conversation with a friend who had a double mastectomy. Reconstruction will take place same day as surgery. I just need to decide on IMPLANT or DORSI FLAP (where they use muscle from my back to help create a breast). It's not something I can rush. I think Nigel worried I haven't made my mind up. A practical question - can Mr Mallon make me a breast similar size to my left one. I'm thinking implant only as it will be quicker recovery and less scarring. I need to recover as quickly as I can, so I can move to next stage which is treatment and I don't want any delays.

I'm off to Mr Mallon tomorrow with my decision as this will impact on his surgery list. I have some questions needing answered and I'm sure once these are answered I will have my decision.

Opened my mail earlier and letter from hospital confirming surgery on Monday twentieth February. My stomach jumped when I read it it's really happening going back for surgery number two. It's like I'm back at the beginning again. Three weeks ago, I was preparing getting all ready, prep, fasting surgery, recovering exercises and none of it matters must go again. My cancer is bigger and more serious than I had hoped for. Well it is what it is, I need to hit it head on.

SUNDAY, 12 FEBRUARY

I awoke this morning with Nigel showing me a text he had received late last night from Alex. The message said, "I am really worried about mummy" and that he needed to talk. It broke my heart. I don't want him upset. I phoned him cos I needed to talk to him. I didn't say anything about the *text* until he said he had messaged daddy last evening.

He's very worried. I told him not to worry to which he replied, "how can I not worry mummy". One of his questions was "Is it not bad cos they have found cancer in your lymph nodes?". "Why are you worried about that?" I asked he replied, "well if it is there it is spreading mummy." I tried to reassure him that all was being done at this time to make me better. So difficult. He's a clever boy and his mind is racing and yes that's exactly one of my many thoughts too!

MONDAY, 13 FEBRUARY

Just back from consultation with Mr Mallon.

Nigel & I both went in to see him. It went well. Cathy the breast nurse was present in the room. I asked Mr Mallon about my choices

1. Implant only
2. Dursi flap (muscle from my back)

If I proceed with implant can he create one very similar to my left breast.

I know they say your own tissue is better that then pushes towards dorsi flap. We spoke about my spine, Nigel brought it up what with me having a weak spine and previous spinal surgery. Would having back muscle removed weaken the area further? I know I need to recover as quickly as possible, so I can move to treatment phase don't want any unnecessary delays.

There were further discussions about choice later, way down the line if more breast corrective surgery required. Mr Mallon clearly explained all options with ease of understanding there was nothing left to say.

So, I had made up my mind. I knew how I wanted to proceed. It was my decision and I honestly felt like I mattered, I was a person not just a patient. I was Wendy making an informed decision and that was a nice feeling. It's gonna be reconstruction by *implant* only. I'm good with the decision.

It's now only one week away.

Mr Mallon went on to explain some other post op stuff, so I wouldn't be scared things like the *drains* I would have post-surgery. My new breast might look strange in the beginning cos of drains but not to be alarmed. He shook our hands and we left. I did give him a hard time *again* about his time keeping but he had redeemed himself he was sitting waiting on me today!

Cathy my breast nurse asked if I had any further questions and explained some post op stuff care with my implant exercises nothing too strenuous for four to six weeks and that I would need to have a *heart check* before chemotherapy commences and that would be arranged. She told me she would organise that before I got to see Oncologist *(cancer doctor)* and that treatment normally starts four to six weeks after surgery. Oh, and one other thing Mr Mallon said was that I might need radiotherapy as well as chemotherapy. It will depend on pathology results.

Gosh, the goal posts keep moving just when you think you've got it all and you know the plan it changes. I guess you must be prepared to move with the developments.

I am doing ok. I am devastated at the enormity but need to keep going. I will beat this. I'm not going anywhere. I want to grow old with my family. I want to see my boys develop and grow and see them through their lives and be part of it!

Tonight, I had a great get together. My dearest friend Jill offered to be host, cook dinner for me and two other dear school friends Valerie & Doreen so they could see me. So, we all got together. It was an emotional evening and we all cried a little. Two friends who have surprised me, pleasantly of course. They have been an incredible support. Little messages appear on my phone just simply saying they were thinking of me or they were praying for me and offering support. I'm bowled over, such compassion and great to have these lovely people in my life.

I just love Valerie for her frankness, views and opinions. She's really a big softie! Big heart, very funny and great craic and lovely to be around. She was at my wedding all those years ago (twenty-eight) and still very much in my life, and I'm grateful for that.

We had a great night. They all listened to me attentively. We had some great laughs and we chatted about the perils of turning *fifty* something we all had done. I have no doubt these wonderful ladies will walk with me as I continue this road.

TUESDAY, 14 FEBRUARY

I made a very big decision to day and decided to have my hair cut. My long beautiful blond hair that I have always loved. I was renowned across the countryside for my big hair. Mummy drove me to my hairdressers, Escapades in Moira. My hairdresser Jill was wonderful so considerate. I had brought some pictures of possible styles.

We had a good discussion, both a little emotional.

Jill said she was nervous at cutting my hair off. I saw my blond hair drop onto the floor behind me and onto the chair I was sitting on. I was ok tried to look at the positive I was getting a new style. I had planned that this was the first cut and I would continue to have it cut shorter as I moved towards treatment. I need to be control and this was just one step. I just didn't think I could cope waking up one day and my long locks of hair lying on the pillow. That would just have been too much to deal with.

Sensible and practical all the way eh! My new style looked fab, refreshing, made me feel good. Thank-you Jill - *the girl did good.*

Ironically it was Valentine's day and whilst I don't celebrate it, think it's a total waste of time a nonsense, as every day is special in my house and I get spoilt all the time. Nigel asked if I would like to do something special or go anywhere.

Yes, I did. I choose my favourite Indian restaurant and off we went for a lovely meal and some nice quality time together away from everything.

I decided this morning to write down everyone's name who had been in touch with me, so I wouldn't forget anyone. Those who have been so considerate. It filled *three* pages of my journal. Overwhelming when you see it on paper. This doesn't include my mummy, my dear sister, my brothers, my husband, my boys.

A big thank you to you all.

MONDAY, 20 FEBRUARY – SURGERY NUMBER TWO

I'm now back in Belfast City hospital.

It's seven thirty in the morning. Nigel has just left the ward that was emotional saying good bye. The nurse is doing the admissions process. I can't believe I'm doing this again. It's exactly four weeks since I was last here and ironically the same bed and position in the ward. The board above my bed says I am *second* on Mr Mallon's list.

Hopefully I won't have to wait as long this time. Lots of activity around my bed. Mr Mallon has been in to see me signed my consent and he has drawn all over me, all around my breast marking the edges drawing arrows and prepping me for surgery. Ward doctor has just been round. I have asked for something to be prescribed for *bowels* as post op it's a disaster.

Into bed now, gown on, stockings on, blanket on and I guess I'm ready to go.

Not sure how I am feeling lying here - well it's like my goodness I am here again. This is surreal. The lovely nurse Julie-Ann who looked after me four weeks ago is here, got to see her. I had brought her some chocolates to say thank you for last time.

I'm calm. I guess I'm resigned to fact this must happen. I need them to get the cancer removed and I need to move on, get treatment started. I want to be well again and get on with my life whatever that will be.

The past week was so busy, so many people wanting to see me, so many cards and flowers.

Yesterday was a bit manic as so many people came to visit.

I showed my sister my breast just to let her see the scarring and how I had recovered post-surgery as I knew she would always wonder. I think she was pleasantly surprised at how well I had healed.

Got to chat with Matthew & Alex last night by video calls. Good to see each other. Matthew was very tearful. He's very emotional has a lot going on in his life poor pet, but he will get over his break up with girlfriend and not look back.

Bigger and better things to come that I'm sure of. Alex was good, great wee chat.

That's it, I'm ready to go for surgery.

Nine weeks after my breast cancer diagnosis I'm now going to have my right breast totally removed. My beautiful breast will be gone when I get back to writing in my journal.

WEDNESDAY, 22 FEBRUARY

It's now a couple of days since surgery. Nine forty on the ward.

Oh my, what a forty-eight hours I have had. Surgery behind me. I understand it took between three and four hours. When I opened my eyes in recovery a lovely lady from church Linda Kelso *recovery ward nurse* was at my bedside speaking with me. How kind. She knew I was in her recovery ward and came to see me. She said she would phone Nigel and tell him I was awake.

Just amazing people in my life and crossing my path. Jennifer Ard the nursing sister in the ward appeared again squeezing my hand. They are so lovely.

Have had a peek down at my breast. It's all bandaged so can't see how it looks. It's hard as a rock! I have three drains attached which are taking fluid mostly blood away from the breast and armpit area. Yes, there's a shape to the breast looking pert! Now left one pointing south, right sticking out!

Pain has kicked in big time.

Moved to Ward five. Mummy & Shirley came in to see me. They said I looked great yeah right! Lovely to see them and I was bright when they arrived but had just got my *morphine*. Lena from church came to visit too, she's just amazing.

By the time they left my pain was horrendous and that pretty much continued until night staff came on. A lovely nurse called Sharon Porter was my saviour. I was so distressed about the pain I burst out crying. One of my drains had come apart and that made me cry too. A cannula was reinserted in the back of my hand, IV paracetamol given, more morphine and I settled and slept quite well. I have now got the meds regulated properly to give me no breakthrough pain.

My breast nurse came in yesterday morning along with Mr Mallon. He was happy all had gone to plan in surgery. Siobhan my breast nurse was brilliant. I had a cry. She comforted me told everything was ok Advised to get my bra on for support and oh boy it was tight.

Katherine Carlisle my breast nurse came in this morning that's all five of the breast care nurses I have seen and each one of them wonderful. Again, I was so emotional and just cried. I don't know what's wrong with me think so much happening and so much to deal with. Katherine told me to calm down. It was all very normal to feel like this. She gave me some advice, got me more pain relief and everything just seemed a little better.

Oh, my goodness the first of the three drains had to come out. I was so anxious and not looking forward to it. Laura the nurse was looking after me. She said it would happen at the bedside. People has told me it is a painful procedure to have it removed. Horrendous! I sat on the edge of bed as it was removed. She pulled and pulled the tube as I tried to breathe, not nice, not pleasant just awful, but you know what it must happen, you've got to endure it. *One* down *two* more to go - oh dear!

Well the rest of the morning resulted in me lying in bed feeling a bit off. Pain relief much better this morning.

Lots of messages coming through on my phone just not up to responding just yet.

THURSDAY, 23 FEBRUARY

Day three post-surgery. Pain under control getting correct meds. Pain in my armpit not good and pain at my sternum equally bad. Surgical team been visiting and appears happy with everything including two other drains which are still filling up. Been for a brief wash, can't shower yet but got my knickers changed, jammies changed, teeth brushed, face washed, face cream on *(of course)* just makes you feel a little more human. Lisa the nurse has been and recharged my drains new bottles on this morning. Seventy mil in both. Fluid still flowing. She also took my bandages off didn't feel so well when that happened. Just tried some exercises as required to do.

I'm struggling a bit to write as my right arm is painful to move.

Sometimes the weirdest things can happen in your life. As I sat on the bedside just after eleven with everyone else resting on the ward, I looked up and saw a lady walk towards me. I had no idea who until she got close to my bed then I realised it was *Julia Hanna*. A blast from the past. A few years ago, I was her manager and looked after her after her young husband died of cancer. She was coming to see me in an *official capacity*. She is a complimentary therapist working from the Macmillan Centre. My breast nurse had referred me for some therapy. It was clear Julia was shocked it was the same *Wendy Walker* she knew from old. She told me she had seen the name but never imagined it was me. Lovely to see each other. How bizarre I had been thinking about her recently as I knew she had changed jobs and was now helping people with cancer. Now here she was to help me! I got treated to some reflexology at my bedside. A wonderful service, very relaxing and just what I needed. I never got to say goodbye as I feel asleep. She left me a little pot of cream for later - *Bliss*.

Today has been tough with pain and emotions.

Alex has passed all his first year exams at University. I'm so very proud of him. He kept going pushed on all the while handling his fear and concerns for me that's my boy. Matthews results also coming in and has passed his exams too. How good is that.

They are both fantastic boys so brave, so I sent them this little verse

"You are my greatest blessings and I love you more than words can ever say. May your challenges be small ones, and your blessings and victories huge"

I'm just crying now.

Tonight's visitors were Jill, Valerie & Doreen. Great to see the girls and some craic, a wonderful distraction. Nigel came in bringing me some *food treats* and my clean washing - I'm spoilt.

FRIDAY, 24 FEBRUARY

It's now Friday and I am still in hospital. Surgical team been around to see me drains still filling so not being removed. I'm not getting home.

Was back in the bathroom of the ward trying to wash (not a great success as I can't shower yet with drains still in). So little exhausts me. I stripped off and looked in the mirror, I could clearly see my new breast very different to the left one. The bandages all gone and some steri stitches still there. The scars are the same ones as surgery four weeks ago. Will have to wait and see how they settle and what my results say.

Handwriting is a mess as armpit so painful. I'm struggling but I'll keep going.

Mr Mallon came to the bedside this evening to see me and advised another doctor would be covering for him over weekend and as he left, he said he would be back to see me. I thought that's great. He came back at around half five pulled the curtains around and sat down on the bed. He proceeded to tell me the results were back.

Oh, my goodness that was fast. He had a file with him, and he proceeded to say that pathology had done their investigations *(now what I am about to write is not in any logical order just what I heard)*. For the first time since this journey started, I was on my own, Nigel not with me for these results.

Eight lymph nodes removed in total and cancer just in the first one,not in any that was removed on Monday. That's good news. He said for survival and recurrence *(words they use that scares the life out of you)*. It means cancer has not spread on up through lymph nodes and just at number one. He confirmed all breast tissue taken away and that they had found *another* tumour in a different area of the breast. *What?* your joking me - no he wasn't. I asked what he was saying? another *cancer nodule* to the right of the first area, same size of tumour 1.5 cm and it was *invasive ductal breast cancer* same as tumour number one so that was *two* tumours, DCIS and cancer in one lymph node.

I couldn't believe what he was saying about the *second tumour.*

He told me everything had been taken away and now time for me to recover from surgery and that the Oncologist will see me in a few weeks to discuss treatment plan. It was so overwhelming to hear all this.

The rest is a bit of a muddle. I asked if I needed to have chemotherapy he said, "you are young Wendy your healthy". I was confused what he was trying to say, do I need chemo or not? I think he thought I was indicating I didn't want it. That's not the case. I just need to know with all these results is it a given. I will take whatever I have to get to give myself the best chance. I asked about radiotherapy and he said the Oncology team would decide on this.

So much to deal with and more cancer mentioned *crap.*

Gosh where would I have been in a few months' time if the *second* tumour had not been detected. Had I not of complained about my chest area so good Mr Mallon checked the area this could have been more disastrous.

He left the bedside told me he would see me in a few weeks' time to check reconstruction.

When he left, I can honestly say I was in a state of *shock* and *panic* set in. Had I heard everything right. I needed to speak to my breast nurse but they had finished until Monday. By the time Nigel arrived long with mummy and Shirley I was so emotional and had to tell them. Such mixed emotions. There were gasps as I mentioned another *tumour* but relief at lymph node results.

I know each of them are struggling as they walk this with me so much to take in. Not sure how Nigel felt when I started telling him. He was practical though saying lymph node result good.

We just keep getting result after result - it's never ending.

Mr Mallon did previously discuss with me about when you decide to remove a breast it may be an overkill when you don't know what will or will not be found, but, on this occasion, right thing to do for sure with the amount of cancer in my right breast best to get it out, remove it, banish this cancer from my breast.

I spoke to Nigel on the phone when he got home. He told me he had cried when he left and was sad. He doesn't want any more of these results. He wants me home where he can look after me. He was upset he wasn't there for me getting those results to hold my hand and say comforting things. Not his fault it's just the way it happened.

A good cry always helps and that's just what I've done.

Spoke to Jill and Valerie that helped too. Weird thing this week is the hot flushes are less frequent why is that? Is it the drugs I'm on? What my body has been through this week not surprised they are *hiding* somewhere! No doubt they will come back as bad as ever.

SATURDAY, 25 FEBRUARY

Awoke this morning and form ok. Slept ok with plenty of meds.

Yesterday still playing on my mind mainly did I hear it right? Have I understood everything correctly? Both drains still in, ninety & thirty millilitres going down a little, maybe get one more out today.

Toilet patterns a disaster! Suppository didn't work, double dose of laxative now taken need to hurry up or I am going to explode!

I left a message with breast nurse need to talk to them some questions needing answered.

This morning a bit of reflection and quiet time.

'I will say of the Lord, he is my refuge and my fortress, my God, in whom I trust'. Psalm 91:2

More visitors today. Toni Hannigan, Jill and her boy Adam. So good to see them all, they are all very special.

My drains are changing going from running clear *that must be a good sign* to then bright red blood. The change of colour happened after I took a sharp stabbing pain in my breast, a strange pain, I haven't had that before.

I might get one out today but no consultant here yet.

Nigel came into see me and we just chatted about lovely things. He brought me a *surprise*. A cheque from work. I apparently had been paying into a scheme since I joined the police which covered *critical illness*. I didn't realise but heh a pleasant surprise.

We spoke about the future and that we were going to live our lives differently take no *crap* from anyone, no silly distractions or other people's issues. Their problems are theirs and we are not going to sort or resolve for them. I'm up for that, as I no longer can be bothered with *small minded self-centred pain in the arse people* this is about me. This is my walk, focus on me getting better, live my life.

Mummy's been speaking to my mother in law and being totally negative about me always the *pessimist*. Mummy needs to be stronger and deal with this. I can't be worrying about her. I don't want any negative people around me. I know it's challenging watching your daughter suffer but she needs to deal with it. I want to scream. I'm not dealing with this. I phoned mummy telling her that her negativity would have to stop, leave it be, everyone is trying to deal with my diagnosis, and she needs to be more positive and keep her thoughts to herself. It's upsetting for others - there she's been told.

MONDAY, 27 FEBRUARY

Breast nurse my *ground angel* came to see me at eight. I told her about my results and had some questions. She couldn't answer as she hadn't seen the results. She came back to me later and explained everything clearly and it was correct as I had picked up from Mr Mallon. Katherine says the Oncologist will discuss my treatment plan in due course.

A more settled day not as emotional and not as tearful, feel nothing today.

Some lovely messages coming in on my phone. Doreen sent me another message. This was a very heartfelt one so amazing and unexpected. This girl has been incredible these last few weeks. I will reply to her as it needs a proper reply, I just can't do it now.

Talking of weeks, it is now *ten* so much has happened. Found a lump, diagnosed with breast cancer, tests, results, tests, results, surgery, results, surgery, results. UNBELIEVABLE roller-coaster! The breast nurse gave me more reading material. I like reading material it empowers me. This time it's about treatment. chemotherapy, radiotherapy, hair loss(OMG) tamoxifen, menopausal symptoms oh my! Lots to read - this is all very real.

The next step once I recover from surgery bring it on! I need to be better.

They brought a lady onto the ward earlier who had had surgery. As I looked across, I could see she had no *hair,* quite disturbing for me to see it. It was like a reality check. She needed help to find her glasses as her movement was limited. I went across to assist. She got me to check her bag and as I opened it, I put my hand into the pocket of the bag and onto her *wig.* It stopped me in my tracks I was so shocked at what I had touched, but I carried on trying not to show any emotion outwardly but inwardly I was *rumbled.* This could be me in a few weeks. I thought no hair a *wig,* but you know I thought who cares - I don't. I just need to be better. I want them to give me whatever they must for best chance of survival.

Today I felt a little calmer although quite tearful, but I'm determined that I'll kick this cancer!

Surgical team around again. They won't take final drain out as still fluid coming away (oh drain two wasn't as painful as first one so that was good). I so want to go home. Doctor said he'll see how next twenty-four hours go. They don't like to keep the drains in too long as run risk of an infection, but it needs to be there for now. The drain bottle to be changed and the suction had been removed from the bottle. He agreed to revisit at teatime today. Whoopee - this girl might just be going home tonight.

My lovely minister Rev Trueman came in at lunchtime to see me so very kind and thoughtful. I so needed his presence. His prayers always help. I always feel God closer when someone else prays with me. I feel the stillness. I had been reading some scripture this morning. I'm behind in my *Bible in one year plan* just could not lift it to read. They are just words on the page, and nothing being digested. Today he held my hand as we prayed that was so sweet and very important to me.

Had my dear friend Judy in to see me this afternoon. Just so nice to see her and had a good natter talking about normal stuff in this abnormal situation. She made me laugh lots to the point of hurting my wounds. She stayed until nearly five. I thought the staff were going to throw her out.

I'm now back home. Last night final drain removed. I was so anxious about getting it taken out, but it was so okay not painful at all. Nurse Danielle handled the situation very well. surgical team came around, happy for it to be removed and I could go home. I was so happy. Nine days in hospital this time. I have never been in a hospital for that long even when having my babies. As I lay on the ward, I kept thinking I could help fix this ward and the issues they are experiencing, get me onto the ward and I would manage it for sure. The *matron* would be back.

Anyway, home with my meds.

There was a few emotional farewells to those in my wee ward. I had been with three out of the four ladies for the whole nine days so we all had seen ups and downs. Each one of us with our own battles and we had supported each other. The doctors and nurses on *ward five south* at Belfast City Hospital were so wonderful. I had had some *low* days particularly when I got the last set of *results*. I've cried a lot with a little laughter thrown in. Nigel walked each day with me as close as close can be. I couldn't do it without him. I love him so much.

The house is peaceful and quiet I love being home.

My first night in bed, my own bed was a bit strange post-surgery. Bedroom so dark and quiet. Struggled to get comfortable. It wasn't easy, pillows everywhere. Mum gave me her 'V' pillow. It's helping.

THURSDAY, 2 MARCH

I have considerable pain still needing lots of pain relief. I'm very nervous about my new breast restricted movement, tired and sleeping a lot but that's ok I can do that. I so wanted to have shower so Nigel to the rescue. I wondered how he would handle the NEW boobie and seeing me naked and clearly looking different. He never flinched, clearly didn't matter to him. He has continually said it's just a breast he wants me, not the breast. I want my breast though. I want everything to go back to the way it was but not possible! He dried my fragile body from head to toe. As I look at my new breast its different but bizarrely, I still have my cleavage.

You know mummy has been wonderful over the last ten weeks. I know she has her moments. There's been lots of crying and some stupid comments, but I understand her. I'm her little girl - she's feeling my pain. She keeps saying she wished it was her with the cancer not me but that's not how it works. Gods plan for me is to have this disease not mummy. I'm glad it's not her she sure couldn't cope not strong enough to deal with cancer and for years she has been terrified about such a disease almost fixated on the fear of getting it, well she didn't - I did! She's very practical and a doer, cleans and cleans that's her way of helping. She knows I like Shanroe (that's what our house is called) kept in ship shape. I love her dearly and you can only imagine how difficult it is for her child to have cancer and not really know what's going to happen.

Sleeping continues to be a bit of a bugger. I can't get comfortable. I have had to sleep on my back. I don't normally do that. You take so many things for granted in life and simple things become very difficult.

Went to see my GP this morning to drop off my discharge letter. Glad I got to see Dr McCandless - she's lovely. She's been so supportive since my diagnosis. You know I believe she was shocked that my *lump* was cancer. Yes, so true. It's a game changer. She examined me and was concerned my new breast a little hot and an antibiotic might be best and some stronger pain relief. Pain is quite bad in the breast chest area and my armpit. I have no feeling in my armpit. It's quite clear they have cut or severed nerves in that area. I did ask one of the doctors in hospital about it and apparently the numbness is normal and a price you might have to pay when having Lymph Nodes removed. Not sure if the feeling will ever return to my arm but let's see its early days.

So, trip to doctors went fine prescription in hand I left.

Many visitors calling at the door and I continue to receive cards, flowers, food, chocolates, fruit, you name it I'm getting it.

Oh, my HOT flushes are just crazy. I thought they had disappeared after surgery but boy oh boy they are very present. They come and go so fast, well probably lasts about five minutes and then it's gone. I can feel them starting, I get fidgety and then hot, back of my neck gets wet with perspiration then my forehead is soaking wet, whole body feels hot, my skin hot and then it's gone!

SATURDAY, 4 MARCH

I slept well last night got myself into a comfortable position propped up with lots of pillows and I didn't move. I didn't wake for pain relief so that's good too. Got up and showered myself more progress! My paper stitches are still holding firm. I wish they were off, so I could get a good wash but not ready yet to drop off. I can see lots of hardened blood under the stitches and the breast is looking very bruised and swollen. It's throbbing and stinging but I guess that's normal too.

I have just had a Chinese meal with a glass of wine. I haven't had any alcohol, since Christmas day. I just decided I wanted to be free from any alcohol in my body not that I drank lots but love a glass of wine and maybe on occasions a little gin. I suppose from my cancer diagnosis I have changed some habits wanting to do things to assist my body where possible and abstaining from alcohol is one of them. There's mind games cos each time I thought I could really do with a glass of wine I thought no its bad for me (is it really?) just wanted my body to be free from toxins that could interfere with the fight. You read so much literature about good and bad. I'm not sure how I will deal with it as I move forward. I have looked at my diet through a different set of eyes conscious of the implications of food. It's strange how it all plays on your mind. Can I do something that will help in making me better? I honestly don't know having read lots does it makes any difference? I have given up caffeine and I loved my TEA drank maybe up to eight cups a day, but it hasn't been difficult. I have stopped eating red meat, reduced my chocolate intake (although my brother Cecil had bought me some last night naughty!)

Nigel the chef has been wonderful in the kitchen with new menus, new foods being introduced especially fish which I was never keen on and I'm finding surprisingly very nice. I'm eating lots and lots of greens so I'm doing my bit. Oh, and a huge development I've had *no* fizzy drinks since the nineteenth December and I loved my daily can. No idea if this will help but I will try anything to give myself the best chance.

SUNDAY, 5 MARCH

Awful night.

Pain very bad continues to throb and sting in the breast, chest and armpit areas. Impossible to get comfortable. I'm lying up in bed with an abundance of pillows around me. HOT flushes in abundance so bad.

Today is another momentous day. I'm going to my hairdressers at half one. Jill has asked me to be her model as the staff within the salon are having some training provided by someone previously trained by Vidal Sassoon. Jill knows I am planning to cut my hair again. That's me controlling this little bit. I want to have it short before I start treatment. Hopefully get a funky style even if just for a few weeks.

Hair cut!

What a day a lovely experience.

I like my new style. Jill was very nervous I know not only the fact she was taking my locks off, but she was being overseen by a lady who had trained with Toni & Guy and Vidal Sassoon salons - nerve wrecking. She did just fine such a nice thing for her to have me as her model today. The girls in the hair salon were all lovely to me and when my new style was completed, I cried lots. Nigel said he loved it. I looked gorgeous (apparently) much younger, every cloud eh! I called to let mummy see it and I sent a pic through WhatsApp to a few friends. Everyone positive. I guess they can't say anything else! Just something I needed to do and glad I did it.

I need to speak about my friend Jill, a dear old friend who has been in my life for a long time she was my bridesmaid almost twenty-eight years ago. You know when your back is against the wall you really know who is special in your life. Don't get me wrong I have lots of very special people in my life who have been amazing, but Jill is something else. I knew she had taken my diagnosis very bad and she's been emotional from the night I told her. She has been there every single day. I knew the night I told her I had totally shocked and rocked her. Not a day goes by she doesn't message or call. She's at the end of the phone morning and night. She's brought me food, books, scarves, fruit, meals for Nigel & I just so attentive. She feels the pain I know she does. There's a sadness when I look at her. She's offered to drive me here, there and everywhere. Our friendship if possible has gone to another whole new level. She has come to the house, hugged me, sat with me, rubbed my legs. She is hurting for Nigel too, always asks after him. She knows he loves me so much. I am grateful for her friendship, I need it and I need Jill in my life. I told her today this road is going to get bumpy and to be prepared - she says she will.

TUESDAY, 7 MARCH

Pain continues to be awful nothing more I can say. The worst thing of all is having to wear my bra all the time - I hate that. It's involving a lot of bra changes for freshness. I always took my bra off at night.

Tomorrow is a massively important day in my cancer journey. I'm going to see the oncologist (the cancer doctor) another first for us. I'm nervous but equally relieved I've got to this stage. It's now eleven weeks and so much has happened. I'm not sure what to expect but perhaps I'll know the future pathway and clear direction. Right now, though two weeks after surgery it has totally floored me this time. I'm not strong enough physically anymore. Two surgeries within four weeks has taken its toll. Too much pain and too fatigued!

Saw my lovely friend Valerie today. She came down and spent some time with me. Brought me goodies the ever practical Val. I'm privileged to have her in my life.

WEDNESDAY, 8 MARCH

What is it about the eighth of each month? Eighth February was result day, worst news ever. Now eighth March I'm with the Oncologist.

Nigel & I arrived at the Cancer Centre. First time we both walked through the doors looking for Belvoir Park suite. It's a busy place. People coming and going everywhere. I checked in and waited on my turn. I met a couple we knew lady going through similar journey to me. She confirmed she was starting her treatment soon. My turn to see Oncologist.

My letter stated Dr McCarty. I have no idea man or woman!

A nurse came to get us and as we walked into the consulting room Dr McCarty was a *woman* very pleasant and personable. She explained everything in easy language going through all my results and types of treatment and what I would be needing. Not dictorial very down to earth although everything she was saying I already had read about it so made it so much easier. I also knew all my results so there was no shocks or surprises today. She said that as a Doctor she liked someone like me as a patient. I think what she meant I was well informed. I know what's going on and what's happening. I'm ready to move forward let's do *this my mantra!* Results were as follows: *Hormone Therapy* a MUST (*my cancer is hormone driven*). Radiotherapy still to be discussed and will come after chemotherapy. Chemotherapy will be happening and will give me the best chance to move on with life and a better survival chance my interpretation. Dr McCarty examined me and was happy with what she found. I need to provide some blood for testing, have a chest X-ray and a heart echo will be required before treatment starts.

She talked about pain provided a letter for some other pain relief. It was very interesting to hear her say the fact that I had been on HRT for twelve years made no difference because women exact same age as me with their ovaries would be producing same levels of Oestrogen, as me taking HRT so I was not to dwell on or consider HRT as having caused my cancer. Gosh I have worried about that and to hear this reassured me a little more.

Dr McCarty was lovely, and it was reassuring as I was now moving to a whole new set of professionals who were taking over my care.

I feel ok about it all no shocks today well except one - the treatment would be starting on twenty-first March. Oh, my goodness that's quick and I don't feel so well post-surgery. It's just been *two* weeks and I am in pain. I suppose a little scared I'll not be ready to handle chemotherapy need to be strong and well. I want to move on as quickly as possible to move this forward, so I can get better and back to living my life with some normality. I was gonna say like before my diagnosis, but I know it will never be the same again! Today mummy took me back to the hairdressers. How mad am I but I want to go more *blond* just for a little while with this new hairstyle. Yes, mad I know, but I don't care and it's my decision to have it all whacked off. My hairdresser Jill did good has cut it again much nicer than Sunday trendier cut and yes, I'm blonder and I love it!

Oh, mummy's driving makes me laugh. She thinks she's driving just fine, and I think she's all over the road and I'm holding on tight to the car seat. She pulls out of junctions so slowly I tell her off and she just ignores me says nothing keeps driving. It makes me laugh so much. She's just wonderful been so good to me and drives me mad all at the same time. I know she continues to be sad about me and doesn't cope very well with this. I think she has forgotten about all her issues whilst concentrating on me another positive. She continues to walk with me on this journey and as I move forward into the treatment stage, I'm sure she will be here.

SUNDAY, 12 MARCH

I decided when I woke up this morning, I was going to church determined to go, needed to go. I got dressed and off we went. If I'm honest I struggled with Gods word. I've needed it read my bible and I kept focused but for many weeks it's just words nothing going in nothing being digested, but I've kept reading and praying. I've listened to some Christian music, talked to God daily and prayed and prayed. And then just little rays shone through like todays verse of the day. God is so important to me, but all the words are jumbled up and fuzzy. But I keep reading for signs of support and guidance and that lets me know God is still with me.

So, whilst today I wasn't very fit to go out to church, but I needed to do it and glad I did. A bit overwhelmed when I entered church. I sat down and prayed. There was a calmness just being in Gods house. It allowed me to feel a little closer to him and I wanted to see if it would make a difference as I hadn't been since my surgeries.

I don't know but I certainly feel more content.

Nigel & I went for a little drive in the car this afternoon. It was lovely a trip down memory lane certainly for Nigel. We ended up in Forkhill, South Armagh, Northern Ireland somewhere were Nigel worked years ago. Hopefully it was not too painful for him and it was certainly nice for me to see where he had worked.

We ended our day with dinner at a nice restaurant.

I was absolutely shattered but happy.

MONDAY, 12 MARCH

Twelve weeks now.

It seems like forever so much has happened in such a short space of time three weeks through second surgery and one week away from Chemotherapy starting. My pain has decreased. I am having strange pains though and skin on my breast a bit sore. My armpit feels weird. It's totally numb, my upper arm inside and out is numb also. I continue to wear my bra 24/7 and I hate it but it's necessary yes pain more manageable the nerve pain relief meds interesting quite an experience not helped by the fact I think I took a double doze oops! It took me on a trip of relaxation to the point I felt nothing not even my legs. When Nigel arrived home, I was out of my tree.

I'm still doing my exercises daily. I want as much flexibility in my arm and chest area. I had my friend Zelda call today that was nice, a lovely distraction.

Cora my other dear friend called on Friday that was equally a lovely visit. She is such a great long time loyal friend. Very lucky to have all these people in my life. Alison Smyth from church came today bringing flowers so kind of her. So, kind of her to think about me, as she has some worries of her own. Her young son is dealing with a very serious health matter, so they are all on a journey of their own right now.

Been thinking about my review appointment with Mr Mallon next Wednesday. I have a few questions for him (no surprise there then!)

My little piece of scripture from day

"Be strong in the Lord and in his mighty Power" Ephesians 6:10

TUESDAY, 14 MARCH

What a nice day I have had.

Judy took me to the Slieve Donard Hotel in Newcastle, County Down *(beautiful hotel)* for *Afternoon Tea* just lovely. We headed off from home took a drive through my home town of Rathfriland and arrived at the hotel. It was just as beautiful as I remembered (I had my wedding reception there in 1989).

Afternoon Tea was superb such a treat and lovely conversation great company and a welcome distraction. As we drove back, we stopped at a little farm shop in Bryansford as Judy *(who loves her bees)* spotted *honey* for sale. So after a quick stop off, honey bought, and the little man who served us gave us *two duck eggs*! So, we had a dilemma, we had to get the two eggs home and we were miles away. We decided to nurse them on our laps. We laughed so much, and Judy told me if we get stopped by the police, we can say this is a *new fertility method* we are trying out.

Some nice *Grahams* ice cream ended our lovely day. It was just fantastic.

How lucky am I to have such great friends?

Oh, and I took *no* pain relief today. How good is that. Though clearly now in need of some, just not there yet with the pain.

Tomorrow I see Mr Mallon. Night night …

WEDNESDAY, 15 MARCH

I arrived at *Wing A* at Belfast City Hospital with Nigel. I've had so many appointments here. It's not so busy this morning.

Mr Mallon in Room eleven. Oh - never been in that room.

Of course my ten fifteen appointment not on time.

Hopefully not too long to wait.

Appointment went great. I had not too long to wait.

Had to strip off to the waist put on a little gown and just before Mr Mallon came in to see me Nigel said I looked *good*. I felt little emotional and tearful not sure why maybe just that this bit of the journey was ending. I would not be back in this area again *(hopefully not!)*

I can't say I have come away unscathed by this, but I've got this far.

In came Mr Mallon told me I was looking well as I patted a few tears away from my face. He said, "not happy to see me?" we had a laugh. He asked how I had been, asked to see my breast and was impressed at my wounds and how well they were healing *(good skin eh!)* I showed him a little area at the side I was concerned about. It was as I thought the end of the implant close to my arm pit and it was *normal*.

Now for my questions (I think he has got used to this when seeing me. I come armed with my piece of paper)

- Did you or pathologist find my second tumour?
- Why would all the mammograms not have picked up my two tumours?
- How long would all the cancer found have been in my breast?
- Stage of the cancer?
- Was the tumours a progression of the DCIS?
- Reviews – will I get regular check-ups?

He answered all my questions and I was more than happy with the answers. Consultation over.

My time with Mr Mallon at an end *(hopefully)*

He asked about oncology appointment and I explained it had been put back a week. He advised it would not make a difference so not to be concerned saying chemotherapy is all about *survival* and *prolonging life* for me.

The cancer has been removed it's now *belt & braces* stuff, all about stopping it returning.

It was time to say farewell to Mr Mallon.

I had bought him a little gift to acknowledge his kindness, support, courtesy and his personable delivery. What a nice man, been very attentive nothing ever a bother. Perfect gentleman. The *Belfast Health Trust* are lucky to have him.

You know sometimes I feel consultants can be so cold in their delivery and all you want and need is politeness, warmth and for them to see you as a person in turmoil not just a patient or a number. That was NOT Mr Mallon. As I hugged Mr Mallon *(probably scared the life out of him with my affection)* said "see you soon" then realised what I had said and quickly said "oh I hope not to see you again soon". We had a chuckle.

Mr Mallon – Thank you for removing all my cancer, thank you for listening to me when I told you something was going on in my chest area and I felt something wasn't just right. Thank you for creating a new boobie for me, and oh thank you for allowing me to retain my cleavage.

Goodbye Wing A.

I honestly and truly pray I never have to return.

A lot of visitors today everyone so kind, such great people. Girlies from work Kelly Anne and *awesome* Patricia. All my department colleagues had bought me a gift so thoughtful and kind. Toni came to see me too. I had Aunt Vera, Geoffrey and Meryle so many visitors for one day. I did have a few tears along the *way (never have cried as much)*. I can't help getting emotional. I am overwhelmed with kindness.

I'm feeling better. I think I have turned the corner with pain, and I think I'm doing good.

Last week I had a considerable number of visitors. They kept calling. It was hectic but just lovely the kindness and support has been quite unbelievable. I was exhausted by the end of the week.

I'm tired so very tired. I think I am recovering well physically my wounds are doing well. I continue to have severe pain in my armpit and its down my arm. It feels like everything inside my arm under the skin is way too tight like too short in the inside and when I do the exercises advised it's so painful. I'm presuming its cos of what they cut in my armpit to get the lymph nodes and remove them.

Sometimes it can take a diagnosis like cancer to bring down our walls and let people love us.

I got a lovely card today from a lovely girl from church called Claire. How kind. Some lovely comments and at the bottom it was written John 14: 27. I wasn't sure what the verse was so got out my bible and as I read it, I recognised the words;

"Peace I leave with you; my peace I give you. I do not give to you as the world gives. Do not let your hearts be troubled and do not be afraid."

I have asked God over the last twelve weeks to walk with me be close to me give me strength, give me grace. I have read his word. I have prayed. I've needed him close as I came to terms with my illness and walk this personal journey.

Visitors continue to come. Today I was been treated to *afternoon tea* here at home. My sister in law Wendy and my niece Jenna came armed with a *cake stand* full of goodies.

My mummy continues to be my housekeeper. I'm truly grateful.

TUESDAY, 21 MARCH

Today my breast care nurse Catherine Carlisle telephoned. An unexpected call but nevertheless it was pleasant and allowed me to ask a couple of questions. It was just a follow up call. What a great service and a support which I have truly valued.

THURSDAY, 23 MARCH

I had a *heart scan* at the City hospital today. The appointment was at nine. A bit crazy getting there in rush hour traffic. Cardiac ward level ten. Wasn't sure what to expect and just another test for me. They put jelly on the device and run it over the area being tested. I'm told it must take place before my chemotherapy commences as you need to have a good *'ticker'* before you start or maybe it's to check I have a *heart*! Was straightforward procedure no more than twenty minutes. A lovely pleasant girl completed the test. Clearly well informed as she appeared to know I was starting treatment for cancer. Couple of wires attached to me, few measurements taken on the machine she clicked moved the device around and chatted with me. Nigel was with me and got to watch the procedure. It was fascinating for him for both of us learning something new. At the end the girl says, "everything looks fine". She told me the results will go back to Doctor McCarty by Tuesday in fact probably be back later in the day. All over painless.

Talking of pain my arm is so painful, really bad in last four to five days where everything has gotten so tight under the skin pulling sensation. It's running down the inside of my arm. It has got worse and pain very acute so I went to the physio department at the cancer centre to see if anyone could help. I got to see a lovely physio called Joanna. She knew immediately what was wrong just by looking at my arm! She told me she could it! See what, I couldn't. Well she started to work on my arm, oh my, what pain I was shouting as she pressed and pressed on my arm - horrendous pain. I wanted to shout out loud "how much more pain do I have to endure". Joanna explained it was *cording*. What on earth is cording? *(Axillary web syndrome, also known as cording, sometimes develops as a side effect of sentinel lymph node biopsy or axillary lymph node dissection, Rope or cord like areas that develop just under the skin in the area under your arm. It may also extend partially down the arm. In very rare cases, it can extend all the way down to your wrist.)* Well whatever it is, its bloody painful!

Another appointment made to see her again next week.

I knew something wasn't right in my arm!

Nigel & I called into the Macmillan Support Centre cos my breast care nurse suggested I do so and speak to them about a *WIG*. An appointment made to discuss options. I felt a bit overwhelmed talking about wigs, and of course I'm not sure if it's something I want to consider as I move forward. I need to think about it and see what's involved.

As we left Macmillan, I suggested to Nigel we go visit a wig shop I had heard of. I wanted to look at the wigs and feel one. We went to the shop walked in and all I'm going to say is it was the *worst* experience for me. I felt the staff were unapproachable standoffish and clearly in sales mode. The woman that spoke with me asked for my name to check appointment time and I advised I didn't have one that I had been at the hospital and wanted to come see wigs and feel one. The lady told me they were *private* nothing to do with the hospital (I knew that). She told me I needed to make an appointment and the consultation fee was twenty-five pounds which is then taken off total cost of a purchase WOW! NO WARMTH or COMPASSION there! In fact the staff I felt the staff were so cold and clinical. I felt so awkward and embarrassed about being there clearly interrupting them. (they had a dog sitting on a sofa when I walked in, remember thinking that's not very hygienic with variety of women that may attend the shop). There was no offer by any of them to allow me to touch a wig or to ask me any questions. I just stepped forward and touched a long wig sitting high on a shelf.

Thus far in my journey having met so many people these three females today made me feel awful and my visit to this shop was not pleasant. It took so much courage to walk into the shop. I was so nervous. Nigel was so brave coming in with me. They did little to reassure me in fact made it worse.

As I looked round Nigel had walked out. I left the shop. When I got outside, he said, "well you'll not be buying from that shop". I had heard of the shop, my hairdresser even recommended them and offered to visit with me if I wanted to, and yet here I was in this awful situation. I feel they need to look at their approach and consider women like me walking through the door and be a little more considerate! Nigel's right, I won't be back.

Had a little away day today with my dear friend Jill. She called it our *road trip* and that's just what it was. Spent the day together and went down memory lane back at home. Some retail therapy and finished off with some ice-cream (it always helps). What a great day!

Mummy continues to clean. She has been so wonderful. A lady of her age with her own health issues, but she wants to do it and I think it helps her.

Visitors continue to drop by. Today Pauline Shields called with me, an old boss who is so amazing and very attentive. Just a delightful lady.

Another friend Claire called in. Just lovely to see her.

My niece Megan left a little gift for me today. It was a willow tree figurine called *Courage*. The message within "bringing a triumphant spirit, inspiration and courage". How kind and sweet.

MOTHERING SUNDAY

Well its Mother's Day I've had a kind of lazy day. Sun is shining brightly. I'm not sure how I feel today and I'm not even sure how to explain it. I miss Alex it's the first Mother's Day I won't see him.

My unit is NOT complete.

The boys bought me a beautiful ROSE for my garden it's called *Mum in a million Rose*. A fabulous fragrant pink colour my favourite and very apt PINK for breast cancer. I look forward to planting it in my garden. Really lovely and poignant right now.

It's the last Sunday before my treatment starts and now at a juncture in the road as I am about to start eighteen weeks of chemotherapy. I don't really know what to expect. I am aware of many ladies walking this before me and not feeling very well and feeling crap, but I must keep going.

It's peaceful at home.

Matthew at home and Nigel cooking dinner.

I did drive my car this morning as I wanted to go see mummy. She is only two miles. I did it, that's progress. A little nervous driving cos of pain in my arm but I managed slowly!

A wee call from Alex that's cheered me up. He always calls me when he's walking home from his wee part time job on a Sunday it's our special time.

Well I'm nearly there.

Chemo starts Tuesday. It's all feeling very real now next stage approaching. I'm nervous but ok. I need to have this treatment for survival.

Got to spend some time today with Shirley that was lovely.

A visit from my dear old school friends Jill and Joy. We've been friends from Primary six at school. They were twins and I loved them dearly. They came to my school at primary six and their mummy Daisy asked me to look after them and gave me *fifty pence* to do so. Forty something years later we still love each other's company. At high school we were a threesome. I always sat between them both and we had a ball. They are five days older than me and I never let them forget it. We don't see each other often enough but today was so wonderful. They are crazy chicks and I love them. Some lovely pics taken how special. I think my diagnosis has affected them both.

MONDAY, 27 MARCH - NIGHT BEFORE CHEMOTHERAPY

My dear friend Jill called earlier. Just a little visit before this new phase starts. She handed me a card and a little box a little red ring box! She had mentioned about doing something special. This was very special! I opened the box and there was a Diamond & Ruby ring. A ring Jill wants me to wear on my right hand on my third finger, an eternity ring from her to me. WOW! I was so emotional buckets of tears, and we just hugged each other what a special thing to do. I could not read the card in front of her, way too tearful and emotional we hugged again, and she left. I sat alone and read the card …

TO: My darling friend Wendy

With all my love here and to Eternity Jill X

She had written some details on the meaning of each coloured diamond. I will treasure the ring until the end of my life. Each time I wear it I will have Jill close by - four rubies and six clear diamonds,so beautiful.

It's bedtime and I'm nervous about tomorrow not sure what to expect. I'm ready physically ok some discomfort in my breast but I'm ok coping fine the pain in my arm is giving me the most bother the *cording*. Let's get this treatment under way. I'm ready. It's time, lets smash this once and for all.

I haven't cried in a few days. I mean just me crying alone. I did cry when the twins left today as they cried but I'm feeling a bit stronger think just need to do this that's me need to push on. This is gonna be tough, but I can do tough things bring it on!

In Sophie Sabbage book The Cancer Whisperer she writes;

"Grief passes through our lives like a river through mountains or the flow of blood through our veins, it is emotional oxygen as vital to our spiritual health and wellbeing as the air we breathe and the water we drink. It is our best most appropriate response to regret, loss, bereavement, hurt, privation, disappointment and change. It is the transitional bridge from the life we wanted or expected to live, to the life we are actually living the one riddled with out-of-the blue setbacks and let downs."

TUESDAY, 28 MARCH

Awake at six thirty.

Well I didn't sleep very well was nervous about today. So many thoughts not really knowing what to expect today. First day of Chemotherapy. I need to be at the city hospital for eight thirty as I'm going to see the physio about the cording in my arm before I go to Bridgewater suite. Shit the cording is so painful. Hoping she can help me. Nigel and I hit the road at seven twenty trying to beat the traffic, it's so unpredictable and I hate being late!

Got to the hospital just after eight such good time. I had my bags all sorted a lunch box for both of us so we don't go hungry as I don't know how long we will be at hospital. Some herbal tea, reading material to keep me occupied most likely a lot of waiting around to be done and of course my journal so I can keep up to date. Joanna the physio on time takes me into the room and Nigel gets to come in too so see what she's doing to my arm in case he may be able to help at home. Oh, my goodness what pain so sore *screaming sore stuff* it's awful, but with her work I felt some ease. She's says she will see me again when I'm back for cycle two of chemo.

Nigel and I arrive at the Bridgewater suite *(cancer treatment unit)* at eight forty-five. Saw the couple from Hillsborough who has been on the same journey as us.

I checked in to reception. A little nervous. It's all so new. A new location, new people moving around. I'm given a little pager device that will beep when it's my turn. We sit in the waiting area.

My pager sounds. Nigel & I walked forward. My heart beating faster. I'm greeted by a nurse. A lovely friendly face. She takes us to the *blood room*. Nigel comes in sees the surroundings and says he'll go and wait outside. It's busy so many people coming and going. I give some blood from my left arm (can't give blood from the right after the surgery) the nurse is so friendly and makes me settle down. She explains what's going to happen and that each time I come for treatment I will get my bloods taken first. That's to check all is ok with them and treatment able to go ahead. It's all straightforward no dramas. The nurse is very complimentary to me about how well I'm looking (outward images not always the true state of affairs!) how nice my figure is, my new breast through my clothing looking well. I struggle to take the compliments as I have been through so much and don't feel perhaps like I look losing my breast, scars, pain, cutting my lovely hair (my choice) The nurse weighs me and takes my height - you're wondering why? well when you get chemo treatment it's made up personally for you so all these stats are important. Doctor is waiting and takes me to the consulting room. I bring in Nigel. Again, another friendly face a lovely nurse present, her name is Hayley Lowry. She stays with me throughout the whole procedure. Doctor goes through all the formalities explains all the scary stuff! Like risks side effects and so on. Then gets me to sign consent for chemotherapy process. He turns to the nurse and says is chemo happening today?

At which I stare at them both thinking that's why I am here is it not?

The nurse says she'll go check comes back in in and says no not today WHAT? Your joking me. I have the letter saying it was twenty-eighth March. NO, it's not happening cos today is all about procedures and tests. It's only a pre-assessment that's crap. I'm so disappointed. We both are. Nigel has taken a day off work to be with me. He looks gutted I'm not getting it today. I didn't sleep last night thinking it was happening. The doctor asks to see my wounds and they were happy with what they saw. The nurse was so young and lovely Hayley was from County Tyrone. She took us to a room to discuss whole process explain things give us a tour of the suite and she was upset for us saying the delay of first cycle needs to be better explained. Pre-assessment comes first and not to build up patients hopes. It's not her fault, but I totally agree tell us this in the letter, so we know. That way it will better manage cancer patient expectations. It's a huge mental thing preparing for this day.

I had to go for an ECG of my heart. No issues all ok. Nurse advised bloods back and all good.

That's it. I'm going home. No treatment today. I am returning in the morning at ten fifteen for cycle one of chemotherapy.

I'm exhausted.

Before I go the lady, who provides the wigs to patients popped in to see me and offered to show me some of the wigs on offer. *Gosh,* I guess I should avail of the appointment with her. She's called Judy and such a lovely girl so warm and friendly.

She took Nigel and I to a private quiet room with her little suitcase. When we she opened it was full of little white boxes and yes inside them were *WIGS* lots of them. I never thought I would be looking at such things and having to decide like this. She opened the first box with what she thought would suit and you know what I was quite impressed similar style to how my hair is today cut short. It was not how I imagined it to be much better quality. She clearly had studied me up. She placed it on my head. It was a great fit, colour great and it looked ok. First one a possibility. I only tried two others on. One was not right the other quite good too, but I went back to the first one, happy with it. I said I would take it but honestly not sure if I will every use it when my hair falls out but at least I'll have it just in case, and I will be able to make the choice. It was *free.* It cost me nothing and Judy says I'm entitled to another one in September.

How good a service is that for a cancer patient.

It was a comfortable experience. I felt ok and thanked Judy for making the it bearable. Nigel was just brilliant in the room offering sound advice. He's always so calm and reassuring making me feel number one and special. Nothing ever a bother. *Love you Nigel Walker.*

So, we left with the wig in the box. It's called *Elizabeth*! That's what it says on the side of the box! All *three* of us headed home. I think she will stay in the box for a while.

It's now bedtime glad to be getting into bed. I get so tried. Slept most of afternoon away, just exhausted.

Tomorrows another day let's hope it goes to plan!

WEDNESDAY, 29 MARCH

We left home at nine for a stop off in Moira to pick up some medication from the doctors. Then off to City Hospital hopefully for cycle one.

My treatment will consist of six chemotherapy cycles of twenty-one days. I will receive three drugs on day one of the first three cycles and a new drug on day one of the last three cycles.

Arrived in good time checked in took a seat. Such a busy place. So many people sitting around people coming and going everywhere. This *cancer* is affecting a lot of people for sure!

Got my little pager again and we were called quickly this morning. Armed with my journal I was taken into the treatment area. Given a chair and Nigel got to sit with me. It was cold in the *bay* as they called it. My blood pressure and pulse taken all ok. I saw the lovely Hayley Lowry the nurse from yesterday. She told me she would see me shortly. The bay I'm in has six big reclining chairs PINK *(my favourite colour!)* all very clinical. Each chair has a television screen above it. There's one lady already in a chair. Hayley came in and told me she would be looking after me today and administering my treatment. Oh, that's so good. Her delivery and kindness so warm and important for me. She moved me to another chair so there would be more room to walk around the chair and make me more comfortable. Again, Nigel is sitting close by.

The first thing to be done is a needle needs to go into the vein in my left arm, my forearm. That's how the treatment will be given. Hayley starts the procedure but it's difficult and she can't get the needle in. She tells me its normal that's why it's good to consider a PICC line *(peripherally inserted central catheter)*. I read about the PICC last night, and not sure about it! All the practicalities and inconvenience of being in my arm for up to six months.

Hayley had to go get a colleague to try procedure as clearly not working for her this morning. She comes back with Grainne another nurse who manages to get it into the vein *bingo!* Thank goodness as it's getting painful.

They do so many checks and balances which is good to see. One is they push some saline through the needle to ensure everything working ok before moving to the chemo. I took a strange pain in my arm and then it started swelling up clearly a problem! Saline not running through vein but into my arm. Device had failed and had to come out.

I was so upset. This was proving difficult and I haven't even got started yet!

Hayley got Grainne back to try again and I felt so overwhelmed. I just started sobbing. Why was I crying? Just about everything the enormity of it all, what I'm going through and what I must still go through.

Grainne was wonderful she just stopped everything held my arm said it was good to cry and get it out. She told me that this was an enormous difficult thing happening to me, but it was for my future. She advised me that I should seriously consider the PICC one less thing to endure on each cycle.

Third attempt successful thank goodness

This was it up and going - day one of chemotherapy.

Hayley the nurse did all her checks and balances. She had another nurse with her who was a new nurse on the ward and who would be observing Hayley.

The chemotherapy drugs were in 5 syringes. The first three were huge syringes and the liquid within was red in colour. Hayley explained this was the stuff that made your hair fall out. *Just brilliant!* The fluids went through the vein smoothly didn't appear to be any dramas.

After syringe three I really needed a pee, so toilet break to be had.

The whole process of chemo going into my body took from eleven thirteen to twelve thirty-six almost one and a half hours. Hayley told me that was good reasonably fast.

I didn't feel any different as it was being administered maybe just a coldness in my arm. Syringe number four is the one that gives you the metallic taste in your mouth. I didn't experience it as I came prepared and ate a banana while it was going in. Syringe number five gives you a strange feeling in your nose like going under water and the water going into your nose. Yes, I did experience that just a little and it went after five minutes of having treatment.

I am lying on a big pink recliner chair on Wednesday twenty-nineth March having had my first cycle of chemotherapy. This starts a new chapter!

Nigel and I left the hospital and came home.

I felt very tired but nothing other than that. Mentally I was very calm and together no issues. I decided to sleep when I got in just lay down in the sunroom where it was warm and cosy. When I awoke felt headachy and just a little strange but not ill or anything. The hospital had provided lots of meds to come home with. I had some anti sickness to take. I was also given an *Oncology Advice Helpline number* in case of emergencies. They also provided a *thermometer.* Such a clever idea and great service. Very sensible to be provided with such a tool, although, I had one in medicine cupboard the boys one.

I was starting to feel more unwell very sick in my stomach. At nine I went to bed and at nine fifteen some fifteen minutes later oh boy I was sick, physically, violently sick.

Thought I'd better call the advice line!

It was a smooth operation. Got a call back within minutes from a lovely nurse. She went through a checklist with me got me to check my temperature which was thirty-five point nine. Advised to take another anti sickness and let's monitor as the hours go by.

What a night! I sat up from two to six just so very sick.

Is this it, is this what to expect? Am I going to feel this ill all the time? Shit this is crap, and I've just started chemo.

It's not getting any easier.

Temperature taken again at eight fifty. Thirty-five point nine just sitting under what's preferred as the norm. You know it's unbelievable what you learn as you walk this pathway you become so informed as I have.

Well day one over, it would need to get better!

Day two post treatment. I feel crap such a headache and sick stomach. No more projectile vomiting like last night. Temp is now sitting at thirty-six which is a slight improvement and basically normal. So tired but it's the general feeling of being unwell. I just need to keep lying down. I need to close my eyes and hope and pray when I wake up it will be ok, and I'll feel better.

Sorry my dear journal I can't talk to you. I'm too unwell I can't do anything.

Day three

Day four

Day five

SUNDAY, 2 APRIL

Day six. I got up this morning after another crap night. *HOT* flushes in abundance. Hoping today will be the day I'll feel more normal whatever normal is these days!

I haven't written anything down in days. Just could not pick up my pen just couldn't do anything. I had nothing to give physically or mentally.

This also makes me very sad but I haven't spent any time with God. No time given, no prayers. My chats to God, has stopped, how bad is that? I just can't. My bible has remained untouched. No scripture, no words, no prayers, no nothing. I can't explain it. I just couldn't do it.

Got into the shower good to have a wash. I want to just feel normal. I managed tea and toast but boy oh boy I felt sick with no real change.

The sun was shining outside. I could see my beautiful garden. It is frustrating as I can't do anything in it. I put my shoes and coat on and off I went for a walk hoping the fresh air would make me feel normal *desperate* I now am!

No, it didn't work. I couldn't even appreciate the emerging beautiful spring garden.

Now I was feeling really shit. Things not good. I know I'm not well. I kept drinking lots of water as I always be concerned about dehydration. Thought I would take my temperature as I felt shivery, sick and generally crap. My temp was thirty-four point nine. Oh my that's a bit lower than it should be! I told Nigel I needed to phone advice line at the Cancer Centre cos I don't feel well at all.

Phoned the helpline.

Again, such a quick excellent service provided. Adele Henry was the lovely nurse. She went through the checklist they use and immediately said, "Wendy you'll need to see someone", She told me she would make a couple of phone calls and get back to me which she did.

I had to go to hospital. I got upset.

Today is my beautiful boy Matthew's twenty-first birthday. That's all I could think about now, how ill I was not wanting to spoil his day, and now I must go to hospital. I had organised delivery of his birthday cake *(my sister was bringing it shortly as her lovely neighbour had baked it)*. I wanted to be in the house with him to celebrate.

My sister arrived at the door with my niece, and when Shirley saw me, she was so shocked saying I looked so bad. She kept asking me if I was going to faint *(clearly a nice sight!)* I was such a bad colour white as a ghost apparently!

Both my boys appeared to be very concerned when they looked at me. In fact, Alex my nineteen year-old sat on my knee hugged and kissed me saying it would be ok.

Nigel and I left for the hospital. I never spoke through the journey just couldn't felt so unwell. The difficulty is I don't know what is normal with this chemotherapy.

Twenty minutes later I'm in the Cancer Centre.

The nurse was waiting on me and within ten minutes I have a line into my vein in my *good arm,* bloods taken, antibiotic given, injection for sickness, x-ray for chest and abdomen and doctor was coming to speak with me.

No messing about here clearly taking no chances!

Temp still below thirty-six, blood pressure a little low but nothing crazy. I'm now lying in a little room with Nigel by my side.

I did get a spin in a wheelchair when they whizzed me off for x-ray. The corridors all very quiet and empty cos it's a Sunday.

I knew I wasn't well. I felt so awful.

I got an ice lolly as my mouth was very dry.

Then came the news. They were keeping me in hospital. I was being admitted not getting home needing to take all precautions. IV fluid going up, IV antibiotics going in. They said they need to look after me.

Please please make me feel better.

I'm not wanting to stay as it's Matthew birthday. I need to be home, but they say *no.*

You know what's bizarre, and a crazy correlation twenty-one years ago today, I was in the Jubilee Maternity Hospital which is now the new Cancer Centre building giving birth to Matthew how weird is that!

They moved me to Ward 2B in the cancer centre. I was given a single room. A big spacious room. Into bed and over the next few hours I got lots of meds.

They threw everything at me to try and fix this.

DAY SEVEN - POST CHEMO

It's Monday morning and I've woke up in Ward 2B. at the Cancer Centre. Goodness still saying those words stops me in my tracks, I've had a reasonable night all things considered. Nurse was in and out checking on me more antibiotic, more saline, sixteen hours of fluids by IV and anti-sickness in abundance.

I have had some breakfast.

Doctor came around said they would repeat my bloods and they would keep doing what they were doing and see how things are tomorrow. I feel bad lying here in hospital. My boys are at home and I totally missed Matthew's birthday yesterday. The boys and a friend are going down to our home in Spain today for a pre-planned break and a treat for Matthew. Daddy Nigel has it all sorted, everything in hand.

My energy levels are low. I have just lay and chilled, listened to some music.

I'm feeling hungry. I haven't felt hungry since last Wednesday. Nigel brought me a subway last night and I did eat it. Loved all the flavours. I'm having weird cravings!

Sickness easing not feeling as bad.

Judy came in to see me. Loved having her around.

Got some more bloods taken.

Nigel came to see me in the afternoon and physio came to see me and did some work on my arm cording. I've developed a new big cord high up on my arm. It's so painful.

Whilst Nigel with me my oncologist Dr McCarty came in to see me. We had a good chat. She went through everything I'd gone through since cycle one. Good news is my blood markers are fine which is good apparently! Dr McCarty is of the belief that the ill health is due to chemotherapy and nothing more sinister going on.

Great news in a weird kind of way. Great it's nothing more serious, but it's been crap for the last few days and how my treatment has made me this ill.

She gave me some great news by saying I could go home I asked her when? She told me now. *Wow* I'm going home. She told me I may continue to feel rough, but all would be ok, and she would give more meds to help.

I did tell her about a new *lump* I have found in my armpit. She didn't appear concerned about it. I asked about session two and what would happen. She said she didn't plan to make any real changes in respect of chemo dose but would look at anti sickness meds.

So, off home with my *sweeties* from the medicine trolley - it's working!

I've turned the corner. Gosh I'm feeling better, feeling different, feeling hungry. I've got my tastes back. Food appealing again, still craving things I haven't eaten in a while, sugar puffs, baked beans *(cold)* what's going on? Energy levels up. I'm feeling a LITTLE MORE NORMAL. I've been to the toilet without any stress that's progress too.

I got really irritated yesterday so clearly feeling more normal! A little angry over an administration blunder with my medical insurance provider. I ate the head of a guy on the telephone cos they hadn't paid my bill to my consultant.

I then fractured with mum over the washing taken from the clothes line. She had gone to put it in the hot press, and I shouted at her for taking it off the line too soon. She fusses too much and goes at a hundred miles an hour. She never said a word, just left me down the hall and went to put the kettle on. *Tea* always helps. I just need people to understand I'm ill. Please just understand this is difficult and some days I get it tough. I must be improving, clearly feeling better, as I have feelings again. I have emotions and the last three months have felt nothing.

So, to recap on week one of chemotherapy. It was *bloody awful* and by the Sunday I was on my knees so unwell. I kept hoping that each day would be better than the one just past, but it didn't come. I had no appetite, no energy, no nothing. I said to myself over and over I want to *rewind* I don't want to do this. I was scared. I thought I can't do it. How can I cope with this? I'm not gonna be able to do it and nobody understands how I'm feeling. I thought this is just the first session and it will get worse I'm sure. I didn't want to get up. I could not physically. Have had to push myself. I felt lonely.

On Friday Nigel and I had *words* the first cross words since my diagnosis. It really upset me. He said to me "you're not being active enough and I'm worried about you getting DVT (*Deep Vein Thrombosis*) or as I know it clots. The hospital had mentioned this as a risk. Well, I responded *(not so well)* by saying which *marathon* would he like me to go out and run? In fairness Nigel just didn't know how unwell I was. I was so annoyed with him with what he had said. I know he cares and worries but bad timing! He has since apologised for his comments as he clearly knows now how ill I was with a hospital admission on Sunday! He said when apologising he didn't want to lose me to a *clot* when I'm fighting a much bigger and tougher battle *cancer.*

Well I've survived cycle one and feeling more positive now. It's nice to feel a bit more normal. The sky was blue today. The sun was shining. My garden was pretty. My house felt like home again. I'm going to enjoy the next few days and not think about cycle two just yet.

It honestly scares me, but I must keep going.

Week two of cycle one and I feel much better. Got to go out into the garden with Nigel and potter around. Have a little more energy but still very tired and do need naps but just feel better. I am delighted about that and give thanks to God.

On reflection side effects from cycle one were sickness (including vomiting) low temp, shivery, diarrhoea, headache, tiredness, sore gums, loss of appetite, foods having no flavour.

It's so good to want to get out of bed, get up and face the day, eat breakfast. To do little chores around the house. I had been constipated for weeks and weeks and weeks. I am now not taking any pain relief or laxatives and able to go to the loo.

Week three post chemo continued much like week two. A good week well a better week. I do get very tired and really feel effects of dehydration. I'm drinking lots of water otherwise I get a stinking headache.

TUESDAY, 11 APRIL

Tonight Nigel & I were chilling together and as I lay on the sofa with my legs across him, he turned to look at me and I saw a strange expression on his face. It made me sad the way he looked at me it was one of those moments I saw something in his face, and I started to cry. I couldn't speak, and he kept asking me what was wrong, and I needed to tell him. I spoke through my tears saying I just seen in his face pity towards me it was so clear. He said straight back "it isn't pity". He doesn't pity me. He feels sorry and sad about what I am going through. Oh,I get that I could see it in him. I know him so well and we have been together for so long. He is my life I know him, I get him. The conversation then went on to one of *survival* me surviving cancer. What will the future be for us both.?

WEDNESDAY, 12 APRIL - LOSING MY HAIR

"Your hair the gown you never take off, it speaks for you every day, your mood maker"

Day fifteen of cycle one. I have just put my hand into my hair at the back of my head, the nape of my neck and a handful of hair has come away.

Oh, my goodness it's happening.

It's really happening my hair is falling out.

In disbelief I ran both my hands through my hair and yes, it is. My beautiful treasured amazing hair that I always loved, that so many people for years spoke about is falling out. Day fifteen boy that was quick! I have known that my hair would go with my treatment. I talked about it to others. I've read enough literature to know it would go. I prepared myself by having it cut from long to short. It took fifteen days from they gave me those *red* syringes of chemo. My lovely nurse who administered the first cycle of chemo said, "this is the one that makes your hair fall out" Look, it's still such a shock even though you know it's coming it's now *real*. I said all along I would go with it. It's part of this process to give me the best chance of survival of getting through cancer and becoming well again. I'm now thinking how's this gonna work. How fast will it go from my head? Is it going to be patchy or thinner until there's none? I just don't know? how do I manage it disappearing?

THURSDAY, 13 APRIL

I awoke this morning expecting all my hair to be lying on the pillow but no it hasn't happened, in fact only a couple of hairs on my pillow. As I run my fingers through my hair, it is coming away in my hands. It's coming away from all over my head now. Last night my head, my scalp became very sore to the touch, weird sensation, quite painful when I touch it. I guess another side effect! Over the last week the texture of my hair changed just hasn't felt the same and it's not as bright and shiny. Alex said to me a couple of days ago it has lost its brightness. There's a lot dropping out today.

Spent a couple of hours with Jill and Katie lovely distraction.

FRIDAY, 14 APRIL

I awoke to such pain in my scalp bloody nightmare! So very sore to the touch. I can't believe this new pain. No one told me about this or warned me that my scalp would hurt. It's painful to put my head on the pillow or a cushion. Oh, my days it's awful coping with this as well as hair falling out. My hair is dropping everywhere. I'm casting, hair falling over the floor, sofa, everywhere not easy to watch. My beautiful hair well actually no this is not my hair. It's getting unrecognisable texture changed. It's not *Wendy's* hair anymore.

Each day brings something new. How bad is this gonna get?

SATURDAY, 15 APRIL

My hair continues to drop out. Today I have a bald spot developing right at the front where my parting starts. It looks so bad. Hair everywhere in the house hoover is in overdrive! I've had to hoover the bed each morning. Thankfully staying at my side and not annoying Nigel. He has been wonderful about my hair loss just like my breast he says "its only hair Wendy it doesn't change you", how sweet is that. He has offered to shave it off. Even my beautiful Alex has said "shave it off mummy" the intelligent reasoned Alex has said to me "'you know mummy it's clear your chemo is working as your hair is dying off its killing the hair cells so it will be working on any cancer killing it too". He's a wee gem.

I have been thinking today about my hairdresser Jill wondering what she would think of my "big hair" now going, and bizarrely I got a text from her offering to come around next week and do whatever is required. What about that!

SUNDAY, 16 APRIL - EASTER SUNDAY

Today's Bible verse of the day

I am the Resurrection and the life John 11:25

Today's prayer:

Lord may my eyes only look at things that light up the inside. Fill me today with your Holy Spirit. May my heart be filled with generosity, justice and the love of God.

I do give thanks for this great day.

However, I have awakened to find so much hair on my pillow and all over my pyjamas it's awful. I feel rotten. This is so bad, and my scalp is so painful the only thing keeping me sane this morning is that Alex said last night for me to google *sore scalp whilst on chemotherapy* doh! Why didn't I think of that? Well brain not working can't deal with logical thinking. I'm normally very in control. Not right now.

So, getting back to googling the phrase yes of course. Oh, my goodness I'm not a freak lots of ladies on a forum speaking about sore scalps its normal! Whoopee. I'm not so different. Ladies saying the pain started for them at days twelve and fourteen for me day fifteen. How these ladies coped and their solution was for them to shave their remaining hair off and it gave them relief *REALLY*! You know it's unbelievable what you can find on the Internet. *(I would say always be careful where you read from and when researching about cancer stick to safe reputable sites.)* This reassures me. The option to shave of my hair is becoming very real. As I sip my tea and I fear moving in the chair as hair is dropping everywhere, Nigel is looking at me feeling so sorry for me and he again says, "I'll shave it off if you want me to". That's a big thing for your husband to say its huge! But he takes it all in his stride. Having earlier looked in the mirror I see it's not a good look could not be much worse well maybe it could! I got up went to the bathroom looked in the mirror took a picture of myself horrible to see. That was it. Time to do it. Time to shave my hair off. One of the most difficult things I've decided. Though it will never surpass losing my right breast the biggest of all, but this next step is huge.

Nigel got out the razor prepared a seating area in the dressing room for me. I stripped off totally naked and took a seat. I was so cold not sure if it was how I was feeling or the trepidation of what was about to happen. Nigel stood behind me and asked if I was ready.

He started. I began to cry and cry.

I sat there feeling so vulnerable, so sad, weird feelings like I was being cleansed. It immediately made me think of those people in days gone by in refugee camps having their heads shaved just cause. Nigel did call me his *GI Wendy*. I was so cold he wrapped me in a towel, and I watched my hair fall to the floor so much hair but not my normal hair. Nigel gave me a clean cotton handkerchief as I continued to cry and needed to blow my nose.

There was a couple of funny moments amid this madness and we did have a chuckle. I said, "Love is...when you are married twenty-eight years and your husband is shaving your head giving you a number two all over." He told me I had a scar on my head. A scar where? And awh yes, I remember. My brother Cecil throwing a hair brush at me when I was like twelve and splitting my head open. Blood went everywhere all over my nice clean school uniform *(mum was so angry with him)*. Thanks Cecil.

Nigel then says "it's unbelievable you have such a lovely shape of head so perfect with no hair." Aye right! He's just being kind but no kept saying my head was such a great shape. "You are beautiful". All the right things said at all the right times eh! I know he loves me dearly. It took forty minutes and I was sporting a new look. I ran my hands over my head it felt prickly but neat all very tidy. I had to go look in the mirror. I knew it would be tough to do so. As my hair was being shaved off my scalp was so painful. Nigel could see what was going on with my scalp. He was able to touch it and ask me if it was painful in different locations. Oh yes its painful. I asked what he was seeing. He described my scalp as very red in colour where I was experiencing the pain and very swollen and raised clearly inflamed. It honestly was so painful. I hadn't slept properly for two days cos of the pain.

All my hair lay on the floor.

I went to the bathroom and stopped to look in the mirror. Oh my days my hair is gone. I wasn't devastated more relieved, strange viewing me almost bald but not quite this little bit of hair left. Nigel's right my head shape is good in fact totally proportionate every cloud eh!

I showered and let the hot water pour over me used some medicated cream on my scalp and it felt so good. It still hurt but not just as much. I know the online forum talked about *inflamed follicles* and *hair weight* causing the pain.

I totally related to that.

Nigel removed a few more straggles always the perfectionist! Job done. Hair removed no more nonsense. One less thing to worry about, and it won't distract me.

The cording, the pain in my breast and preparing for cycle two, that's enough to be getting on with. I'm sad I've lost my hair some say its brave, but it's not brave, it just dealing with all the things and the conditions that comes with having cancer and treatment. You know 'short term pain for long term gain'. I've coped fine with hair gone. It's funny I've said to the boys I look like Kojak of course they have no idea who I mean way too young to remember him! My head gets very cold. I'm wearing a bright pink beanie that Nigel bought me. The stubble on my head continues to fall out. Nigel keeps saying I have this perfect head for no hair.

My sister and my lovely niece Zoe called to see me. I don't think they were too shocked told me I suited no hair I had the perfect shape head really, where have I heard that before! I think they are all just being kind although maybe not as they all would just be *very* honest whether I like it or not. Alex will certainly just tell you how it is!

I have gone out into the garden and pottered around since the shaving. Beanie on beanie off hot then cold. Little anxious as I don't want to get a cold.

When I look in the mirror, I still see Wendy she's still there. I think looking a little older, but I have also lost a lot of weight so that might have something to do with it.

I am wondering if my hair will ever grow back and what will it be like if it does. What texture it will be, what colour will it be? You know there is so much more important stuff than my hair.

I want to do so much with Nigel. I have so many plans and we want to travel. I pray to God it can happen. I want to see our boys progressing in their lives. Nigel and me growing old together.

My scalp pain has eased greatly so much better still tender in some places but much better thank goodness. What has been astonishing was the speed my hair fell out. It was rapid once it started at day fifteen. You need to be prepared but its ok honestly it is. My mother in law said it wasn't my hair when she seen me the other evening. She saw a bald spot and had never seen my hair looking like that so there its best it's gone. I look healthier without it wasn't a good look!

TUESDAY, 18 APRIL

I got a card today from my dear friend Valerie who has been wonderful to me these last four months a true friend indeed a constant! Today's card was so lovely.

I got so many cards over the last four months. I have put all my cards in a box just as I was about to start chemotherapy. For me, the end of one chapter, and the start of another. Important for me to put them away right now for the mind and soul. was running out of space for them. Those cards clearly showed the shock experienced by those who sent them along with such support. I will never forget those people who did so. You know who you are and so do I. You've helped me get this far. Today's card from Valerie said; *'It takes a long time to grow an old friend!'* What wonderful true words with a very personal message inside but on the back was this little verse

'Life should NOT be a journey to the grave with the intention of arriving safely in an attractive and well-preserved body but rather to skid in sideways chocolate in one hand wine in the other totally worn out and screaming. Woo Hooooooo what a ride! I wanna go around again! Anon

What a lovely friend to have. How lucky am I. What fab words how true. I suppose though for me I think of life as much more spiritual and my love for God knowing one day, I'm off to a better place with eternal life … the light will never be switched off.

Went out today with mummy and Shirley first day going out in public with NO hair (I still have a little stubble) I also put some make up on. My friend Jill had bought me a piece of headgear a lovely floral bandana, so I matched a jacket with it (of course must match) and off we went. My sister said 'shit you look well, she said no matter what way you are you've no hair and you look great' how sweet of her to say that. You know what NOT ONE member of the public did I catch staring at me not one. No one turned to look no gasps no shockers. I was just another shopper. I blended in just fine. I felt ok too. I did look at people to see if they stared back but nothing. I wanted to gauge their reactions not one! A bit of me wants to have nothing on my head no hiding away just be who I am right now. I've no hair get over it who gives a dam!

A few callers since Sunday have now seen me without my tresses mixed bag of reactions! My sister in law Wendy who I have honestly never seen cry got very emotional when I removed my beanie in the kitchen. She was visibly upset could not speak for a few moments and hugged me tightly. She doesn't normally do hugs, but did today. Others reacted by giving me a hug saying I looked well. Others said I had perfect shape of head for no hair! That makes me laugh when they say that. I guess some people have crazy shapes of heads and it might be wacky just to see them bald. Everyone is starting to ask me about *WIGS*.

Am I going to have one? what am I going to do?

I'm not sure if I want to wear a wig. I know I'm starting to look like an alien as I'm bald but wearing a wig for me seems a bit dishonest in a way. I am not ashamed of how I look that's who I am right now. I've never wanted the *sympathy vote* or a feeling that people feel sorry for me No one needs to cos I don't feel sorry for me so don't expect anyone else too!

I opened the door today to Jill the half of Jill & Joy with such a bunch of tulips some chocolates *naughty* and strawberries along with a heavy *COLD*. She said "I can't come in cos I've got this cold" and I say "yes you can't come in with that cold cos I don't want it".

I couldn't even hug or kiss her. We stand six feet apart. She just wanted to see me before session two. How kind of dear Jill. I'm annoyed we can't spend time together, but I really don't want her cold as it might delay my next cycle of treatment. Our chat ended on the doorstep. We will have to wait until another day - Thank you my dear friend x.

Cycle two is getting close and I'm apprehensive about this treatment. I've settled now on having a PICC line *(Peripherally Inserted Central Catheter)* inserted for ease of getting treatment. I just can't go through process each time of finding a vein and I'm worried about having none left worth anything. It is a thin soft long wire that will be inserted and positioned in a large vein that carries blood to the heart. It will be used to give me my treatment and will stay in place until the treatment is completed. It is given using a local anaesthetic. They use a scanning machine to do it and then a chest X-ray to make sure it's in the right place. So that's what I'm going to have done next week It's not getting the treatment that's making me anxious it's the feeling afterwards let's pray it will be better.

THURSDAY, 20 APRIL

I rang the hospital to check if my session two will go ahead on Tuesday twenty fifth Just a bit concerned it will be like last time and delayed to day after. They confirmed it's happening on Tuesday *good news*. Arrangements firmed up about getting PICC in at eleven after my pre-assessment on Tuesday. It will be a long day but good to get it all done on one day. Nigel able to be with me - MY ROCK.

MONDAY, 24 APRIL

A bit sad today. Alex returns to University and I have so loved having him at home. I've felt ok and been able to do some normal stuff. My arm is very painful. I see physio tomorrow. I'm sporting my new hair style *(no hair)*. *T*he stubble is going fast but so has the scalp pain.

On Saturday past I went to Hillsborough with mummy to a little shop called the Cheshire Cat. I had been told they sold headscarves. They did and I bought three. Well a girl needs to be trendy!

TUESDAY, 25 APRIL - CYCLE TWO

I awoke at six twenty. A little before my alarm. Said a little prayer and went for a shower. Didn't have any feelings this morning. I'm ready for cycle two.

We left home at seven twenty and got to hospital in good time. Booked into the Bridgewater suite and given my little pager. Spoke to the girl who I see on each visit. We have a catch up. It appears she has had a rough Post cycle one too! I was a bit surprised she still had her hair. She was wearing a hat with long straggly strands hanging from it. She's holding onto it doesn't want to let go. Her hair is very important to her. I don't care and have no issues about mine. I think I'm healthier looking without my hair.

Pager goes.

I'm off for bloods, they weigh and measure my height. I've got this routine now!

I have put a few pounds on but heh ho I don't care have been eating lots in latter stage of cycle one.

Back in waiting area.

I had worn my little beanie hat this morning. I would prefer to wear nothing, but I am sensitive to those around me not wanting to upset anyone although this is about me and not others. I took it off when chatting to the girl I knew, and she said you have a great shape of head *(not the 1st person to say that!)* I put it back on then told Nigel I wish I could just take it off. He told me to and reminded me we were in the *cancer centre* all very normal. So, I just pulled if off he turned to me and said, "your beautiful" and "I am so proud of you". Honestly, I am so ok with my baldness.

Got called to see the Doctor. It wasn't Dr McCarty. It was a female foreign lady think maybe Spanish. *Hola!* I had been sitting a while with her and she told me they didn't have my notes. "What do you mean you don't have my notes?" "Where are they?" They don't know might be something to do with my admission to Cancer Centre after cycle one and notes not back where they should be. *Brilliant!* She went through health check, told me blood markers all good, sounded my chest no issues and advised chemo would go ahead today *hooray.* I told her about the lump in my armpit and how it concerns me a little. She examined me. She stated she would arrange an ultra sound *(not today but another date).* I asked about anti sickness due to horrible effects of Cycle one. She stated they would be providing more anti sickness in the days following cycle two.

Off now to have the PICC line procedure completed.

Met two lovely nurses called Janine and Mary. They explained the procedure told me it was straightforward and it will take twenty minutes.

Oh, my goodness NOTHING straightforward for me one of the nurses was in training learning how to complete PICC insertions. It took an age and had to be restarted. I had a *hot* flush in the middle of the whole process whilst lying on the bed. I did panic as I lay there thinking oh, I hope they don't pierce my vein, and is this going to work but *BINGO* procedure finished. I was sweating on the inside and calm exterior. Look I know people must learn new procedures but why me today? They were lovely and very apologetic for my procedure which took forty-five minutes! I was the guinea pig for the nurse.

I was provided with sleeves to put over PICC when showering and a pack of dressings *(it has been inserted into my upper left arm.)*

Back to Bridgewater with my notes. Advised chemo will be at three and I could go have lunch. I have my physio at two thirty, that's good all perfect timing. I had made a packed lunch for us both so went and had lunch. I so want to have plenty in my tummy, so I don't feel sick. Seen Joanna my physio my arm is still very painful, the cording still there and really annoying me although my movement in the arm is better. I showed her the two lumps that had appeared on my arm. She's unaware what they are. She did some stretching advising me to add ice to the lumps, go gentler on my arm exercises and she'll see me again in a couple of weeks. She assures me this will get better in time. Oh, I want relief from it, would be one less thing to have to deal with.

Back to Bridgewater for my chemo. It's taking an age to be called and I am so tired been a long day and Nigel has nodded off beside me he's exhausted. He's so supportive and a constant in my life, but I know he gets tired.

I'm thinking again about the PICC line procedure earlier and had a quiet chuckle to myself. As I was hooked to the ultra-scan machine, the monitor makes a sound. I look and see it has a line running across it as it detects what's going on next thing it *flat lines* out. Now when I watch Casualty on the TV once the machines flat lines, they call the time of death! Oh my please no. Mary the nurse says, "I think we will turn that off and on again don't listen to it". Hard NOT too!

Three forty-five I get called to the treatment room cycle two is almost underway.

NOPE they just want to give me a new anti-sickness drug and another one hour before chemo starts. Back to the waiting area. Four forty-five called forward for treatment.

Into the big *pink* chair, reclined back. I'm a little nervous about the PICC line, will it work?

The bay is busy with three other ladies already there. My obs completed.

Blood pressure taken over where my PICC line is attached and I get them to stop it as it's too painful. I think it was just tender due to all the fuss getting it in. Moved down the arm and retaken. No issues all good to go. The nurse today was called Victoria Campbell. What a beautiful nurse she turned out to be, warm, courteous, friendly explained everything as she went along. We chatted lots. All meds given PICC line working perfectly. Continued with all the checks and balances which is very reassuring. At five cycle 2 started and at five thirty-seven completed WOW! That was quick. Thirty-seven minutes. Unbelievable! That's because of the PICC line *(really recommend it cycle one took one and a half hours)*. NO pain or discomfort worked well. Five syringes in. That was it, ready for home. I get my bag of meds and we were good to go. What along day it has been for both of us.

This evening has gone okay. I am tired but NO vomiting. A little anxious as I'm waiting for what happened after last cycle.

I am now comfortable on my sofa in the sunroom wrapped up in my big blanket mum gave me. I am drinking lots of water. I have just told Nigel if I fall asleep soundly to leave me there.

WEDNESDAY, 26 APRIL

Reasonable night. Slept on the sofa. Had everything close by including my *sick bucket* just in case, but I didn't need it. Had lots of meds to take. Felt a little nauseous. They gave me a new drug in my bags of meds yesterday. It's new stuff and Victoria the nurse said it's an expensive drug and not everyone is prescribed it. Glad I did! I'm on three anti-sickness along with steroids for a couple of days and taking pain relief for headaches.

Very tired and just going to sleep. Rest and listen to my body.

Keeping a check on all side effects. Have told everyone I just want to be alone for next wee while to see how cycle two goes.

Day going ok no vomiting. Face swollen and high coloured *(steroids)*. Drinking lots of water, eaten a little and taste buds ok right now. Taking anti sickness and nervous this sickness gonna start like last time.

Tired gonna sleep.

THURSDAY, 27 APRIL

Another reasonable night. Again, slept on the sofa. When I take my evening meds, I fall into a sound sleep, so don't want disturbed. I'm left where I am sleeping cos, I'm comfortable. I've been peeing lots and lots and me staying in the sunroom allows Nigel to get some unbroken sleep.

No vomiting! perhaps now not going to happen. Meds working, I think! Temp is up and down. Thirty-six then thirty-five keeping an eye on it. My PICC line is ok not giving me any bother. A bit inconvenient having a shower need to keep it dry wearing the sleeve along with some cling film.

Tired and sleeping lots.

Today was ok thankfully sickness not severe.

FRIDAY, 28 APRIL

Not able to formulate words to tell you how I am feeling. It's so bad I would scare you best not to know!

SATURDAY, 29 APRIL

Got a surprise this morning doorbell rang at eight thirty and there on the doorstep was my number one son Matthew. He flew home from Edinburgh as a surprise how lovely! Will be nice having him in the house for the weekend, although I'm not in great shape there will be no partying for sure! This was also the first time he saw me with *NO HAIR* he appeared ok with it. I just carried on as normal exposing my baldness not covering it up accepting it. Matthew just said, "I'm sorry mummy" and went on to say he hadn't coped well with me losing my hair and how sick I am. He's not sure what to say or how to handle it. He struggles a bit hearing about procedures. I think PICC line is an issue for him doesn't like stuff like that. It's hard for my boys I know. I wish I didn't have to expose them to such difficult matters.

SUNDAY, 30 APRIL

All sickness meds now taken. They certainly helped and made a difference from cycle one. Today was bad. I felt rotten. Crazy side effects like a strange feeling in my head. As I bend down strange feeling in my throat like full feeling. Pain in my left leg. A little sick but not bad just feel shit really. Didn't sleep well exhausted. The whole day totally wiped out tough when you feel so out of sorts.

Lots of people are messaging who are so kind but I haven't been able to respond. I've nothing good to say right now. I don't want to be a bother to anyone. This is gonna be a long road. I want everyone just to get on with their lives not to worry about me.

Oh, got a message that has annoyed me just a little irritating. It came from someone who has been very kind to me over the last few months but their message a little insensitive. They said they had seen a photo Nigel sent them it was me at session two sporting no hair or lack of it! They said I looked good and in the next sentence said "Get the wig you'll be good and don't worry" now what the heck does that mean? Obviously, I don't look good when I need to get the wig! Everyone will know I've made the decision about wigs. My views are for me it would just be like dishonest in that not the real me and I don't want to be someone I'm not right now. Poor Nigel felt so bad when I shared message with him. He said, "Wendy I can't help people's insensitivities what can I say." Clearly not a great message to send to someone. I wouldn't dare say such a thing but then you need to walk this path to fully understand what's involved!

MONDAY, 1 MAY

My scripture today was

"So do not fear for I am with you, do not dismayed for I am your God. I will strengthen you and help you. I will uphold you with my righteous right hand." Isaiah 41:10

WEDNESDAY, 3 MAY

Yesterday saw the introduction of the District Nurse making a visit. A lovely nurse called Felicity. She will visit each Monday to deal with the PICC line.

We are calling her 'Pippa the PICC' It needs cleaning each week. So glad to see the nurse as the PICC is annoying me a little. I don't how bad my arm is under the bandaging after the experience of getting it in. It is very bruised that I can see and certainly needs cleaning. I had a lot of questions to answer as Felicity prepared my new file. Got it all cleaned and flushed, and all was ok. Although I was more aware of it and it irritated a bit during the day. Just think I need to get used to it.

Got to sit out in the garden on a chair for a little while today. It was just lovely. I have absolutely no energy. My appetite is good, but I am craving BAD foods. I think its stuff I want to put in my tummy, so I don't feel sick. Ah yes, it came again I needed ice cream yes ice cream, so Nigel took me to my favourite ice cream shop Grahams to have one of their lovely cones. It was delicious. So nice. Helped my sore mouth, gums and bottom lip which is swollen. Nigel reminded me that exactly 4 weeks ago same day I needed ice cream. Crazy cravings. I watched a movie late into the night in bed thinking I wouldn't sleep but I did and got 5 hours. Woke today feeling much improved first good day where I felt more normal so pleased the first in a week. I was able to do some small tasks around the house which was wonderful too. Mum came out bringing ICE CREAM and ice lollies so kind. She had heard me say I needed ice cream so came armed! Had a lovely afternoon with mummy and she did some bits around the house for me. I took a little walk on the road not far though cos I have absolutely no energy but something I needed to try. It's been a tough week whilst sickness not as bad I still felt awful very tough. I'm on my knees so low so many things to deal with side effects new things like pain in my left leg, strange feeling in my throat, tiredness constipation, diarrhoea, sick BUT I've survived cycle two yippee. A third of the way through now well nearly.

Not pleasant no point glossing it up. It's a tough road but you gotta walk it, strips you right back makes you nervous thinking can you do it?

I MUST and I want to get back living with my family.

THURSDAY, 4 MAY

Have awoke having not too bad a night on the sleep front.

Went to bed don't know how to explain it. A little LOW, feeling down, apprehensive annoyed why are you asking? I have an appointment today back at the breast clinic with Mr Mallon. Why you're asking? Well during my Oncologist assessment at cycle two they asked if I had any health issues and I mentioned my concern about a lump under my arm in my right armpit. I think it's all to do with post-surgery maybe scar tissue or something like that but it's annoying me. I can feel it every time I move and there is clearly so much going on in my breast and armpit areas that it's hard to separate all the pains and issues. The Oncologist wants it checked and has referred me for a scan, and I now have an appointment with Mr Mallon so they obviously want the breast team to look at it again. I had truly hoped I would never have to see him again other than for yearly check-ups, so it makes me sad and stirs up emotions. Anyway, it's a positive that the health system is really looking after me and I'm truly grateful. So yes went to bed with that on my mind, and I am also annoyed as my new breast is changing since surgery, which I totally expect and get. It needs to settle and there's clearly scar tissue at the scar in my armpit as its extremely tight and pulling which is changing the shape of my breast it's like distorting the shape. Look I know it's not going to be perfect, but it stills annoys me.

Jill came to get me as she was taking me to the appointment today. This is the first one that Nigel is not coming with me, but I'm ok about that as I don't feel he needs to. I was very emotional when Jill arrived just a build of everything. I showed her my breast hoping it wouldn't shock her. Not a bother to Jill never flinched and she thought my new boob looked good and to remember it was early days for recovery. I know that too.

We arrived at the city hospital and back to Wing A flash backs for sure so much has happened since December and here I was back again. My appt was for one forty-five and I got called quite quickly. Jill came in with me and I was worried about her coming in as I know she worries a lot and gets upset when things are affecting me. Mr Mallon came in. I told him I had hoped I wouldn't see him again. He said I was looking well asked how I was doing, and he was aware of my referral and why I was there. A *lump* in my armpit! I got undressed and he examined me and without me even having to identify where I had found the lump, he was able to put his fingers right on it and boy oh boy it was painful. He checked my breast and how the implant was sitting at the side of my armpit. All normal and that everything would still be healing, settling and recovering.

Back to the *lump* Mr Mallon advised it could be a *Seroma* but that a scan would confirm this. He did briefly mention lymph nodes and maybe one raised but a scan would confirm everything. So off I went to the X-ray department. I know the process so well now into the cubicle, strip off to the waist, put the gown on and into the waiting area.

In the treatment room a lovely male consultant radiographer came to see me introductions and pleasantries. He asked me to identify where I had found the lump. He put the scanning probe onto my armpit, and he watched the screen. I'm lying on the bed nervous and thinking "I can't be here again" He says I don't see anything then he moved the probe. I felt him on it at this point and then he confirmed, "Oh yes I see it I see it" My heart missed a beat. He had found something this was real! I knew there was something in my armpit. He pressed a few buttons and then said "that's a Cyst". I said "what?" He said a "Cyst or a Seroma." Oh really! Mr Mallon mentioned that word a short time ago. I asked what a Seroma was?

An area filled with fluid and can happen after this type of surgery.
I said, "what type of fluid blood or clear?" he said, "a mixture." He
then just calmly says ok I'm gonna drain it – like what your gonna
drain it right now like here, like here now? He said he was gonna
drain it with a needle syringe and he had it in his hand says you will
feel a little prick indeed I did! NO pain relief just straight in and
within seconds he says that's it. I asked if he had got something,
he told me he had and showed me the syringe. There was a
considerable amount of fluid *straw* like colour. I couldn't believe it.
It all happened so fast. He said that's it, but it could need draining
again as it can refill. All over RESULT and a much better one than
I was expecting. Got dressed and back over to see Mr Mallon. I
came out of the department and Jill just looked at me. I told her I
had got the lump drained. I told her what had happened, and she just
looked at me and me at her. Jill came in with me to the consultation
with Mr Mallon. He confirmed it was a *seroma* and *straw like liquid*
was removed no *infection* and all good. He did say it might happen
again, to keep an eye on it and speak to GP if necessary and they
would bring me back. To look out for swelling of arm and pain. I
shook his hand and thanked him before leaving just before I left the
room, he said to me "you are doing well, your eyes are very bright
you're doing well" he just gave me a look, a real reassuring look,
positive look - so nice. I guess he saw something in my eyes. I'm
assuming the brightness in my eyes the white of the eyes are clear
maybe that's a sign!

I told him it wasn't easy this journey was tough he said he
understood. I also told him that I was sporting a new look and
pointed to my head he said, "it's only temporary". There that
was ok. I was nervous about today and what would develop. It
did concern me that something was not right and again proves I
do know my body. I can tell when something is just not right.
You know there is so much to cope with. Obstacles continue to be
thrown at me, but I'm ok. I can do this. It's bloody tough but I can
do tough things, strips you of everything you need to be strong,
weakness will tear you down. You need to keep positive push on,
ups and downs rough and smooth but this is all about me and my

life. I'm fifty years old so much more I want to do in my life. I have a *bucket list*. I want to work down that list, live life, laugh lots, be happy, spend time with my loved ones - so bring it on.

I spent the rest of the day with Jill. A lovely day finishing off with another naughty ice cream! Jill looked tired at the end of the day. I think it was tough for her being with me she feels my pain. I was tired too very tired - an emotional day as you just don't know what results are gonna bring. This time nothing serious.

I continue to feel a little better post chemo cycle. I'm tired. PICC line really annoying me but things better than last week.

SATURDAY, 6 MAY

Today Nigel and I had a wonderful day together. I'm feeling ok better than last week, but I know it's only temporary as I prepare for Cycle three which I have trepidation about but it's just cos I feel so ill after each treatment and spend a full week on my knees.

Anyway, today we went to a lovely garden centre. I bought a tree a little more expensive than I would normally pay for a tree, but this was going to be a special tree. A copper beech with a spectacular peculiar design. We decided it was going to be known as my *chemo tree* and we would plant it in a special place in our lovely beautiful garden. God willing I'll be around to watch it grow and develop for years to come with only good memories.

SUNDAY, 7 MAY

I had an amazing day Nigel and I had planned to go for a drive in the car just the two of us. I had suggested Donegal in Southern Ireland. We headed off at nine. It was a glorious day made even more special cos the weather was amazing sunshine all the way. Nigel had suggested we pack an overnight bag and maybe stay over somewhere, but I put a spanner in the works saying the District Nurse calls on a Monday to refresh my PICC line drat - that plan scuppered. Well what a wonderful day we had. Lunch in a little cliff top restaurant, the *Gaslight Inn* in Rossnowlagh looking out across Donegal Bay. I did well, felt ok apart from a pain that had developed in my left arm. Had it now for a few days just another drama! I took some pain relief, but it just doesn't feel right its swollen and painful lower part of arm. I think its related to my first cycle of chemo which was given through a cannula into my vein in lower left arm. The pain runs down the arm in a direct line like where the vein is which took the liquids on cycle one. I would say my poor vein didn't like that bad stuff!

Anyway, a wonderful day we spent together making memories. I was so tired when I got home but it was so worth it … thank you Nigel x

MONDAY, 8 MAY

Awoke today feeling ok still improving. District nurse due to call. I'm planning to go out into garden today not able to do anything but just to be outside will be wonderful. I direct operations the forewoman! Still have this silly pain in my left arm swollen and painful. PICC line has annoyed me all week irritating me, but it is not infected just annoying! This last week I've felt very emotional and cried a little more. Not sure why I feel positive and fighting hard but just get tearful when we speak about stuff. Just can be normal family stuff and I just well up.

Oh, my days! Another drama my district nurse Felicity arrived dealt with my PICC line. I showed her my arm and how sore and swollen it was. She could see the way it was and said to me she was a little concerned. She suggested I contact the Oncology advice line and speak to them about it. Felicity mentioned a CLOT and that my arm needs checking. *SHIT* a *CLOT*, it's only a sore arm its cos of my chemo I kept saying, but now worried as the nurse is worried! I hadn't panicked about the pain since I took it but maybe I should be panicking now! I rang the advice line spoke to lovely nurse Eve, told her my issues and the concerns the district nurse had. She listened attentively re-assuring me saying it sounds like what I was thinking it was the vein in my arm not liking the chemo its known as *tracking*, but she would speak with the doctor and call me back. Within minutes a call back saying doctor wanted to see me at the Bridgewater suite to check me out. *Crap* here I go again a trip to the hospital. Nigel's day in the garden ended abruptly. He wouldn't let me go alone to hospital. Arrived at Bridgewater checked in and very quickly my little pager went off, time to see the doc. I bumped into a lovely girl who had been in hospital having surgery same time as me. We had a quick catch up. She's starting her treatment tomorrow.

Saw a lovely doctor called Ronan McLaughlin and a lovely nurse Grace Dowds. He examined me and was satisfied it wasn't a *clot* but concurred it was as I believed the vein in my arm just hadn't liked the chemo going through it and now reacting. No scan required he was happy. I was *happy*. Advised to use a heat pack and given some hydrocortisone to put on the arm around the pain. This word CLOT unnerves me don't like it being talked about.

Another trip to hospital over. Hospital team were wonderful again. They reassured me and made me calm. Thank you to the medical team.

SUNDAY, 14 MAY

My last week was good after my trip to the hospital. I'm certainly feeling more human and normal still having issues with the cording in my right arm have been back seeing physio Joanna and she worked on my arm. She said the fact I got seroma drained might give me some relief with the cording. I agree it's a little less painful in upper arm but lower arm a nightmare so painful so tight. Joanna provided me with a new bra, a compression bra quite a piece of kit! High sides that will help the area in armpit where the seroma is located. She says if it needs draining again get the bra on immediately. Yes, I will for sure. It's just like, a good sports bra and its comfortable. Left arm continues to be painful with this "tracking". Joanna the physio says I need to be exercising the left arm as well. Here we go another thing to deal with!

PICC line hasn't been as annoying although almost three weeks later the area around it on my upper arm is still very bruised.

My hair has gone on my head no stubble left, but no pain in the scalp it's gone too.

I've got myself some more new scarves and little hats. Nigel has also been buying me some too. I've been out to the shops wearing my new items. No issues although it does get hot under them. I can't wait to get it off when I get home. I think my eyebrows are going this week and my eyelashes not as thick they may be reducing too. It's a bit funny the hair on my VJJ *(my pet name for my private area)* is going too it's not quite bald but certainly has its bald spots. Armpit hair and leg hair basically gone every cloud eh! Form good, well much more human than last two weeks. I'm now thinking about cycle three and to be honest a little anxious about it. I think Nigel is too as he sees how ill I am post treatment, but it must happen I need to go through this. It's just the unknown. I have a couple of questions for the oncologist this time

1. Do I have to have Radiotherapy?
2. At the end of the treatment do they body scan me?
3. After each cycle of treatment would it be a good idea to wear DVT stockings to help prevent clots?
4. Do I get my Bone Density checked with having my HRT stopped and lack of Oestrogen?

I had a lovely day today with my friend Judy. I spent afternoon with her and her lovely Mike. She made me lunch and we chilled. She took me to Shanes Castle where there is an Apiary. Judy is doing a bee keeping course. She's mad about bees and I got to see some hives. She's very special to me and a great friend. I'm very blessed!

Tried a walk up our road today. Nigel came with me. I'm always pleased when I can walk albeit just a little and wasn't easy with energy levels. Don't feel strong but I tried. It's good for the soul!

Well it's close to Tuesday now CHEMO day Cycle three.

Oh, my dear journal - I'll check in with you on Tuesday. You'll continue to be with me like you have been since nineteenth December.

TUESDAY, 16 MAY

Had a late-night last night and didn't sleep so good woke a few times. I guess today is on my mind. I think I also worry about sleeping in and missing my appointment. We must leave home so early to get to hospital for treatment. We are now getting our travelling fine-tuned proper time to leave to beat the mad motorway traffic.

Checked in at the hospital and got my pager. Got called very quickly to have my bloods taken, weighed and back to await call from doctor. Pager went off quickly. Oh, all very fast this morning.

We go into the consultation room and it was a female doctor from the Oncology team. She immediately said to me "your chemo won't be going ahead today" WHAT, WHY? She proceeded to explain that my white blood cell count is down and not at appropriate levels to give me my chemotherapy. It is them that helps me fight infection. SHIT I couldn't believe it. I was so disappointed. I need this to move on get through this bit. She asked how I had been. I told her first ten days was a disaster not good at all. I told her anti-sickness helping but I had a new pain in my leg. She seemed to be very interested in development.

I told her about my seroma and having it drained. She wasn't impressed! Oh dear! stating, she didn't like needles being inserted while I'm on chemo and that they should have consulted her team. I told her it was Oncology who referred me for a scan for my armpit. She told me it only should be drained if causing pain, I told her it was really causing pain, a lot of pain for weeks. That upset me that both departments hadn't talked to each other. Surely my breast surgeon would know what's safe and not safe. I totally trust Mr Mallon. I got a bit anxious as I thought had this procedure caused my current health problems internally resulting in my chemo being delayed. I did want to scream out loud *"You guys are the professionals for goodness sake."* She examined me, sounded my chest after I told her it felt like I was taking a cold or chest infection. It felt a bit different and more laboured. She then announced she wanted me to have a CT scan to check the chest area. She raised the matter of pain in left leg and mentioned a *clot*. Not this *clot* word again! I'm at the mercy of the professionals to check me and make sure I'm ok and well.

Letter for GP antibiotic required and a scan to be organised.

Doctor left the room for brief time and I just started to cry couldn't believe it. Nigel was so supportive, and I knew his heart broke for me. He squeezed my hand whilst I sat in the chair.

So that's it I'm off home Cycle number three not happening. How am I feeling? Disappointed and sad. This just knocks back end date and that's something that I continue to focus on. I'm trying to be positive and make plans although I clearly live a day at a time and haven't been able to look too far ahead to be honest. I want to be positive think ahead get through this treatment.

A goal I have is to be well enough to travel down to my home in Spain. To rest, recover, build up my strength and allow the chemotherapy to leave my body. Total relaxation with no disruptions or distractions that's my *goal*.

So many people had messaged me saying good luck for today thinking about me and hoping it goes well. Now I will have so many replies saying it didn't happen. It makes everyone anxious. They are all so attentive and care so much. I held off telling boys as too early to annoy them they are in exam mode. I'm always truthful with them. I know it will upset them so first call to mum she was so disappointed for me. I rang Shirley, Jill and Judy. Told my dear school friends Doreen & Valerie in a WhatsApp message.

To cheer myself up I got Nigel to take me to JJ Shannon's a Jewellers in Lisburn. I wanted to spend my birthday money that the Gracey family *(my family)* had given me. I hadn't got around to spending it, then circumstances took over and it wasn't a priority anymore. So today I treated myself to a new watch a little *Tag Heuer*. It certainly lifted my low mood even if just for a little while.

Thank you, to my wonderful family. I will treasure it always.

Phone call from Bridgewater.

CT scan arranged for Thursday eighteenth at 1pm that's quick!

Another test what news will this one bring? A CT scan well that should show up everything I suppose. It's ironic as one of Nigel's questions is, will they body scan me after treatment? I'm getting it quicker than expected. I still have pain in my leg. I thought it wasn't here anymore, but it is. It's like a cramp pain. Doctor had asked me if it was swollen, red or a lump present. I don't see any of that just this weird feeling pain like thing.

THURSDAY, 18 MAY

Hospital for one for CT scan. Made good time. Arrived early. Made my way to Cancer Centre Radiology department for CT scan of Chest and Lung area. Taken to examination room. A big cold and clinical room. Lady was nice. I had a gown on stripped from waist up and had to lie on the bed that goes into this huge scanning machine.

Felt a little overwhelmed thinking another test another concern another worry and I felt lonely. Nigel outside and not able to come in. The tears just ran down my cheeks. Lady came back put device into my PICC line. She asked if I was ok. I just replied yes. Test was straightforward. Over very quickly. She told me all went ok. She would get a doctor to see me to explain results, but a full report would be completed. Back to the cubicle to get dressed.

Oh, my I've been in a lot of those cubicles in last six months.

Got back to waiting room. Nigel there, always there for me always supportive, always by my side. I know he loves me so much. It's so tough for him. His calmness works for me.

Our wedding anniversary is on Saturday twentieth May two days away. Twenty-eight years I did buy a card and it said;

To My Husband – my soulmate – On our Anniversary I'm so glad we found each other. I love you to Eternity.

Back in the waiting room I said to Nigel I thought I would have had my leg scanned cos of the pain I have in it. Nigel said "right we are going back to Bridgewater to see a doctor not going home when you have this pain". We see the same doctor from last time Dr McLaughlin. Such a nice guy, very attentive wonderful bedside manner. He said, "I can see your calf swollen through your jeans." *Shit*, I didn't think it was swollen. He examined me and then said he had small scanner which he was going to use to check but he would want me to have a large full scan by the department. So, I had to remove my trousers and lie on the bed getting good at this! Nigel with me scan began, and Doctor said he believed he could see something that wasn't just right. He indicated a possible *clot* not that *clot* word again! This is serious stuff another obstacle!

He told me he would go organise full scan which would provide full prognosis.

He left the room and Nigel & I just looked at each other. Doctor came back in saying it's *not* happening today. No appointments available. I need to come back in the morning. In the meantime, I would be given an Anticoagulant injection to reduce risk and could also help with concern at my lungs.

That's just *crap*.

I mentioned to him my seroma that it was filling again and painful. I told him last doctor was not happy about getting it drained. He said it's about comfort for me. He left room came back and said Mr Mallon would see me downstairs.

Off to Breast Clinic. Oh, my days, I am getting around today!

I got taken straight away no hanging around. Mr Mallon came to see me. Hello again it's me! Pleasantries then he feels the seroma and immediately tells me that they will get it drained. Such a nice guy.

Off I go to other side of clinic. I know this place so well now and how everything works. Nigel not allowed in. He gets so far then it's no further *Mr Walker*. So, I go alone into cubicle to change, waiting area to wait and treatment room to have procedure. In comes the same guy from two weeks ago the radiographer person nice guy. No messing around. Scan the armpit found the seroma needle in, liquid out not as much as last time and it was bloodier in appearance this time. I asked why he told me probably because they had been in poking at it in last two weeks. *Job done!* Hopefully I will get some ease. I got to see it disappear on the ultra-scan machine as he used the needle to drain it.

When I get back out to Nigel, he tells me Dr McLaughlin has been down looking for me, and they are waiting upstairs to give me the anti-coagulant injection, so we rush back. I get some more blood taken and then the nurse gives me the jab into my tummy. I get to have Nigel with me for this procedure. I'm glad he can see what needs done. Apparently if confirmed as a clot I will have to inject myself for months.

Ok that's me ready for home what a day! I'm totally exhausted such a rollercoaster and from what the doctor has said it appears to be a clot in my lower leg this is not easy. I'm certainly being tested but I here in my head the scripture;

Be still and know that I am God. Psalm 46:10

FRIDAY, 19 MAY

I left home with Nigel to make my eleven o'clock appointment. I'm having a full leg scan today to confirm if it is a *clot* in my left leg. I'm also getting my CT chest scan result too. Look I'll deal with whatever is thrown at me today just another obstacle just another step in this journey. Difficult things being thrown at me but its ok I can deal with it.

Arrived at the LORIMER suite for the scan. This is in the Tower Block at Belfast City hospital. Got taken into room for procedure, trousers off and into bed, the room is so cold. Why are all these scanning rooms so cold?

In comes a guy who introduces himself and gets down to business. I'm just lying there waiting on the confirmation. He appears thorough and doesn't say very much just scans and measures and keeps his eye on the screen. The scan involves him picking up the large vein at my groin area. The vein runs down my leg right to the ankle area splits and divides into two. This vein runs to the heart, well veins clearly take blood to the heart that's obviously the worry eh! And I suppose this *clot* can travel which makes the bugger dangerous! When he gets to my calf area, he spends quite a bit of time with the scanning device. He hits a few buttons on the machine says nothing scans a bit more takes a few more measurements and then asks me to confirm where I'm having the pain. I tell and show him. I'm holding my breath at this point waiting on the result - he then speaks and says "everything looks fine I see no clot" what?

seriously I don't have a CLOT really honestly - he confirms he doesn't see a thing to be concerned about. Oh, my days I couldn't believe what I was hearing. He couldn't explain swelling and pain in my leg, but No *clot*. He said if leg continues to swell or gets red, they will rescan in ten to twelve days. I just couldn't believe it I could have kissed him *(a step too far I'd say!)* Such wonderful positive news couldn't wait to get dressed and go tell Nigel who was waiting outside.

Got dressed, had a pee and rushed to tell him. He was as shocked as me as we both thought it was a cert and was just being confirmed this morning like a formality. Now it's just great I felt like skipping from the Lorimer suite back to the see Dr McLaughlin in the Bridgewater to get my Chest results. I see the doc. He just appeared by my side like my *'doctor angel'*. He asked if I had got my results Yes, *NO CLOT* he said, "brilliant I got it wrong yesterday". I told him I was so pleased and then asked about my lung and chest area he said it was clear. That was me finished at the hospital.

Such a crazy two days a real rollercoaster. I'm shattered. Nigel was smiling and clearly relieved. More good news we were so happy. Doc told me my blood results back and my white cell count going up it was nought point four on Tuesday its now one needs to be one point five so in forty-eight hours going in right direction so hopefully I will get cycle three next Tuesday.

Lots of prayer needed.

Again, the staff at the hospital are amazing so attentive even the sister in charge was just so nice. She told Nigel he was right not letting me go home without getting leg checked out that's what they are there for, so good.

Yesterday while we were with Dr Ronan as I call him, we had a chat about life and living your life. I had told him I had given up lots of stuff since diagnosis including *wine* and *gin* my two wee favourite tipples. He asked me why? He told me I had to live no point only existing and that having a gin or glass of wine would do me no harm everything in moderation of course. I was telling him about a colleague from work having bought me a bottle of *Belfast Jaw box gin* and that I could have it at the end of this journey. Doc told me I could have one now. I know he wasn't encouraging consumption of alcohol certainly not. I knew what he was saying *chocolate, wine* whatever my pleasure I should have it. This is a tough journey. He told me I didn't need to punish myself. I guess I just wanted to have my body as pure as it can be not letting anything interfere with the healing process and giving myself the best chance.

Oh, I think I'll have a glass of wine after the week I've had. Just a little treat I deserve it!

Now here's a wee story. The doctor and us was talking about *gin* and he asked where he could buy some honeycomb. He had a bought a bottle of fine gin for his mum's birthday and was going home to Donegal to see her at the weekend. We didn't know the answer straight off and told him that. When we left the suite Nigel & I thought, let's see where we could source it for him. He's been so kind and attentive to me and it would be a nice wee gesture just to say thank you for my care. I found Aunt Sandra's on the Castlereagh Road in Belfast. We drove across the city. I went into the shop. A lovely little man called *Ron* a German served me. We had a great wee chat. He had had cancer too and was a survivor. He went in the back and came out with four speciality truffles for me as a little gift how kind! So, honeycomb bought, a stop of at the supermarket to get three limes and I returned to the hospital gift bag in hand on a mission to deliver the *package*. I found Dr Ronan. He was clearly so shocked. He told me I should be home resting. I told him it was something I wanted to do for him. He was gobsmacked. We hugged each other. I said thank you for looking after me. *Mission accomplished.*

SATURDAY, 20 MAY

It was our Wedding Anniversary today. Twenty-eight years married to my wonderful, beautiful, kind, considerate, supportive, loving, sweet man.

Nigel, I love you so much.

I don't think he knows just how much. He really is my *soulmate*. We didn't go out. I didn't want to, but we had a lovely Indian Takeaway. So good I thoroughly enjoyed the meal and my evening.

MONDAY, 22 MAY

Last week wasn't easy emotionally. Very tough from Tuesday when I didn't get my chemo. That set me back.

CT for chest, draining of seroma and scan of my leg, suspect clot though all ok. I survived it. White blood cell count on way up. Let's hope its continuing to rise and tomorrow chemo will go ahead!

TUESDAY, 22 MAY - CYCLE THREE

I slept ok last night. It was close to one in the morning when I turned the light off. Been building a jigsaw hard to pull away from it. It has been a great distraction for me and lets me focus and concentrate on something else. Though I can't do anything in the first ten days or so with it.

Awake at seven and into the shower. It looks like a beautiful morning.

Traffic report says collision on motorway, brilliant just what I need to hear, will be fun getting into the city. My appointment is nine twenty. A crazy time for travelling to the hospital. I have taken another green smoothie this morning. I'm trying to boost my blood cell count and green smoothies just might help. *(Broccoli, spinach & peas yummy NOT!)* Sometimes you just need to do these things and I will if it helps.

Off we go to the Bridgewater suite hopefully for cycle number three. Arrived at hospital in good time its eight fifty-six. Traffic was awful. Checked in and got myself a tea, my own tea. I've got good at carrying my herbal teas with me. Today's is *ginger & manuka honey.* Just waiting to be called for my bloods.

Pager sounding that's me. I'm off. Fingers crossed.

I met the lovely heavily pregnant nurse Grace again this morning. She greeted me saying "you are looking well, love your outfit" awh bless her that's sweet. Quick catch up telling her about my last week's drama cos she had been off. Bloods taken.

Back to waiting area. Oh, *please* let them be all ok, so I can get this treatment over. Waiting room getting very busy, people everywhere all with their own worries and concerns. All ages, genders, people with hair, no hair, wigs, scarves, concern on faces, people reading, on mobile phones, all so normal and yet there's nothing normal about the *Bridgewater suite* full of sick people! Nigel is by my side as always standing firm with me as supportive as ever. It's a long day for him but he never complains never ever.

Gosh pager has gone off that's quick this morning.

As I turned the corner, I saw the Doctor standing waiting on me. The same oncology doctor I seen last week, Dr Sinead. We go in sit down she asks me how I've been and then asks if Dr McLaughlin had discussed my results with me, the CT results. I told her yes no *clot*. She starts talking then saying yes there was no clot *but* - shit I hate *buts*.

The scan has shown something else. A *nodule* at the bottom of my lung. I couldn't believe what she was saying to me. I really wasn't expecting any such results. Now she's telling me I have a *nodule* on my lung. Inwardly that's what I'm saying, outwardly I don't speak then I become matter of fact processing what she is saying and asking questions. The doctor does tell me there could be any number of reasons there is a nodule. Infection, chemotherapy, been there for years or nothing. The fact I have *cancer* they need to carry out further investigations and complete another scan, but the scan will not take place for another three months as they need to leave it and then compare it to this scan just taken. I was so shocked. I didn't even ask what lung or what size the nodule was? I did ask though if it something sinister like, if its *cancer* in my *lung* would or could my chemotherapy help deal with it. She said yes if its breast cancer in my lung then anything lurking there, chemo could help!

I call it, they call it *belt & braces* stuff with chemo. I didn't even look at Nigel and he didn't look at me. We just kept our focus on the doctor. I asked her would it be normal for my cancer to have gone to my lung. Reply was more probable in other areas. We were both very matter of fact. Nigel spoke asking when the scan would take place and he asked at the end of chemo would I get a full body scan? The answer is *NO*. Doctor then asked how I was feeling what about my chest? Do I have any flame or spit? *No no no* I don't. She told me to keep an eye on my body any concerns speak to them. She said my bloods were back and the levels were two point six up from nought point four so that's good still waiting on more blood results but chemo most likely going ahead.

The doctor then said I would be getting an injection today if chemo going ahead to assist in boosting *bone marrow* and *white cell* stuff. She explained how it would affect me; zapped of energy, pains through my body, feel flu like, can take pain relief but check temperature before doing so. She explained how I will need an injection. District Nurse will give me day after treatment. This will happen at cycle four too.

She spoke about cycle four and the changeover drug. Energy levels will go down dramatically, and steroids will be given along with meds for white blood cell renewal. Oh, my days! This is still a tough road and I think it's gonna get bumpier! My head is spinning. So much information to absorb. I'm so glad Nigel with me to pick up on all the info as I'll not remember. I'm still taking in the news about the nodule.

It's getting scary.

If I have cancer in my lung that's not good but let's pray it's nothing just a little blip with just everything that's going on.

I'm wondering what Nigel is thinking. He will be inwardly devastated about the news. He keeps saying he *can't do life without me*. Another *bombshell* though there is nothing we can do right now. I need to put it to the side and deal with the matters in hand. I hope and pray all will be okay.

So back to chemotherapy today, doc asks if I was going for a coffee and that she would contact me if blood tests *not* ok. Mobile number given and we leave the consulting room to await the results. If no phone call, we must return at three-thirty. She was a nice doctor very factual, a bit *cold* in her delivery, but I get it she deals with this stuff every day. She was very clear and understood everything she told us.

We decided we were going home for a few hours, so I could have a rest.

On the way out spot a girl selling headgear so I go have a look. Go to buy one and Nigel says take two. *Why not!*

We left hospital and on our way to car park Nigel just stopped turned and gave me the biggest tightest hug and said all he could think of when doctor mentioned nodule what more can they throw at us! True very true. We chatted it through in the car made sure we both on the same page, had a cry and said let's just carry on with what we do know right now. Let's get through treatment and we will deal with whatever else at the end of this bit of the journey.

We returned home, and, on the way, I get a call from my dear friend Judy. I break down with her just hearing her voice and told her the latest news. I knew she was upset. I could hear it in her voice. I think she was crying. We composed ourselves and she said, "I'm ringing with some lovely news, good news" *(oh I could do with that!)* she told me she had taken a call from my boss Gillian who had got a call from my *big boss* in my organisation the delightful Mr B. He wanted to put my name forward to Buckingham Palace for me to be invited to the Royal Garden Party at Hillsborough Castle in June or September. *No way,* how lovely how kind of him to think of me. I'm speechless. What a gesture! Judy thought it would best in September but wanted to check with me. I'd love that and yes September might be best. Mr B needed an answer today as Buckingham Palace needs to be provided with list from the Service. I can't believe it. I can't believe someone would think of me like that. How special. I'm very grateful. *Mr & Mrs Walker* might be going to a Garden Party! Let's pray I'm fit and well enough in September to make this special event as I'd so like to attend and a nice treat for Nigel. When I hung up from Judy, I told Nigel. He was shocked and I saw he was holding back tears and a bit overwhelmed. I know I was. Oh, my goodness an excuse to buy a *frock* and something for my *bald head!*

Three in the afternoon and back at the hospital. Treatment going ahead. Hooray thank goodness you know I can't believe I'm excited about having this awful treatment, but for me it's about moving ahead let's get this done give myself best chance of survival. Three twenty-five sickness tablet given. I must wait one hour before treatment.

Chatted to another girl I now know who is also having her treatment same time as me, but she doesn't appear to be having all these extra crappy things happening. I'm really pleased for her no clots or seromas through her surgery and treatment. At sixteen thirty-two cycle three underway. Delivered today by Kelli Marsden a lovely nurse. It was straightforward no issues. Given anti sickness and steroids before it started and at five o'clock all done brilliant! My little bag of sweeties, *meds* provided and we are off home.

Called mum to tell her it went ahead today she appeared relieved. Updates to Shirley, Jill & Judy and of course my beautiful boys. Now tea time for me and Nigel.

During dinner Nigel just started to cry, very difficult to watch. He rarely cries. He says he can't do it without me, *life* that is. I guess so disappointed with new development. We are so positive and have been pushing forward trying to think of end game and more reality and normalness in our home.

We hugged. Nigel held me close.

I know this is tough for him it's tough for me too - a long tough day.

Sleepy now. Let's see how next few days go.

WEDNESDAY, 24 MAY

Slept on my big sofa in the sunroom with my blanky and v-pillow mum gave me. I just get comfortable and stay there. That's what I want. Reasonable night felt a bit sick at seven thirty so had some breakfast and got my meds sorted and taken. A little headachy and thankfully been to the toilet to do number twos *phew relief* cos that's a difficult thing right now!

Temperature steady and a reasonable day overall post treatment.

I keep waiting on the dip coming cos it's awful.

THURSDAY, 25 MAY

A reasonable day, a bit headachy not too sick at all meds seems to be working. Very tired waiting on nurse to come give me the injection I must have in my tummy.

Felicity my lovely nurse arrived and told me I was not going to feel very well later after she gives the injection. I told her I know I've been told. Just a little prick into tummy easy and straightforward. Now I await to see how this develops.

Yesterday I told mummy about needing further tests on my lung and the nodule which I now know is on my right lung and its 5.5 mm not big but still worrying. I always feel bad when I hold back details from her as I want to be honest with no deceit or pretending but I must balance it all with mum as she is such a worrier and a real fear of cancer and what it brings. She doesn't cope well with news. She often repeats what you tell her but clearly hasn't heard or interpreted correctly which is concerning.

I haven't told the boys about the *nodule. T*hey are still attending lectures in Uni. I don't want to further upset them just yet.

I told mummy cos you should be able to tell her anything. I then worry about her being alone and thinking about all I have told her. She's not good at going the distance. I think she feels it should be over now. We've done that, let's move on and yet there's such a road to go. It's so not over, and therefore I need to be upfront and honest and do what's best for me!

Those around me need to be able to handle this themselves as I can't do it for them.

I got my gorgeous boy home from Edinburgh today. He has finished his year at Uni. It was a quick *hi, cuddle* and *bye* as he's away to do what he loves best *Agriculture*, contracting driving big tractors and trailers. It's *silage time*.

I went into the garden today with Nigel. It was a beautiful day weather was glorious. I need to be careful with the sun as super sensitive when having chemo. Threw off my headgear needing sun cream on my bald head. My brother Cecil calls it my *chrome dome*.

I'm not able to do anything in the garden and it frustrates me, and I just follow Nigel around like his family pet. Escaped to my sun house in the garden and had a nap another one!

Sent my sister a message this morning just hope you are ok message to start up a conversation as I want to tell her about my further tests on the lung. They are so busy on the farm and she does not always reply so quickly, and this time she didn't reply. When she did get back to me, she was sad as some problems with animals on the farm, so I decided not to tell her my latest news. It would keep to another time. She'll not want to hear my latest, she has enough going on.

FRIDAY, 26 MAY

Fell asleep on my big sofa shattered as I couldn't sleep all day spent night on sofa what a night with *hot* flushes. Had five through the night and they were bad lasted longer than normal but I survived them! Did sleep and woke at eight. I felt ok not too bad wiggled my body to see how sore it was but no big pains I can hardly believe it. I'm waiting on this cracker of nightmares. Look I don't feel on top of the world or couldn't climb a mountain, no marathons *(not that I would be doing such a thing!)* but it's ok I'm surviving this.

Taking all my meds which is clearly important and a *must*!

Had a lovely visit from Jill nice lunch and catch up. Also, a visit from my mum and niece the lovely Zoe that was nice too.

I read a little piece from a book this morning. It was one my dear mother in law had bought me;

God Will carry you through by Max Lucado

"God knows what you need and where you'll be. Trust him ... Fretting over tomorrows problems today siphons the strength you need for now leaving you anaemic and weak."

WEDNESDAY, 31 MAY

I've just picked up my journal today nothing from last Friday.

I guess that tells you all without saying anything more!

YES, it's been bad and TOUGH. It started on Friday night at 11pm.

I took the pains that they had warned me about. Weird strange pains up the back of my neck and into my head, into the base of my skull, oh so sore also in my chest bones *(this is the injection given by district nurse post treatment)*. Well that made for a *bad* Saturday. I felt rotten awful so many pains, no energy, lethargic, felt yucky not sick but just rotten. The whole day wiped out. Sunday not much better and just slept a lot. Awoke in early afternoon from a sleep and it started another disastrous few days.

When I got out of bed, I had a strange feeling in my left arm some pain but as I looked at it, I realised above the elbow it was a blue colour strange! I thought I was imagining it looked a bit bigger than right but certainly not a good colour. I tried to move it up and down feeling pain in shoulder area. I got up ate some food and it didn't change. I went to Matthew and asked him if he could see any difference in my arms he looked and said, "your left arm is blue, and I think you need to do something about that". Oops ok then! I think I might need to ring Oncology helpline. Guess what - they needed to see me. Brilliant another trip to the Cancer Centre. Examination, questions, bloods taken which of course, could *NOT* be taken from my PICC line this time, as they were concerned of a *CLOT* at the PICC line site. So back of the hands for the blood. My poor veins. They are struggling on the left arm. I got a spin in a wheel chair for an X-ray and an injection into my belly for clot prevention.

Monday evening back to hospital, more bloods and another injection into belly and they wanted me back again on Tuesday to run a scan on my arm to check and see what's going on.

I was exhausted by this all.

It's tough up and down to the hospital each day and I had only had my chemo on Tuesday. This is the worst week ever to have to attend hospital.

Back on Tuesday arm scanned. This is the third time in two weeks for scans. I just thought I had fallen asleep on Sunday and lay heavy on my arm leaving it a bit numb and off colour and hear I was having a scan to check for clots. I found this one more difficult to deal with. I was so frustrated as I wasn't feeling well. Tired and this all makes it more exhausting. Anyway, scan was completed *NO* clot at my PICC line another Hooray! I was so relieved and just very tired.

Poor Nigel he looked tired and exhausted. I know he worries so much about me. It was all dealt with and I got back home.

I had a fuzzy feeling in my head. I think it was just tiredness and exhaustion.

Anyway, back to today, I feel a little emotional and have had a bit of a cry not sure why? A little overwhelmed, I think. The treatment is tough to endure without all the other crap that's being thrown at me.

I had Shirley round for lunch that was nice as we don't get enough time like that. Then Jill called and then my brother and niece. Even my lovely neighbour Freda called in with some flowers - everyone continues to be so kind and caring. I'm still getting daily messages from great people. I thank each one of them.

THURSDAY, 1 JUNE

Gosh I can't believe it's the first of June what a six months' that has been and it has gone by so quickly. So much has happened. Diagnosed with cancer, two major breast surgeries, three sessions of chemotherapy and everything else in between one heck of a trip!

Feeling more human today coming up out of session three. A great feeling when you realise you are a little more well and ever so grateful.

Hopefully some more normal days ahead.

WEDNESDAY, 7 JUNE

Well I am into my third week of cycle three.

I've had a great few normal days feeling more human. Got to go out of the house and spend some time with my family and friends which has been lovely.

We took my sister to a lovely little place Ballydougan Pottery for lunch as it was her birthday this week. Gosh I got so emotional when I went to pay for the bill *(my treat cos they have all been so good to me)* The lady at the till an older attractive lady with lovely blond hair funny how you notice such things was processing my transaction. She turned to me and said, "you look beautiful as you walked towards me" a little surprised I said, "oh thank you". I smiled at her and said "I haven't been very well these recent months" she looked at me again and said "well you looked beautiful as you came towards me" I was a bit overwhelmed at this stranger saying something so lovely and kind. I had one of my headscarf's on and my bandage covering my PICC line was visible, so it was obviously evident something was going on with me. I said to her "I'm fighting hard right now". I didn't say I had cancer and didn't say anything else as I was now *fighting hard* to hold back the tears, such a lovely thing to say to me. A total stranger. She spoke again to me saying "Well you keep fighting hard as you look beautiful". I took my card said thank you and as I walked back to the table the tears ran down my cheeks. I felt so emotional such warm sentiments. I grabbed my bag and my mum and sister were a bit taken back asking me what was wrong but I couldn't speak. Shirley just said "Leave it mummy" she'll be ok. When I composed myself, I shared what had happened.

I got to spend a few hours with the girls from my department at work; Carol Anne, Kelly Anne and Patricia. CA had arranged tea and scones at hers. What a wonderful morning. Craic was mighty. Again, I found it difficult and very emotional as the girls were asking questions about my health and what I had endured to date and what was still to come but nevertheless I had a super morning with them they are all *mad* but *fab*.

Talking of friends, I also got to spend a few hours with Jill at her house. A wee cuppa and a catch up. She's a real gem - very precious to me.

My dear friends Jill, Valerie and Doreen arranged for us to go to Carlingford in the Republic of Ireland for a lovely day together. It was for Doreen's fiftieth birthday A wee treat for her but I honestly felt they did it for me. I got to spend time with these special girls. A bit of retail therapy and a lovely leisurely lunch with lots of craic. So good to spend time with people who clearly care so much about me. Of course, it was a bit emotional. I think we all had a cry as they chatted about my journey. I shared with Valerie & Doreen the little discovery of the nodule on my lung. Valerie had tears in her eyes bless her! Such a pet.

MONDAY, 12 JUNE

Wow! what a lovely weekend I've just had. Lee my brother in law such a lovely guy and always has been booked a two-night stay in a cottage at Castle Leslie Estate in County Monaghan, Ireland for my sister's birthday. A surprise for Shirley and he included me in the treat too as he said I have been through a tough time recently. How *sweet,* how *caring*! We headed off on Friday afternoon and had the most amazing relaxing weekend. My sister, mum, niece and I. Just what the doctor ordered! We had a ball. Great to spend time with these special girls in my life wonderful time such great memories made - thank you Lee.

Well, it's now the day before cycle four. I am apprehensive about this cycle as I will be getting the *changeover* drug that the Oncologist spoke about. I will get this one for next three cycles. I have been told my energy levels will be depleted.

I started the drugs this morning given to me by the hospital after cycle three. Required to be taken before cycle four starts *Eight* tablets daily. I have another eight tomorrow. Then on Wednesday post cycle four a further eight. They are steroids and normally they make my face swell and go red so let's see! Whatever it takes I don't care.

I've been drinking my green smoothies in the run up to this next cycle yuk! Not pleasant spinach, broccoli, peas with real honey just to sweeten. I've also been trying to do some walking *(not going great)* but I just want to be fit to handle all this. I've tried a one point seven mile walk and did double the distance *(I know it's pushing myself, but I don't care).*

I pray that tomorrow goes ok, that my levels are all good and treatment goes ahead.

Nigel & I had planned that in two thousand and seventeen we were going to carry out and complete some home improvements around the house It has been put off since my diagnosis. Today I got very excited. We've had our kitchen designer McGowan Brooks from Killinchy, County Down out to discuss changes we want to make. Oh, it was exciting, and I can't wait to move it all forward something nice to look forward to.

My sister sent me a little WhatsApp message today a little verse by Helen Steiner Rice and the message within was so positive and spiritual. It made me cry - happy tears.

'The Bend in the Road''

Sometimes we come to life's crossroads, and we view what we think is the end. But God has a much wider vision and he knows it's only a bend – The road will go on and get smoother and after we've stopped for a rest, the path that lies hidden beyond us is often the path that is best. So, rest and relax and grow stronger, let go and let God share your load and have faith in a bright tomorrow you've just come to a bend in the road. Helen Steiner Rice

TUESDAY, 13 JUNE

Well that wasn't a great night's sleep. Lights out at one and up at six.

Its cycle four today. It's on my mind for sure. I pray it goes ahead and all is good to go.

We left home for the commute through heavy traffic to the hospital although surprisingly light today. Made good time, checked in, took my pager and a seat. Bloods taken, back to waiting area and very quickly called forward. This time it was a male doctor from the Oncology team. A very nice guy. Very officious, clear and concise. Quite a long consultation with me this morning nothing left to chance. He detailed everything. I said to him about how I was feeling including constipation, anti-sickness meds, general health, way forward. They are *not* planning to reduce chemo dosage due to my overall health. We had a chat about the *nodule* on my right lung, the *scan* results and what they intend doing. Radiotherapy also discussed today. Doctor looked at my file told me he would discuss with my oncologist Dr McCarty and the way ahead. Hormone Therapy will start at the end of my chemotherapy. He left the room as he wanted to discuss with Dr McCarty. He came back a short time later and advised Dr McCarty would be changing post chemo meds *anti-sickness* giving me new ones today.

There will be a CT scan at the end of chemotherapy.

Consideration still to be given re radiotherapy.

My bloods good today, white cells at twenty-six point four. He discussed side effects of cycle four. Lots of pain, fatigue, sickness maybe? The doctor today provided me with so much information which I love. It informs me greatly and I like knowing.

He spoke about treatments and my pathway. Getting me to the *ten-year* mark for *survival* but you can live thirty or forty years. All very direct but I prefer that. It's all a bit scary when they speak and use the words *survival* and *number* of years but it's true!

So that's me to come back at three-thirty for cycle four and will be getting the *D drug (Docetaxel)*. Nigel and I gonna go do some nice things, normal things, something to eat then Nigel wants to go car shopping thinking of a new purchase. Oh, I'm so pleased for him he so deserves a treat and a new car would just be the thing. Then gonna go buy some fabric to cover an old rocking chair his mum has given him. Arrived back at hospital. Oh, I realised why my sleep not great last night. The drugs I took at seven-thirty. I should have taken them at lunchtime the second set of steroids oops! No wonder I was like a rabbit in the headlights. Anyway, into the big pink chair and this time the chemo is in a bag and not syringes like the first three! It's a clear liquid drug and apparently takes an hour to run through. Blood pressure and obs normal. All good to go chemo cycle started at three thirty-five. Buzzer provided to call nurse if I feel or take unwell. I got to see nurse Hayley today. That was nurse who I saw on day one at Bridgewater suite. She's lovely. She can't believe I'm now at cycle four. I can't believe I'm now at cycle four! My nurse today was Alison another super girl very friendly and explained everything so well. Nigel is on the little seat right beside me. It's now four twenty all going well nothing weird happening, feel fine. I am getting tired, but it's been a long day with little sleep.

My baby coming home tonight from Southampton can't wait to see Alex. That will be both boys back in the nest. Four forty-five all done cycle four given and administered let's see how this goes over the next few days!

WEDNESDAY, 14 JUNE -DAY ONE AFTER CYCLE FOUR

Slept ok and not feeling too rough. Had some breakfast ate two breakfasts some frosties then porridge with orange juice weird crazy appetite. I'm eating more rubbish since I started chemo always eating have put some weight on although not up to my previous weight before my cancer diagnosis. Oh, my goodness what tiredness, so tired can't stay up need to get back into bed need to sleep.

I got a call from Alex. He's ran out of petrol on the A1 oh my days! I must drive to him with petrol which I do of course, but I am so tired and driving the car is very difficult but it's a must he's my baby he needs me. I must fix this! Saved the day got it sorted. By the time I got back I was TOTALLY EXHAUSTED. Into bed and slept the afternoon away. Still feeling exhausted taking my meds and sleeping. Nigel made dinner and we had a nice family meal. My nest is full again my boys are home.

THURSDAY, 15 JUNE

I fell asleep last night on my big sofa in the sunroom and awoke at two thirty. I can't keep my eyes open this tiredness is unbelievable. Feeling ok. Nigel offered to make me a tea before he left but I couldn't even sit up to have it. Way too tired, some breakfast and back into bed that was pretty much my day. Teatime and it has brought about pains in my bones. That's the injection from yesterday the pains feel just like last time really bad pain travels up the big bones in my body up into the back of my neck and the base of my skull. I feel the pains in my chest bones as well it's strange and weird and *painful*. Paracetamol taken hopefully that will help. I'm flushing like mad and so tired!

I have come across an article in a Vogue magazine about a girl having cancer and her journey. An amazing read and so much of what she said resonates with me. So true how she explains and details her feelings.

I just need to write this down from the article;

'I wish not for the first time this year that I had been paid an hourly rate for having cancer, strangely it's more like having a job than you might think; block out the diary, draw your eye brows on and just do it, only don't expect to get paid, but there's no shortcut, no credit card for cancer you have to face it and endure it and live every life sucking moment of it and there is a warped sense of achievement in that'

WEDNESDAY, 21 JUNE

Wow oh my! What a week I've had!

Having got my cycle four of chemo last Tuesday it floored me totally.

What I mean by that is the *FATIGUE*. It hit me immediately. Never ever experienced anything like this in my whole life. I spent basically four solid days in bed. I literally had no energy no ability to do anything. I just slept. Though I had no physical sickness the medical team have so sorted this with the medication, but they had warned me about the *pains* oh yes I had them! The only way I can explain them is that if you ever have had flu were your whole body hurts and every bit of you aches. Well that's how I was. I was also given the injection to boost my white blood cells. Those pains I experienced so tough to handle but just got to hit it head on no alternative I must work through this.

I was so scared of getting cycle four as I had read and heard so many stories about the changeover of the chemo drugs at cycle four and how it can be very tough. My oncology team did advise and warn about fatigue and pains and they were so right and on the money. I continue to have the usual side effects with each cycle sore gums, bottom lip swollen, bowel movements awful, swollen red face *(steroids)*.

The weirdest thing this time and is something new is I've taken severe pain in my fingernails! Unbelievable pain started on Sunday. I've held onto my nails thus far and in fact they have looked healthy, but oh so painful. I've been using Vitamin E on them. Putting my hands in hot water is driving me crazy. My nails are hurting. Marigolds a must! Will have to wait and see what develops. A rash has appeared on my hands. I'm assuming its linked to pains in my fingernails.

Went to the dentist today for a check-up. My mouth so sore and tender but Maeve the dentist was lovely and kind and gentle with me and very understanding. It's the little things that makes the difference. The hand on my arm, the compassionate responses, not a pitying response but just that they understand.

Anyway, back to my teeth. Cos of the pain in my mouth and how I have been feeling my dental hygiene has not been as thorough as it could be. So, after my check-up Maeve did a deep clean and descale of my teeth. What a lovely treat and whilst my mouth was sore the dentist was so gentle and at the end of it felt just great. My teeth looked better. Maybe just my imagination, but it gave me a *feel-good factor* (very little of this right now!) Dentist has prescribed a mouthwash to try. Hopefully I get some relief.

Had lunch in the village with my beautiful boys which was lovely although I didn't feel good. I always try to have a bit of normality. By the time I got back I was totally exhausted, and the rest of the day was wiped out - I also found out today my work was going to continue to keep me on full pay and not reduce it to half. I'm so relieved and so grateful to the authorities and to my boss Gillian who has been wonderful in looking after my needs within the workplace. Gillian and my dear friend Judy have been so brilliant a great team who have supported me in all things work administrative.

THURSDAY, 22 JUNE

Last night's sleep not great as my hot flushes are in abundance.

Matthew heading off to Edinburgh for the weekend. I make him a lunch for his travels and see him off.

I have an appointment later at my work Occupational Health & Wellbeing (OHW) department. It's in Belfast at two. Not sure what this will involve or how it will go. I haven't seen them since my diagnosis.

My hands continue to be changing. I have rash on my thumbs and first two fingers on both hands. It's weird and fingernails still painful. I haven't spoken to anyone about it just seeing how this develops. Nigel is off today to come to the appointment with me. *I need him with me.*

The appointment at the OHW went ok. I met a lovely lady called Joanna, very caring, kind and understanding. I was very emotional not how I wanted to be. I wanted to be strong but when she showed me what had been written electronically on the IT system the words were just so powerful it made everything very real when you see it in black and white. The reality of my illness, my cancer. I just started to cry and couldn't stop couldn't hold back the tears they just kept coming. I had to relive everything from the nineteenth December. Joanna was recording on it on the system. That was fine. I understand it must be done. It's important to have it recorded for me. It clearly is still very raw and when you hear it back its quite a huge journey I have travelled thus far. The meeting went well reassuring and very supportive. I think I realise this is tough and I am nowhere near at the end yet much more to come. The meeting took almost two hours and I was exhausted. Nigel said he could see how tough it was for me. He was brilliant too and was able to explain lots of things while I *snattered* into a hankie. I told Joanna my goal was to get better and return to work. I have completed twenty-seven years' service as a police officer. I'm almost there. Thirty years is where I want to get to. I'll be retiring then that's my plan. She asked me was it a full twenty-seven years' service no broken service, no part time hours, no term time working. *NO* none of that. I have worked solid for twenty-seven years as a police officer. She was clearly impressed as it's rare for a female in the force to do such a thing - *don't make them like us girlies anymore!*

I also know I honestly cannot answer how this will end and when my return to work will be?

I'm glad I seen OHW today. I hope they will continue to support me as I move forward.

Well I'm even more exhausted now. It has floored me so very tired. Fingernail pain just not as acute but rash still on fingers and its now itchy but I'm managing it ok.

SATURDAY, 24 JUNE

Over the last few months professional people from the various departments within the hospital would advise when you interacted with them about details of services available to you as a cancer patient. The fact you may be entitled to some help and benefits. They would recommend you apply. The *pack* provided by the hospital team refers to such stuff. I even got a call from a social worker. Such a lovely lady advising of services and the need for me to apply. They clearly worry about your financial situation and advise you can get assistance. For me it has been the last thing on my mind. All this stuff, all these details. I listened to each professional. I read each leaflet when I could. I completed papers and forms as guided when I had the strength to do so. I struggled filling in applications, documents, papers that normally would be straightforward and no bother. I just filled the forms in from my *heart*, told the truth what had happened, how I was and what I was going through. This morning I opened my post and there was confirmation of entitlement to some money, some financial assistance for now. I was so in shock. I rang Nigel and cried my eyes out telling him that I was going to get some money cos I'm *critically ill*. Someone has decided that as I am so ill *(which I am)* that I'm entitled to some money. It was so upsetting. *I really am ill.* Others are acknowledging it now, others that's not my medical team. I cried and cried and cried to Nigel. He couldn't hug me as he was not at home. He told me not to cry. Bittersweet eh! Some extra money which will certainly help us as a family but all these years of working (thirty-three actually) and I have never got anything like this and now cos I'm critically ill I'm getting money for being sick. *It must be bad!*

Alex got a little emotional out in the car with me today. He spoke about how difficult my diagnosis was for him. *I know that.* I don't need reminding. He got tearful as did I. I know it's been a tough six months for him, and it was his first year away at University. I'm so sad about spoiling his first year, but he has done so well such a great positive start. Passed all his exams. I'm so very proud of him. I think he gets scared about my illness. He told me that he and Matthew didn't discuss together my cancer until recently. I asked him why, and he told me it was just too painful for them both. He says it's been so difficult, as we are such a close family of four and for one to be unwell is so sad and worrying. He's right we are exceptionally close (*maybe too close if that's possible*). We just squeezed each other's hand very tightly as we travelled along in the car and both went quiet for little while, gathering our thoughts, lost in our own world - I love him so very much.

I so hope after our chat he feels better.

SUNDAY, 25 JUNE

Spent a lovely day with mummy. Went for a wee drive in the car. Then a visit to see my brother Geoffrey and sister in law Meryle. Always love seeing them, love them very much, such easy company so kind and caring. I hadn't seen them since my chemo started, but they kept in touch by phone. They made me a lovely tea and we had some good craic. When I arrived Meryle cried she was very emotional, and it tore at my heart. Of course, Meryle sent me home with a little gift which are always with so much thought. I hope to see them again soon.

I know mummy worries about me a lot. I'm her daughter it's understandable she worries. She says she's praying lots. I'm thankful for her prayers. I know lots of people are praying for me.

I got a lovely card today from Alison a girl from church. A little handmade card with a verse

'The Lord will fight for you, you need only be still' Exodus 14:14

Wendy stay strong and be assured in the knowledge that you are being held up in prayer Alison xo.

Oh, I hope so.

MONDAY, 26 JUNE

I've awoke this morning with such pain in my arm my *cording*. It raised its ugly head again with vengeance. Right from my armpit to my wrist its awful. I thought it was easing, oh no certainly not. I had just got used to the existing pain and was managing it, but this is a whole new level. I've just applied some hydrocortisone maybe it will help ease the pain please please please maybe its linked to my right breast! Last few days feeling pain on the underside of the new breast. It's painful to touch and works inwards towards my armpit. Quite a pain but no reddening or hotness of the breast so I'm assuming no infection but it's not nice its nasty another pain to deal with! My headache is still here have had it a few days now. I think it might be linked to fact I'm feeling a little sniffly runny nose heavy head. It's funny you know I'm acutely aware of smells and scents in the air around me. My eyes water and I sniffle. I have no hairs left in my nostrils and little or no eyelashes, so I guess all the little bugs or pollen or just what's in the air has open access to the eyes and nose! My chemo has stripped all that away.

Talking of chemo, I'm sure I've said before but if not it's important to acknowledge it's a rough tough treatment its stripes you right down. It's unbelievable. I don't know how to describe it. What I will say is whilst undergoing it you need to remain alert. You need to keep an eye on all that happening to you and any changes. Recognise the signs, the side effects, with all that's going on though that's not easy when you are feeling so awful and often on your knees. Be aware and always check out the effects, deal with them and then move on.

Check in with your medical team.

They are ok about you asking and checking when something develops.

Look I also want you to know if you are walking this pathway you might *NOT* have any of these matters to contend with but it's good to know. I wish I had of known.

My lovely nurse Felicity was in this morning and dealt with my PICC line. It's still working fine but the skin around gets tender and when she washes the skin boy does it sting! She's repositioned the dressing today to allow the air at the very sensitive bit. She is very attentive makes me feel very comfortable.

THURSDAY, 29 JUNE

I didn't sleep well last night mixture of things. Pain in my arm, breast and armpit. I didn't sleep all day yesterday exhausted. Stayed up late the boys were out and I never sleep anyway until they get in cos I worry about their safety.

I took Alex to the dentist *(kind mummy as he had been out socialising last evening).* So whilst in the village I decided to go see my GP about pain in my right breast not getting better in fact it's worse. I know it's different and not normal. I also need to get another sick line for work, I haven't been to the surgery since my surgeries. I've avoided it since chemo started as I am so concerned about picking up a bug or germs that would set me back. Dr McCandless had advised me that she would put a *red flag* on my file so that it highlighted the fact I was on chemo and that I would not to be sitting in the waiting area among other patients.

I've had several telephone consultations with Dr Victoria but no face to face. So, as I enter the surgery, I tell them I want to see her, and the receptionist picks up that I'm not to sit in the waiting area and places me in one of the GP rooms not being used. I'm alone in the doctor's room, just staring around the room reading all the stuff on the walls. I'm hoping they don't forget about me in here. Sat for about twenty minutes then *Dr Victoria* came to the door (personal service!) Consultation went ok. She examined me my breast, armpit, arm, felt the lump in my armpit *seroma.* She believes I have an infection. Checked my oxygen levels it was fine. Prescribed me an antibiotic but said she wanted me to speak to Oncology team to advise them what she has done. Dr McCandless said I looked well. She said I wasn't looking as *gaunt*.

No, I'm not looking well and as for the being gaunt the steroids help that just swell my face *big red head*!

Picked up my prescription from chemist, had breakfast with Alex, took my first antibiotic and then thought about Oncology helpline. Do I really need to call them? No, I won't. Oh yes, I will just to do what doc has advised. I'm very compliant.

I rang helpline, spoke to Louise the nurse, told her reason for calling. She got me to check my temperature its thirty-six point seven. All good. She listens as I tell my symptoms and she advised she will speak to the Doctor at Bridgewater and call me back.

Within minutes she calls me back and advised Doctor wanted to see me at the suite. *No way* this is not necessary, sure I saw my GP but, yes, they wanted to see me. They are so attentive which is great, but it means another car journey to the city, another consultation. Do I have to? Yes, apparently, I do.

So, Nigel at work, boys having a nap and I don't want to wake them. I'm gonna drive myself. Its only twenty-five minutes away.

I messaged Nigel and told him my plans. He didn't reply right away must be busy at work. I head to the hospital.

I went to Ward 2A a new ward in the cancer centre. It has just been set up for patients like me with concerns. It's a great new system. I'm impressed.

They are waiting on me when I arrive. Such a slick service. There is other ladies in the ward all with their own issues and being assessed. Lovely nurse called Marie Shannon looked after me very attentive. They are so taking such good care of me. Obs done - blood pressure little low. Bloods taken and then the lovely Dr McLaughlin appeared

Dr Honeycomb. I've told you before about him. He's the lovely doctor I bought the honeycomb for. I told him I had got three weeks without seeing him *whoopee.* We laughed, chatted about the current issues and as he was about to examine me Nigel appeared in the ward. He had rushed to be by my side. I think he was annoyed I had made the journey on my own, but I didn't need to bother anyone I could do this myself.

They examined me. I was sore, very painful confirmed my seroma was raised and clearly filled up. I *was* thinking it was all linked to the ongoing pains. A paracetamol IV was set up and Dr Honeycomb went off to speak with Dr Mallon (breast surgeon) to see what his views were.

So, I got dressed again and sent off to the breast Clinic. Dr Mallon not there so I saw a different female doctor. A pleasant lady but not my surgeon! She examined me and then took me to ultrasound dept where they would again drain the seroma *(brilliant here we go again)* After an hour wait, I had the seroma drained. Today they called it an *Oily Cyst.* 1.6 cm in size. Fluid removed. A little uncomfortable. As usual a yellow coloured liquid taken from armpit not as much as I thought would come away that's now three times this blessed thing has been drained.

Went back to see Doctor. She confirmed the results and didn't know why I was in so much pain. No issues with my breast implant and no infection. No requirement to take the antibiotic prescribed by GP. Believed nothing more sinister. Pain maybe muscle wall pain all very normal. Not concerned it was my bones? She told me if I was concerned anything to do with my bones not to think like that cos its nothing of that nature. *SHIT* I hadn't even thought that way! She gave me my file and I headed back to see Dr McLaughlin. Results confirmed. He appeared a little surprised as thought the draining would have had much more liquid. Still have pain in the areas mentioned but let's see if draining will ease it. I'm not to take antibiotic and to take pain relief and keep an eye on it.

My bloods were good and so that's positive for next Tuesday as my next cycle will take place then. So, four hours later I left the hospital with no reason why I have such pain on the right side and in this discomfort!

FRIDAY, 30 JUNE

Today I went out with my dear friend Jill. We called it our *road trip* when we planned it. I added another dimension by contacting my old school friend Joanne who lives in Kilkeel, County Down and asking if I could come visit her. So, built into our road trip that I could go see her too. Well of course with a shop in Kilkeel both Jill and I love to visit any excuse and so wanted to see Joanne as I normally only correspond by letter and cards throughout the year. We were great pals at High School. She was a year older than me, but we had such great times as young teenagers and even had school photos taken together. I loved her friendship back then. We would have gone to barn dances, dances in our local orange halls and young farmers hall. We always kept in touch by the written word. We've gone a bit more modern these days and now have shared our mobile numbers, so we message each other now and again. One of those special friendships that even with the passing of time we rekindle so easily.

The three of us met up in the little fishing town of Kilkeel and had a lovely lunch together catching up. I had such a good day. It was so good doing normal stuff, time to forget, time to feel more human not thinking about illness or what's happening right now.

I did well and managed ok. I do get so very tired, but I keep going for as long as I can, and I do know my limits.

Thank you, dearest Jill and Joanne for great company making me laugh and making me forget just for a little while, and oh Jill encouraging me to spend money, you, naughty girl!

I'm a little sad. Alex is leaving tomorrow to go on his Podiatry placement to the Isle of Wight, England. I have a heavy heart he's going away for a month. My *nest* is emptying again! I love him at home. He's such a kind thoughtful boy full of life and always great company.

Tonight, he came into my bedroom with the saddest face. I know he's feeling it to having to go away. I knew he needed a hug and so we lay on the bed and had a cuddle and a chat and worked through how he was feeling. I know it's a big thing him going away somewhere new starting over meeting new people, but Alex is so capable and up for such challenges. Combination of emotions me being sick, his brother being away, him going away, all tough, but I know he will be fine, and God will protect him, He's tearful at the thought of not seeing Matthew until Christmas time, such a long time for them both as they are so very close.

I know he will be just fine.

SATURDAY, 1 JULY

I cannot believe it's the first of July. I really don't know where the last six months have gone, but I do know I've had a lot to deal with. Lots of hurdles to get over but you know I'm still going.

Dropped Alex off at airport with such a heavy heart and as we drove the journey home, I dropped a tear or two and not much said on the way back in the car between Nigel and I.

We stopped off at the car garage for Nigel to look at new cars. I felt ok to do it albeit *very* tired. The tiredness is tough. I get so exhausted and fatigued.

We picked up some shopping on the way home. Alex got in touch to say he had arrived safely on the Isle of Wight - Some days I just don't have enough *cotton wool* to wrap him in.

SUNDAY, 2 JULY

I woke today to discover the seroma was up again filled with fluid. They called it on Thursday an oily cyst well whatever it is, its bloody sore and uncomfortable and I still have pain in the underside of my breast, armpit and down my side. They've no idea what that is. Its nasty and very frustrating as I have enough going on with chemo.

I took a walk today just very determined and a little stubborn so pushing myself. Nigel by my side making sure I was ok. I was exhausted when I got back. I want to be healthy, so I can deal with the cycles of chemo and give my body the best chance.

Today was good. Next week won't be I'm sure of that.

MONDAY, 3 JULY

My alarm was set for seven fifty-eight. Alex had asked me to ring him at eight to ensure he did not sleep in on his first day at the hospital.

I've awoke a bit low this morning didn't want to get up and lay longer than normal. Nigel came down to the bedroom to check on me saying I don't normally lie in so long. I just didn't feel like facing the day! I guess it's the thought of tomorrow, tomorrow being cycle number five. I guess I know what's coming or maybe not as I don't know from cycle to cycle how I will react or what I will be enduring but it's always a big day a long draining day. We leave normally at half seven and don't get back to six in the evening. I be totally wiped out and exhausted and then await the reactions of chemo.

I've taken the eight steroid tablets as directed and will take eight more tomorrow before I go to the hospital.

Pain in armpit not nice the seroma feels quite full and causing discomfort. How long will this go on for? My arm continues to be numb in my armpit and outer side of arm. That's as a result of surgery, most likely the nerves in the area has been affected.

Nigel is busy in the garden and I feel frustrated about that too as I cannot help. I just have no energy nor strong enough to do anything.

My lovely district nurse Felicity came in this morning and dealt with my PICC line. Such a sweet girl who is going to have a baby soon. She'll not be with me to the end as she goes off on maternity leave. I'll miss her coming in. We have become close and have had such great chats.

Alex telephoned in the afternoon he had a great first day. All went well and appeared to have enjoyed it. Seen some patients treated some patients. It's now very real for him in the world of Podiatry.

Matthew working away in England. Very busy with his summer job, and so enjoying it. He's now having what they call a *GAP* year. He plans to work and gather experience, make money, build up his little pot and maybe travel a bit before looking for a real job!

I know I've had many many side effects, but I honestly believe I've coped well, pushed through dealt with everything thrown at me. I've talked a lot to God asking for strength, guidance, grace, peace and calmness. I hope he's listening, no he always listens. I do get little signs. My prayers are being answered. *(oh, my I've just had two really bad almost back to back hot flushes so BAD my bald head is dripping with perspiration),* Talking of being bald I now have no eyelashes, no eyebrows, no hair in armpits, no leg hair, arm hair and *NO* pubic hair all gone!

You know it's a funny experience with no pubic hair when you go for a pee. When you pee normally it's like your hair directs your pee but now it goes every which way, yes, I know that's strange! The vaginal dryness is another horrendous daily issue and drying after a pee is interesting! *ok not telling you anymore as you've probably fell off your seat.* Fair to say it's all very different.

Tomorrow is the fourth July no celebrating for me -just another day at the Bridgewater suite. Ok off to sleep. Let's pray that bloods are good, health is good and I'm good to go for cycle five.

TUESDAY, 4 JULY

Awake at five just woke and got up. It's very peaceful. Made myself a cup of herbal tea (*Turmeric Gold*).*S*ince my diagnosis I've given up caffeine. I've also had no fizzy drinks since my diagnosis. Always loved a can and most days had one particularly when at work. Not anymore trying my best to avoid stuff that I think might not be healthy for me. It needs a lot of willpower, but I've done it and I'm proud of myself. I stopped drinking wine and Gin for a while not that I drank a lot but enjoyed a little glass every now and again.

As I was awake early, I decided to listen to one of the Sunday church services that have been coming to me by CD. It was Lena Morrow our lovely pastoral assistant taking the service. She has been so good to me, so attentive and supportive and I know she's praying like many others for me. I've asked for continued prayer.

I haven't been out to church since I started my chemo as I don't want to be exposed to any risk of infection or get a cold or anything that affects my ability to deal with chemo. I miss church and hearing Gods word so having it brought to me at home is just wonderful. Also took time to catch up on some messages. Friends, colleagues and loved ones have been super to me so many kind people who continue to remember me in so many ways. They haven't forgotten about me. I know some don't want to bother me. I understand totally but so many keep the words coming and for that I'm eternally grateful. I could not do this without them they know who they are.

I've tried to restrict the number of visitors to the house again so as not to introduce anything that would affect my ability to deal with this bit of the journey. I have some who walk this daily with me who never fail to call or message not just once a day but several times. Again, they know who they are - many others who have pleasantly surprised me with their support. I'm truly humbled and just didn't realise people cared so much about me. It takes time to respond to messages. Some days I just can't do it. I'm too exhausted or feeling unwell but I always get back to them and week three of each cycle when I am a little stronger the invites are plentiful, and I get taken out and spoilt.

Arrived at hospital at nine. Checked in got my pager. Chatted to a lovely lady sitting beside me who was going to have her third cycle of chemo. She has endometrial cancer and had some bowel cancer previously. She looked amazing was sporting a lovely wig and so very positive. She told me she had been out cycling last week when a dog bite her on the leg. Poor lady needed stitches and so didn't need this while undergoing chemo. She had been given a tetanus and was worried about an infection but remaining positive.

Anyways called for my bloods quickly as usual. Bloods taken and weighed have put some more weight on up to eleven stone that's around half a stone heavier from diagnosis. I lost over one stone, a mixture of worry but more to do with my change of diet since diagnosis lots more fish and green vegetables.

Back to waiting area had a quick chat with the girl who started her journey same time as me albeit different surgeries but same chemo cycles. She's had a tough time too although as I understand it not as many trips to hospital as me between cycles!

Pager off. That's me off to see the doctor. So, pleasantly surprised as I turned the corner and saw my own oncologist Dr McCarty haven't seen her since cycle one. She is such a lovely lady pleasant, so nice, so calm. Her delivery so clear and concise. I always like to see her it reassures me. It was a great consultation plenty of info *(which you know I like)*. Questions answered she spoke about my seroma and that area and asked if she could examine me *(male student in the room today)*. She was satisfied the pain coming from armpit and my breast nothing to do with chemo. The pain in my side could be from the chemo drug, says she was not concerned about it albeit aware it's difficult for me but said "let's get the chemo finished and then the breast team can look at it again and decide what to do." Bloods results back, white blood cells six point five and other five point six so reasonable readings. Still waiting on other liver and kidney bloods but she's happy all is good and good to go with cycle five. Not planning on changing any amounts and not changing my ant sickness drugs as they appear to be working. Discussed the fatigue and she asked if the Friday and Saturday post treatment was bad. I said *oh yes*, bad can hardly move. She confirmed she would wean me off the steroids slowly this time around and that might help.

We then had the discussion about radiotherapy and my need to have it or not. Based on my data and results five years ago she wouldn't be offering it or even discussing but things change. Data viewed differently therefore it's an option and it would be my decision if I wanted to undergo radiotherapy. The radiotherapy would be directed to my breast *(my new BREAST!)* it would be designed to provide a one to two percent increase of non-reoccurrence. This is all worked out cos of the tumours found, grade, type, number of lymph nodes removed and affected, in my case one. If it had of been three or more nodes, then radiotherapy would be a given.

Dr McCarty did say the side effects and risks are greater than the benefit in my case. She talked about if cancer was to come back *(gosh didn't think it could in that breast!)* then further surgery could be had. The side effects mentioned are burning to the skin, discolouration of the skin, hardening of the muscle on that side, implant displaced. She also spoke about side effects that can happen later down the line. She confirmed it would be my decision and having given me all the facts she knew I would make the decision myself and what was right for me.

I told her I needed to digest all she had said and couldn't give my decision now. She totally understood and knew I needed time. It would be discussed in three weeks' time at cycle number six. It's a big decision needing careful thought. She was so direct and so honest with me *(I like that, I need that)*

There was another conversation we needed to have. The *nodule* they have found on my lung! A repeat CT scan required. She confirmed it will take place at the end of chemo. She said she needed to give it time in order to be able to compare the previous scan with a new one a *reasonable test.* I'm ok with that and I understand. Although, it's a little difficult separating it from the cancer I know I have had in my breast. Good to talk to her about it. So, all in all a good consultation. She said she was glad to see me cos she had been getting updates in relation to all that was going on with me, the other issues raising their heads but seeing me I look well - that's good to hear. I said maybe just maybe I'll get a free three weeks in this cycle without having to attend hospital and maybe not have to see Dr McLaughlin. She said maybe and laughed.

Chemo going ahead, back at three-thirty.

We went out of the hospital *(which you can do)* and went to buy Nigel some trainers and another trip to the car garage.

He's still looking! He deserves a treat so maybe he'll make a purchase. He said the other night with what has happened to me and the shock of the diagnosis and the reality of it all, what's he keeping his money for why not spend it - *goooo* Nigel. I do agree he should treat himself it will make me happy for him.

Back at Bridgewater suite for three-thirty. Checked in and waiting.

It's been a long day awake since five.

Three forty-five into the big pink chair. Obs taken and all good.

Treatment hooked up to my PICC line and at five past four cycle five underway. Nigel by my side. I settle into the chair with my journal.

I chat to Nigel and message my friends Judy and Jill. Treatment room busy lots of chatting people coming and going. Chemo finishes at five past five.

The flush through takes place, pushing through any remaining chemo in the tubes *NO WASTE!* Niamh is the lovely nurse today looking after me along with Karen both sweet girls. I'm to get a syringe for anti-sickness *(Ondansetron)* that's new obviously Dr McCarty has directed it.

That's it's all over cycle five has happened. I can't believe I have now had five cycles of chemotherapy. One more to go in three weeks times *hooray!*

So, let's see how the next few days go. I will get my injection tomorrow from the district nurse. It's for boosting my white blood cells. It's the one that gives me such pains in my bones, *yuk!*

Off home.

WEDNESDAY, 5 JULY

Overall slept well quite exhausted from yesterday.

It's always such a long day.

Had breakfast, took my steroids and not feeling too bad.

A bit lethargic and zapped of energy.

Back to bed at ten and slept solid until two in the afternoon. Some lunch and watched Wimbledon – my favourite tournament, it passes a few hours.

District nurse came to give my injection a new young nurse called Sarah.

My injection *Neulasta. T*his is the third one since cycle three to reduce duration of Neutropenia *(low white blood cell count and help with potential febrile neutropenia - low white blood cell count with a fever) which can be caused by Cytotoxic chemotherapy - medicines that destroy rapid growing cells). W*hite blood cells are so important as they help your body fight infection. These cells very sensitive to the effects of chemotherapy. If they fall to a low level not enough then to help fight infection. This injection encourages your bone marrow *(part of the bone which makes blood cells)* to produce more white blood cells that helps fight infection so let's see.

That's it I've got it.

See how next few days go if anything like last time severe pans in neck bones. It's like in the big bones in the body, breast bone area so painful. It normally kicks in about 24 hours after I get it.

There's no advice I can give other than *grin and bear it* and take some pain relief. Paracetamol will take the edge of it. It does come and go after a few days.

The steroids taken for the day post treatment cause swelling to my face and reddening of the face and neck and my flushes increase whilst taking them again just need to go with the flow it passes - I'm so tired off for another nap.

THURSDAY, 6 JULY

I think it's so important to list some of the side effects, so you know what to expect and it's not a shock for you as it was for me. I know I will have maybe said earlier about these so apologies if repeating *(memory crap too)*. As my treatment progresses the side effects continue, and some new ones pops up particularly since the changeover of chemo after cycle three. I'm now on the *D drug*, cycles four, five and six.

Here goes at cycle number five I have -

hiccups

really light headed

pains through my body

fingernail pain

breathless (big difference since changeover drug)

peeing lots and unable to hold it

inflamed hair follicles

glaze over my eye balls like a blurring

rash on my thumbs and first two fingers

loss of hair

swelling of limbs

constipation

hoarse

sore mouth

skin falling off soles of feet

Feeling really really *FATIGUED* this morning so very tired. This is another level.

Have had breakfast taken my meds.

Nausea now being kept at bay with new meds.

Went for a walk around the garden with Nigel. It's quite a walk. It was way too difficult, and I had to stop several times *(that's shocking)* Took my temp thirty-five point eight, a little low I'll keep an eye on it and take it again in a while

Mummy was here today helping do my housework and general chores. She's so very kind and I so appreciate it.

Had a wee visit from my sister and niece Zoe. Another couple of visitors at the door but I'm not fit to meet and greet way too tired and fatigued.

I managed to shower with Nigel in the ensuite to keep any eye on me and ensure I stay safe.

I got some lovely Suki Herbal tea today given by a dear friend from work Mandy *(my favourite favours lemon and ginger)* so kind of her to think of me.

Also, some more beautiful flowers left on the window sill, later to discover from my lovely neighbour Freda who continues to think about me and bring such wonderful flowers.

So many people praying for me and I am so grateful as I am so low that I'm just basically breathing!

I give thanks to God and acknowledge how he is looking after me, guiding me, supporting me and giving me strength to fight my disease.

FRIDAY, 7 JULY

A new day and no real change.

Very tired, few pains, hiccups continue didn't make it to bed last night slept on the sofa.

Taken my meds.

Jill called in to check on me. I think if she sees me, she's happy. I know it's been difficult for her to watch me go through this.

Spent most of the day in bed just couldn't get up taking meds and sleeping, hiccups continue *(bloody awful)*.

I have been thinking today about radiotherapy about my decision. Still not there yet. I have watched a video on the process of radiotherapy. I have listened to Dr McCarty and that the radio will be for three weeks and fifteen sessions and all for a two percent benefit and that it has a great risk of side effects. It will be concentrated on my new breast where my implant is another big consideration.

I'm not there yet as not mentally and physically strong enough to make a sensible coherent rational decision.

SATURDAY, 8 JULY

Another day like yesterday just much the same.

FATIGUE on a whole new level!

The worst thing today is constipation. It's awful. I cannot go to the toilet at all. It's calling for desperate measures. I did start laxatives on Thursday but not working it's getting painful. I need to go, my body wants to go, but nothing happening.

Taste buds up the left again mouth feeling funny and sore, hiccups continue but I'm still hanging on.

Just sleeping and watching the Tennis.

Answered a few messages from lovely kind people who are thinking about me. My three beautiful boys are spoiling me always checking in on me making sure I'm ok. I know it's not nice for them watching me like this, lets pray it gets better and I can eventually make this a *memory*.

SUNDAY, 9 JULY

A restless night.

Bowels playing havoc. Up a couple of times such pain and discomfort *(please please make sure if you must endure this process you get yourself on laxatives in good time DO NOT suffer this awfulness)*.

It's a fine line as chemo can cause diarrhoea and you suffer from constipation, so I always want to be careful with laxatives and not confuse what's happening to my body. My bowel appear to stop working as soon as I get a cycle of chemo. Yesterday I had a total blockage sat on the toilet for ages with no movement and incredible pain and you know in the end *(this is not nice)* I had to assist in the removal *(awful I know)* but couldn't cope with the pain any longer so it required *intervention.* Anyway, up this morning and have spent most of the morning on the toilet. Oh my days! The world is starting to fall from my bottom, such stomach pains. *Omg!* but at least there is movement. I continue to take the *Dulcolax* with breakfast. If I have got it started, I'll keep taking them and keep the movement.

My handwriting is atrocious this morning. I am just struggling cos the fingernail pain is back again. Oh, dear so painful everything you touch the pain in the nails is awful. I cannot bear my hands going into hot water as it causes such pain hopefully this only lasts a few days. My taste buds totally gone, mouth sore and got some more mouthwash from the dentist that has helped for sure *(good stuff)*.

Nearly finished my drugs for this post cycle time. One more day will complete them. Steroids finished, came off them more gradually this time. So, fatigued but I will cope. One of the anti-sickness drugs makes me very sleepy *(Levomepromazine)*. I don't mind that. It helps when going to bed at night time it assists with sleeping.

I weighed myself this morning. I've lost a few pounds now ten stone thirteen, was eleven stone one on Tuesday.

I can hear Nigel hoovering and doing some housework. He's so good an incredible man who just gets on with it. He knows what needs to be done.

He's busy and I'm sitting drinking my *Suki* Tea - delicious!

THURSDAY, 13 JULY

A bit of a gap since I last wrote in my journal. Haven't checked in for a few days.

Well I guess you can work out why?

Tough few days and just not able to put pen to paper.

So many issues to deal with. It's all I can do to function and deal with the issues as they arise. *One day at a time* is my mantra. Handwriting has got a little better as the pain in my fingers is easing. Nails are still on my fingers but all breaking not sure what's going on. Taste buds now slowly returning. Hot flushes in abundance and rash on my hands irritating. Keeping an eye on my right hand just in case skin breaks. I don't need an infection on the right side. I've been using Marigolds as I cannot bear the hot water on my hands.

I have developed a *new* issue in my stomach. I have a discomfort a mix between a pain and like a feeling of burning indigestion. This is different haven't had this stomach problem in the last four cycles. Very uncomfortable. I will keep a check on it.

My hiccups have stopped.

Nigel gets concerned when I try to do some things around the house, but I need to try. I want normality something to keep me sane.

My messages of support continue to come in. I'm truly humbled such caring people.

I told a dear friend back a few months ago when we were chatting that it's at times like this a life changing experience where people will drop into your life make such a difference and *never* leave again along with those whom you will *now* forget and know they are not important to you and not waste your energy on such people.

Thankfully I have very few of those, but in times of reflection everything becomes very clear. It's quite therapeutic a cleansing – what's important and what's not!

TUESDAY, 18 JULY

It's been a few days since I've written anything in my journal.

Reason being Friday and Saturday were tough. What do I mean I hear you ask?

Well, on Friday I was at a such a low ebb, not in a good place mentally and more so emotionally. I just couldn't stop crying. I felt so sad, so low and so empty. I couldn't really explain it but just didn't want to do anything see anyone or be bothered with anything. I know Matthew was unsure of what was going on and I couldn't explain it. What I can say is during each chemo cycle at a certain point in the three weeks I feel like this. I'm sure if I checked it may be the same stage at each cycle.

Just so tearful and emotional.

Well it didn't sit well with mummy who came to the house to do some ironing. Mummy just couldn't understand what was going on and lacked *tactfulness* wondering what on earth would be wrong with me today. *Really!* What on earth is wrong with me - what's wrong? Well, I didn't respond to her very well and we had major fallout and I shouted at her saying, *I was dealing with cancer, maybe that's what's wrong with me.* You know my mum means well but she just sometimes doesn't get it and doesn't think before she speaks. Just not able to work it out and *where its sometimes best to say nothing at all.* She doesn't understand the enormity of the journey.

It's not mum going through this very difficult time it's me! I totally get it that she's upset that her daughter is sick and battling cancer and it's tough to watch, but watching it is very different to *living* it every day. You need to be walking in my shoes!

Well my Friday wasn't good.

My dear friend Judy arrived at the door came in found me on the sofa sobbing. She just held me, hugged me and *said nothing at all.* When she did speak, she said, "come on get up we are going for an ice cream" and we did. She took me out in her car, and we drove to *Rathfriland (the little market town where I grew up and went to school).* We got ice cream and just sat in the car and ate it.

A few tears and some laughter just what the doctor ordered.

She gave me a *Gardeners World* magazine and brought me home. I felt a little better. What a wonderful friend I'm very lucky she's in my life.

I got dressed and went for dinner in the evening with Nigel and Matthew. It was a special meal with Matthew as he was leaving to start his *gap year* adventures. First stop Cambridgeshire to do a harvest.

I kept the tears away.

Saturday, I felt much the same but kept myself busy getting Matthew organised for leaving all the while feeling so very weak with little energy. It's hard to explain. The tears they just come from deep within and I cannot control it.

The cording in my arm is causing excruciating pain worse than ever. I'm feeling it right now down into my wrist and the movement in my arm is restricted again. I seem to move two steps forward and back four. So frustrating and uncomfortable. It doesn't seem to be getting any better. At the same time, I have discomfort in my armpit which is numb just like the upper outside of my right arm. I don't think now it's going to return to normal.

My stomach pain over the weekend has eased that was CRAP too!

My PICC line annoyed me all week.

My mouth has improved mouthwash from the dentist is working.

My annoyance with mummy continues. I just can't believe some of the things she says to me. I'm not going to speak about them but fair to say she just doesn't think about what she says!

My messages of support keep coming in such loyal and attentive friends and people in my life. Cards, flowers, gifts even my neighbour Jenny from over the fields left a cake at my door *delicious* and such a kind thing to do.

Saturday night the doorbell rang and a lovely lady from church Ann Pepper came to visit. She told me she had been thinking about me and just had to come see me and brought a lovely card. Her husband had driven her out - God was directing her - wow what a lovely lady and such a kind thing to do. Thank you Ann and Derek.

Sunday saw Matthew leave for Cambridgeshire.

Early start we got up with him at after five, cup of tea and farewells.

Oh, I will miss him so much but he's excited and happy and off to do something he wants to. Heavy heart I had but after a little cry my tears stopped.

Monday saw my lovely nurse Felicity come in to see me for the last time. She's now going on maternity leave. She has been wonderful these last three months.

I looked forward to our Monday morning chats whilst she deals with my PICC line. A great nurse. I'll have someone new next Monday.

My *hot* flushes continue. The hot weather certainly doesn't help.

Gosh, I looked in the mirror at the weekend and a bald, totally hairless person looked back. I don't even have eyebrows *(mum has bought me an eye pencil so I can draw them on well that's interesting!)*

I've no eyelashes either now that's causing a few issues dry and itchy eyes, watery and swollen eyelids quite unpleasant. I've bought some drops to see if they will help. I'm sure the pollen count is a factor too. There's no protection for my eyes with eyelashes gone. I just look like an *alien* although those closest to me dispute that saying that I have a perfect shape of head for baldness and suit no hair.

I think they are just being kind although it doesn't bother me *NO HAIR*. I run around with my little bald head inside and out. I answer the door to my lovely post man, Paul *(it must have startled him to see me like this, but he's been so kind and unphased)*. Other callers at the door also see my baldness as I forget I've nothing on my head and open the door. I have bought some nice head pieces spoilt myself as I like them coordinating with my clothes. No *wig* worn. I just can't wear one it's not me, being true to myself. I have no hair why pretend. I don't need too.

Today I spent with mummy. She treated me to lunch at Millfarm at Hillsborough. We did a little shopping. It was a lovely *(we've made up, we always do!)*

I get so very tired but getting out of the house helps a lot. Just must pace myself. I get so frustrated I'm not able to do things I did before I got cancer. I can't do anything in my garden. I try to walk in week three of each cycle just pushing myself. Nigel comes walking with me to make sure I'm safe. I must stop on each walk. It's difficult. My pace is really affected, and I feel quite breathless, but I try, and it makes me feel good.

WEDNESDAY, 19 JULY

I had such a lovely day today with Jill & Katie. We did breakfast in Café Marmalade and went shopping after in a little town where I used to work, Warrenpoint in County Down. Jill was looking for an outfit for her son's wedding. Such a privilege for me to be with them both. Was fun and exciting. Fantastic, we found an outfit, and she looks fab in it.

Went to Rathfriland had tea and traybakes and ended our day back at Jill's for some chat and great company. So special and such a lovely day.

THURSDAY, 20 JULY

We have a couple of guys at the house doing some works outside. It's so exciting getting this piece of work completed. Been waiting a while. I know little things make me very happy. Though truthfully, it's a feeling of moving forward, being positive, pushing ahead. Getting on with things Nigel and I had planned before I got sick *fresh beginnings* along with normalness. It's positive and makes me feel good.

We had a walk this morning together well I can't really call it a walk it's a slow stroll requiring lots of stops. I'm really struggling with fitness very fatigued like nothing I can clearly describe. I'm drinking my green smoothies again not the most pleasant to drink but the contents are good for the body and hopefully helping boost my blood count for next Tuesday. The steroids have so increased my appetite it's crazy. I'm eating so much more. I have put some weight on getting close to my normal weight again.

Today I had some visitors. Mandy my work colleague and dear friend came for lunch. I did an afternoon tea for her. It was nice catching up. She's been very supportive throughout. Lena from church called. Both visits were just lovely, and they overlapped with each other so got to chat. This happens often with my constant visitors to the door. I like that very much my friends mixing together.

Alex rang. Had a great chat. His first placement on the Isle of Wight going well. I'm so very proud of him. He's so happy with his choices, such a wise boy!

Matthew's adventure appears to be going well. Again, I'm so pleased and proud of him. He's grown up so much and he's happy.

Jenny from over the fields phoned for a chat *(the lady that makes the lovely cake)*.

Phones calls and messages keep coming.

My friends say I need a secretary to handle all the contact. How lucky am I?

My nail pain has eased although I can see my nails dying before my eyes. They've become so white in colour obviously they are taking a beating but still hanging on which I'm grateful for.

My stomach is sore again today. It's a weird feeling not a severe pain more discomfort like an indigestion type feeling. *Nasty.*

The other weird thing since treatment started when I need to go to the toilet for a pee my bladder struggles to hold. I'm having some near misses! (*I know, how bad is that!*) but I can't help it. It's like I've no control the pee just decides to come oh boy! I hope that corrects itself after chemo finishes.

I'm feeling in better form thank goodness.

FRIDAY, 21 JULY

I awoke today feeling more normal.

Still have all the daily issues but form better.

Not sure if I've said this before but I do have a high pain threshold but it's not an easy path.

I arranged for my mum, sister and my niece to come for lunch. I made an afternoon tea as I wanted to do something nice for them. Then my dear friend twin Jill called with some flowers. She joined us for lunch great craic! My boss Gillian called. We were all together *(overlaps just great)* what a nice afternoon just what I needed.

SATURDAY, 22 JULY

I got to go out today with mum. We met up with my brother and sister in-law so we could help Geoffrey pick a new suit for a wedding they were going to soon. I was so pleased to be able to be with them and help in a normal activity. Made me so happy. Again, I was totally exhausted, but I didn't care.

I had to sleep when I got home.

MONDAY, 24 JULY

Didn't sleep well last night so many HOT flushes they are horrible. Difficult to deal with. Leaves you unsettled and broken sleep which is not good.

Today I had my bosses call with me. Oh, my the Chief Superintendent and the Superintendent. For these guys to take time out of their busy schedule especially on a Monday morning to come see me well I am very humbled indeed. The Supt had visited before, but the Chief Superintendent is new since I've gone off sick. I made morning tea and coffee and some nice little treats. Both the bosses were wonderful, so supportive and kind made me feel it was all about *me*. Well I guess it is! They said I needed to concentrate on me, take time to deal with what's going on right now and not to be thinking about work. The Superintendent did say I was in a very good position where work was concerned with my years' service and that I could *bow out* now if I wanted to. They both know I want to complete thirty years' service, but I could go now at twenty-seven years. Whatever will work for me, my health and my future. I joined the police service to complete thirty years' service that was and is my plan. It's been a wonderful career. I've loved it so much. No job regrets, so fulfilling such a variety of roles.

I cannot say just now what the future will be. Honestly don't know if I'll ever be able to return to work. I hope so, but right now I'm not thinking about it.

Let's get my chemo finished, my tests completed, my further therapy, my recovery and I'll then decide. Work is being wonderful to me. The superintendent said my job remains in my current department if I return. The bosses were honestly lovely and made me feel good today. It was pleasure having them.

My friend Joy called to see me. Oh, I love her so much. She's the other half of Joy and Jill my school friend *twins*. She arrived just as the bosses were leaving (they had stayed with me for over two hours) how amazing.

My district nurse today was new as Felicity now off on maternity leave. Today it was Orla another great girl. Dealt with my PICC. No issues just the usual procedure for cleaning and checking.

I cannot believe tomorrow is cycle six and the last chemotherapy session. *Unbelievable!* I've made it. Where did that time go? Sometimes it feels like yesterday and other times it feels like an eternity. The day before I always feel a little apprehensive cos, I now know what happens and what will come after treatment. I'm always nervous as I worry in case when I get there I'm deemed not fit for treatment and you just want it to happen and be over. Despite me doing everything I can at home to stay fit and healthy things can happen I know that.

Nigel and I now have *chemo day* off pat! I feel a bit different today. I'm excited that tomorrow finishes treatment but a little scared that once treatment finishes what happens next? I feel a little *vulnerable* and *emotional.* You're asking why?

Well I suppose whilst your undergoing treatment you know you're getting something that's hopefully working to kill any cancer *lurking* in my body. So now it's stopping you are on your own! I'm thinking there will be nothing further fighting this *imposter* in my body. Yet I hope all the cancer is gone. It's just gonna be something new after tomorrow and I think tomorrow will be tough.

Emotional for Nigel & I. A milestone reached. It's the end of July.

234

We have been living for this day, working to this date. When we spoke in February about me needing to have chemotherapy it seemed so far away the end of July. Now it's here - just wonderful. This time three weeks I will not be preparing for chemo tomorrow. Then I can move to the next stage of this journey. I know I have a bit to go yet. I need to recover from chemo. I know it takes time, but you just want to be normal again! The nurse today said it can take a year for chemo to go through your body in respect of recovery my goodness a *year!*

Tomorrow I must tell the oncology team my decision about radiotherapy Am I going to have it? I have some questions for my oncology team including about my *Hormone Therapy* and rescanning of my *lung*. Let's pray cycle six goes ahead and that I have the strength both physically and mentally.

I pray Nigel is ok and strong as we reach this milestone.

TUESDAY, 25 JULY - CYCLE SIX

Not too bad a night. Slept ok. Up at seven so I could get breakfast and take my first steroids of the day.

We headed off at eight for the journey to the hospital. Traffic so light we made good time arriving early.

Usual routine, check in, get my pager *last time*, I hope. Saw the girl who has been getting treatment same time as me. Her husband was with her. She will also be having radiotherapy and will move to that next stage in a few weeks' time.

We always have a little catch up and compare notes from cycle to cycle. Like me her road has also been tough though from my interactions with her she has approached her cancer differently. She just doesn't want to think or talk about it. She has had massive issues about losing her hair *(didn't we all but just deal with it differently)*. She doesn't read anything about cancer, her treatments, and I read everything! I think she kept her illness secret for a while. What I do understand is *no two women* are the same. Whilst on this journey we all approach it differently and that's just fine. I never kept my illness a secret. I could not have got this far without my family and friends. Me losing my hair was a necessary evil. I loved my hair. I had fabulous hair, but you know what hopefully it will grow back.

Pager sounding so that's me off for bloods, but as I rounded the corner Dr McCarty my oncologist was standing, so I had to go back and get Nigel.

Consultation first this morning that's different! Great consultation. She asked how the last three weeks had been. We discussed all the issues including new pain in the tummy which she said most likely was coming from additional steroids I'm taking. That's good to know so she's going to prescribe a tablet for the next three weeks to help with tummy.

We talked about my horrible constipation. That's apparently coming as a result of Ondansetron *(anti sickness tablet)*. I stressed how difficult it has been like total blockage and couldn't go to the toilet. I told her I was taking DULCOLAX and she said keep taking it.

More than happy for treatment to go ahead today with no changes. Same dose as last time if my bloods are ok.

She then moved to the subject of *Hormone Therapy*. We discussed that. She explained everything about it or as she called it *anti-hormone* therapy. I will start it in three to four weeks' time. It will be prescribed by the GP (letter provided by Oncologist). I'm going onto *TAMOXIFEN* for two and a half years, then it will be changed to another drug for a further two and a half years, and if it's all going well can maybe be continued for 5 years giving me 10 years on Hormone Therapy. That will be reviewed. I'll take it *orally* each day. Side effects include risk of blood clots in lower leg so keep an eye on this (long-haul flights to be discussed if planning any, but flight to Spain ok thank goodness for that!) long-haul could mean me having to come off the drug to prevent DVT. She did say I could *struggle* with the drug. To try it for two to three months and then it can be reviewed. I can go onto a different drug if it proves too difficult.

Ok the topic of radiotherapy revisited. She wanted to know my decision. My answer is *NO* to radiotherapy. I am not undergoing three weeks, fifteen sessions for a two percent benefit. She looked pleased with my decision. We chatted at length about it and the future. I told her *(quite emotionally)* it's a little scary saying no and I hope I don't regret it. She told me I wouldn't. She told me I had a new breast made, my tumours were not close to chest wall and there were clear margins. I will need to be self-aware as I move forward and if I notice any change or discomfort then I will trigger an appointment or if my lymph nodes in armpit have a swelling or lump.

I'm happy with my decision as she was.

Nigel also very happy and content. I always value his opinion and guidance as he so wise. He has heard all the info and digested it much clearer than me I'm sure.

The CT rescan of my lung will take place at the end of August. An appointment will come out for that.

Dr McCarty said she'd see me again in October for review and happy for me to fly down to Spain in three to four weeks times.

I asked when my PICC line could come out of my arm. Today she said. *whoopee* really that's just fantastic another milestone. The nurses will remove at end of my cycle today. Straightforward procedure I'm told *(it's been there a while now)* so I won't have this thing in my arm some more normality.

So that's it all my questions answered. I had a wee list *today (no surprise there then!)* Well I need answers so make no apologies. I thanked Dr McCarty for all her support and care and told her I hope I didn't see her again in these circumstances, just happy to see her for reviews!

Consultation over.

I will still get the injection again tomorrow by district nurse *(twenty-four hours after chemo).*

We had a few hours to wait so we left the hospital to do a few messages. It's good to do some normal things.

Back at the hospital for one thirty. Checked in with treatment unit but they are running late today. Here's me excited with earlier time for treatment on the last one. I might get out of the hospital sooner. Awh well can't be helped. (I can write in my journal). *Wendy Walker* oh my name has been called at last it's now three fifteen, but I know they are busy its fine.

Into treatment unit for last time, cycle number six. I'm so nearly there. It's a bit surreal and a bit of a blur. Where has the time gone?

Into the big pink chair. All my obs completed. Asked if I felt sick and am I ok? Then they come with the stuff to flush the PICC line preparing it for my chemo. All completed.

Arrival of my last *cocktail*!

The treatment room is quite full today so many people getting treatment. Three thirty-five chemo underway. Nigel by my side as he has been for all my sessions.

In just one hour it will be over all my sessions finished. I started treatment on twenty-nineth March, and it will end today twenty-fifth July.

It's finished *chemo* over. Oh my days!

It's all very calm, very matter of fact, no big shouting or whooping. No fireworks, no bells ringing.

Nurses Hayley and Niamh have been looking after me today. They kept enquiring if I was ok.

They flushed the PICC line which I was excited about as Dr McCarty said it could come out no need to stay in anymore. *Pippa the PICC line* will be leaving me. Nurse Hayley says they need to check notes about removal of PICC line. I confirmed doctor said it could be removed today. Roisin the nurse arrives at my chair saying Dr McCarty had not written it up on my file for removal of PICC line so they can't remove it. No way I said, *please* it's to be removed but they couldn't as there was no written permission. It would have to be another day once checked with doctor. Oh, I want this thing out of my arm please take it out. I know I won't be fit over the next few days when post chemo effects kick in and it will now mean another trip to the hospital for removal. Heh ho that's the way it is, it's not coming out today.

I'm finished.

I want to go home.

Nigel & I are leaving together. He's been so wonderful so supportive, strong, just a great man. I'm very lucky. I left the team at the assessment and treatment units some chocolates just to say thank you. A small token, a very small token as they all have been wonderful during my visits what a great team of people.

WEDNESDAY, 26 JULY

District nurse came in today to give me my injection into my tummy. My final Neulasta injection to boost while blood cells. Again, hopefully last one. I've had four of them, but now know what to expect the severe pains in my bones up into my back of neck and my chest bones.

Today I've been fatigued just like before so very tired just taking my meds and sleeping.

THURSDAY, 27 JULY

Today just like yesterday. So fatigued spent long time in bed just sleeping.

I'm taking my laxatives and did have slight movement but nothing worth talking about. Hopefully that improves and I don't have a repeat of last time!

FRIDAY, 28 JULY

Slept ok. Up just once in the night.

So, fatigued. I tried my stomach tablet differently this morning. Took it one hour before food to see if it would help the discomfort.

Had breakfast and meds.

Rang oncology helpline as no call from hospital about removal of my PICC line. Charlie the nurse rang me back. I explained my enquiry and he said he would check. Called me back within minutes saying come on down to Cancer Centre and they would remove it. *Whoopee.*

I messaged Nigel to work. I know he wanted to take me though I couldn't go right away as I was much too fatigued to leave the house. I need to go back to bed for a while.

I did sleep. Got a few hours just need to build up energy to leave house to make trip to hospital.

Nigel arrived, and we headed to the cancer centre.

When I arrived at Ward 2A two male nurses were waiting on me with my file and a little tray with all the bits in it for removal of PICC Line.

Very smooth and prompt.

I was taken to a bay in the ward. Nigel said he would wait outside I said no I wanted him with me, so we went in together. Nigel took a seat beside the bed I was asked to get up onto. I was so excited about it being removed. Charlie the nurse was all gloved up and started the process for removing. So far so good no dramas *(I thought this would be so easy!)* The device that was in my arm under the skin the wire that ran up through vein to top of heart removed slowly. I didn't feel a thing. It was gone brilliant. Now for the last bit attached to my arm a little orange device like a little heart shaped plastic device nearly an inch long. It's used to keep PICC line in place. It has a wee set of prongs which attaches to skin *(it always irritated me)* District nurse used to help by putting a little bit of padding between it and my arm skin.

Charlie the nurse started to remove it, *BUT* it wasn't moving it wouldn't come out. It was deeply embedded in my arm. My arm had obviously grown round it. It would not budge oh my days! The pain it was awful as he pulled at it the skin on my arm pulled with it. It was hurting. I was squirming, but I tried to stay calm on the bed and took deep breaths. Nurse stopped and took a breath realising this was working. Nigel was standing by bedside watching it holding my hand and I was squeezing his tightly. The other nurse Kieran appeared at my bedside. This time the curtains were around me. A discussion between both nurses the fact the device was clearly embedded in my arm and wouldn't come out. Kieran got gloved up to assist Charlie. I just looked away the pain was immense. I didn't need to see what was going on. Just at that very moment Nigel who was standing at my side says out loud *I don't feel well guys.* I looked at him and he had gone a dreadful bad colour, pale and grey all at once oh my days he's gonna *faint!* The nurse got him onto a chair, head between his knees and they gave him attention while I lay there with this *thing* stuck in my arm. Within a few minutes Nigel was fine. We did have a giggle. I couldn't believe it, as he has endured and dealt with so much with me these last seven months and nothing ever a bother. Blood, wounds, scars, bandage removal and now he decides to faint – so funny. I'm lying on the bed in severe pain and discomfort cos this bloody thing won't come out. Nasty wee bugger. Normal business resumed poor Nigel he's fine now much better colour. So, both nurses got back to job in hand. It was calling for drastic measures! Scissors out to cut device in half one side removed and the other still really stuck. Charlie gave up and let Kieran take over. He applied heavier pressure pushing hard down onto my arm and at last it came out *hallelujah*! Thank God. Everyone sighed with relief not least me. Pain in my arm awful. Kieran put heavy pressure to my arm to stop the bleeding at the sight and held it for five minutes. They then placed a pressure bandage to stop any further bleeding. I was told to keep it on for twenty-four hours and replace with a clean bandage.

I'm not sure how my upper left arm will look when bandage removed but at least it's out. The nurses did say to me that I must have a *high pain threshold* to have endured that procedure. Well, I always said I did have, and I think that proved it for sure! *No kidding.*

SATURDAY, 29 JULY

Today I am zapped. No energy at all. Totally fatigued just needing to sleep and sleep.

Taste buds gone, hiccups in full throttle, lots of pains, nails getting sore again, just the normal stuff like previous sessions. I've had a carrot, celery and apple drink. My dear sister in law Mandy recommends it for a PH drink to keep alkaline levels in the body right. She says the apples seeds are good for B17 so of course I'll try anything to assist my body and this fight against cancer.

SUNDAY, 30 JULY

A new development this morning.

I've had a severe bout of dizziness and feeling faint - nearly lost it in the kitchen was just going to faint, go down Nigel to the rescue just in time! Funny feeling. I'm just not very well this morning. Nigel got me to the sofa and crisis averted. It's the crazy fatigue and tiredness. No capacity to do anything. Can't even dress myself.

You must listen to your body, cannot ignore any signs. The fainting could have been very dangerous if I had been on my own, that's how vulnerable you are. I'm glad Nigel was here. He got me to bed and I slept the afternoon away.

Toilet habits not great! I've been taking two laxatives each night to try and help, but I am very constipated. You know when tiny marbles are popping out that things are not good! I do drink lots and lots of water but still it's difficult, but you know you just need to keep pushing forward and pray it will pass.

My nail pain so bad, oh boy crap crap crap.

In my scripture readings this morning, I had a very powerful prayer

The Prayer

Jesus, I need you! You are my Lord my God my King. You are worthy of all my worship. Help me by your grace, to know you and love you so deeply that the things of this world fade away and grow strangely dim. I need your power, your grace and your love so that no matter what life brings my way I can respond to each situation, each person and each trial the way you would respond – all for your glory. May I find all of my joy in you, may I glorify you in all I do. Lord Jesus grant me your grace, your mercy and your living kindness to enable me to see you, know you, love you and be one with you. Thank you that your word tells me if we ask anything in your name and according to your will that you will do it.

Amen

MONDAY, 31 JULY

The last day of July.

Oh, my goodness. I can't believe it! Its Monday. I'm not feeling so good. Another tough night. I couldn't get over to sleep, so much going around in my head and feeling so awful.

I'm feeling rotten this morning just no energy and so many aches and pains fit for nothing, but I've got to ride this storm. Hopefully things will improve - no more chemo so that's a bonus.

THURSDAY, 10 AUGUST

It's been several days since I've written in my journal just didn't feel like writing.

No energy and no desire.

It has been just about living day to day and dealing with post chemo days.

The *bowel* department, is just now returning to some kind of normality. The usual nasty pattern just awful although for sure the laxatives helped this time.

My hands have suffered again. Pains in the nails so sore and different. Still having great pain and discomfort. A new development this time, right hand thumb and index finger no feeling in the tips of them so weird! Gosh I hope the feeling comes back into them.

The cording in my right arm continues to be a nightmare. It peaks with pain you clearly can see the cording its visible in the arm. It just looks like a cord running under my skin. The skin is taut. The pain is running into the wrist and right up into my armpit.

The fatigue continues. I expect it and understand it will take time.

Over the last week struggling with mummy and frustrated with her, how she is not coping, she does stress me. I must remove myself from it, cos it's not healthy. A good chat with Alex my beautiful boy. He always puts everything into perspective. He gets annoyed when I'm annoyed. I keep thinking about some of the stuff mummy says to me. You know she doesn't realise what comes out of her mouth or maybe sometimes she does know exactly what she's saying!! I do believe she does not totally understand the enormity of cancer!

I plan to visit GP next week. It's my doctor who will be giving me my prescription for *Tamoxifen* the new drug I'm going to be taking for some time. I will start it in around two weeks' time.

The chest rescan date is getting close. It's happening on twenty-third August. I have been thinking about it these last few days. It comes up in conversation when I'm chatting with others as they know I need to have rescan of my lung. I'm thinking what will be the best outcome from the CT scan? Nodule gone, Nodule smaller in size, Nodule same size – no change, Nodule grown *(well clearly that won't be a good thing!)* We'll see.

I haven't done much these last two weeks. I can't. I am so not well enough.

No walking this time at all! I've noticed some different development in my legs. I have new pains in my upper legs frontal area from knees to groin when I walk. I feel so weak like my legs won't carry me. If I go out into the garden to walk, I must stop like I can't go any further. If I draw my legs up when sitting the pains are bad. I guess just another side effect of chemo. Let's hope it lifts and the pains go away.

Struggling with my eyes on two levels; my eyesight just not as good particularly in the evenings and I have water running from them. I need to carry a hanky to dry them. They are so dry and then when I go outside they continually water.

My face skin is itchy and been quite blotchy!

No hair anywhere on my body *all gone*! Though I've noticed on my head there is small hairs appearing happy days! How exciting, a little fine bit of hair. My head is like a duck with downy hair like not even a one centimetre, but definitely a change. During chemo cycles one to three the *(red colour drug)* is the one that makes you lose your hair then cycles four to six is the changeover drug and you don't get the *red* one, so I guess with all the weeks that has passed since cycle three its normal for regrowth *hooray*.

It's comforting to see that as you do wonder if your hair will ever grow back and what colour, texture, thickness it will be?

My breast area continues to cause me discomfort. I've tried to go to bed with the bra on *(which I've worn every day since January and surgery number one)* and trying without a bra wearing a tight vest just to give me a break from bra wearing. I feel it tight and have the discomfort under the new breast and the seroma in my armpit as it's filled up again. It's strange having the *new* breast and it's taking time to get used to it. It's still healing and settling even after all this time.

My visitors continue to come. I'm still getting cards and flowers from such lovely people. My dear friends continue to support me.

I've just had Judy & Mike call on their way to a sheep trial in the South of Ireland. It is always nice to see them.

Jill checks in with me every day.

Mummy rings most days. Some of her calls stresses me, just doesn't think what she saying and other days its fine. I know she cares very much about me. It must be difficult for her. The first three months after diagnosis she was wonderful, a real trooper and did lots of stuff around the house. A good distraction for her but the last three months I've struggled with her cos the focus was back on her and her complaining about her health issues. She feels the need to complain about silly insignificant stuff and tells me all about her illnesses whilst I'm dealing with mine. She is now complaining about a pain in her breast like come on do you really need to. She rings to say she's so tired just wants to sleep all day fit for nothing and wait for it she said, "I just said earlier to myself I'm so tired you'd think I was having chemo" come on how bad is that. I did challenge her and tell her not to say such things out loud and certainly not to anyone else - the thing is you need to walk in my shoes, experience what I've endured then you might not say such ridiculous things cos you *only* tired!

Yesterday I had lunch with my dear friends Valerie, Doreen & Jill. They arranged for us to go to Velvet Rose in Dromore such a lovely lunch with lovely friends.

Today I had a visit form Gillian my manager. When she arrived, she handed me an envelope telling me to open it before I ate my lunch. So, I did, my oh my! Such a lovely surprise inside the envelope. It was the invitation to the *Royal Garden Party*, yes it arrived. It is happening a Royal Garden Party at Hillsborough Castle the official residence of the Northern Ireland Secretary of State. It is where Queen Elizabeth resides when in Northern Ireland. The invitation said,

The Secretary of State for Northern Ireland the Rt Hon James Brokenshire MP requests the honour of the company of Mrs Wendy Walker and Mr Nigel Walker at a Garden Party at Hillsborough Castle on Thursday 7th September 2017 from 3pm to 5pm.

So, in one months' time I'm off to a garden party. I just hope I'm well enough to attend - oh what will I wear? I need a new *frock* and of course I'm thinking what will I wear on my head? I've no hair. Some thought required! I think this treat is lovely for Nigel too, so deserved.

SUNDAY, 13 AUGUST

The weekend was much like the last few days.

Mum took me out on Friday a nice day we had.

My legs are very strange still that pain in upper legs. It's like there's no power in them like *muscle fatigue*. It's difficult to walk any distance really difficult. It's weird, as I didn't experience this in cycles one to five.

My finger nails are now turning white in colour with severe pains in the fingers and thumbs along with my skin has broken out in a rash on my hands, so sore, hurts to touch the hands against anything. They are throbbing. I think I'm going to lose my nails.

WEDNESDAY, 16 AUGUST

Leg pain continues. It's like the muscles in my upper legs are fatigued. I'm struggling to walk. I try to go out into my garden must stop and gather further strength before I continue. Nail pain and discolouration continues and another *new* development *(can there be anymore)*. The skin is falling off the sole of my left foot. My goodness I've never seen anything like this. No pain at all just the skin falling off slightly awful to look at. Alex has had a look (the podiatrist in the making), think he's surprised.

My fingertips continue to be numb with pins and needles. So, I decided to do a bit of online research. I need to know what's going on. I also asked my dear cousin Diane who is also fighting this disease and has gone through her chemotherapy. She confirms she has so much pain post chemo from her shoulders to her toes and her consultant confirmed it's the chemo and that it may improve, may get better or she may have it for rest of her life – oh my days! That's tough.

Online research shows women speak of pains, leg pain, fatigue in the muscles so I guess I'm normal, its normal if you know what I mean!

Alex suggested I google *skin loss on soles of feet after chemo*. So, I did and yes again common side effect of chemotherapy. It lists a condition called *hand-foot* syndrome normally appears two to three months after chemo. Oh boy mine is happening fast then! Again, this is normal. So, what I'm saying is don't panic you've got to go with it. It's just some of the side effects of chemo. Some of the chemo medicines cause stuff to happen.

THURSDAY, 17 AUGUST

This morning I went to see the GP. Took my letter from the Oncologist. This is to get my new Hormone Therapy drug – *Tamoxifen.* Nigel kindly drove me over to surgery which opens at eight forty-five and morning surgery has no appointment system you just go. We arrived at eight thirty-five, and I got the shock of my life to see a long line of people standing outside the surgery waiting on the doors to open. There were *twenty-one* people standing there – yes twenty-one people *crazy.* I was not impressed. I thought of going home as how would I get out there and stand in that queue, and yet if I didn't how many will be ahead of me by the time the doors open. I can't stand for any length of time. I'm much too weak and I don't want to stand among all those people who must be sick! What about the germs? what if I pick up something? I don't want their bugs.

I sat in the car and watched the queue get longer. By the time the doors opened twenty-six people were going in ahead of me.

When I went I inside my record confirmed I'm was not to sit in the waiting room with other patients (my surgery were so good doing that throughout). I was directed to room eight a doctor's consultation room which was empty. I went into the quiet room it was dark with the blinds closed. I took a seat. It was nine o'clock Now a waiting game with twenty-six patients ahead of me! Ten o'clock Dr McCandless came to get me (how kind such a great doctor). She has been brilliant these last eight months, so supportive, understanding and kind. We had a brief chat well actually I gave off about the number of patients standing on the street as I arrived! Then conversation turned to me. I told her how I was keeping. There were far too many things to start talking about. I am just dealing with them daily. I gave her my letter for the new drug I was to get, and then I just started crying, *sobbing*, don't know why!

We just chatted for a few minutes talked about my treatment, my journey, my side effects, my future treatments and recovery. She said I needed to *rest* plenty. It will take time. Discussed possibility of some side effects when I start the Tamoxifen. It can cause joint pain and hot flushes – great can't wait! Dr McCandless was so supportive. She noticed my fingernails before I spoke about them *(observant GP eh!)* She suggested I cut the nails down to a much shorter length, so I don't catch them on anything. I blew my nose tried to compose myself before I left the doctors room. I returned to the car where Nigel was waiting. He clearly saw I had been crying. He just squeezed my hand asking what happened. I said nothing other than my doctor was so kind and supportive and I clearly needed to cry.

I think he was relieved probably scared him thinking what on earth has happened had I got some more bad news – no not today!

Fabulous friends continue to message, call, take me out such wonderful people. They know who they are so caring and supportive. I could not have walked this path without them!

So, I've got my new drug Tamoxifen which I will start on Monday. A *new* chapter, that will be interesting. Let's see how it develops. Hopefully not too many side effects and not too hard to take.

It's getting close to re-scan of my chest area taking in my right lung. It's more on my mind now I guess cos it is getting closer to the date. What is this *nodule*? How will it be three months later. Let's pray everything will be ok. Well it's not something I can control. God has the plan for me. It's down to him and we will deal with whatever the scan reveals.

FRIDAY, 18 AUGUST

I slept well last night although I had taken strong pain relief as I'm full of pains in my legs and now my arms. My arm pain different from the cording pain in my right arm which continues to be a bugger! The arm pain is clearly muscle fatigue.

You know my friend Jill said the other day you just don't realise everything that comes with chemo. That's for sure so many issues that arises. I know I have listed them before from temperatures to sickness, pains, fatigue *(the worst thing ever)* through to fingernail pain they are turning white clearly dying and I have no doubt now they will drop off, skin falling off my feet and everything else in between.

I went out this morning with my mother in law. She had to go to hospital for an appointment, but I didn't go in with her. I sat in the car and waited not wanting to be exposed to patients or run the risk of catching a bug or infection. It is nice spending time with Myrtle. We are very close and always have been. She tells me often *I'm special to her and* the *daughter she never had,* awh bless her. We have always spent lots of time together but these last eight months we haven't.

Talking of eight months it's the nineteenth August tomorrow exactly eight months by date since I was confirmed as having breast cancer. Eight months unbelievable! Where has that time gone and so much has happened since that awful night in December. I said to a friend the other day eight months and I've done nothing with my life in that time to which they said right back to me "you've done nothing, you've been battling cancer look what you have been through." I guess they are right and anyway there's nothing more I could have done. I've been concentrating on what cancer has thrown at me and dealing day to day with all it has presented.

I think about my surgeries about losing my beautiful breast each day. I look at my body. It's a constant reminder. I can only imagine it will always be this way. I'm not the same physically anymore. I'm changed but honestly, it's a small price to pay really for the *gift* of life. I'll trade the *breast* for *life* every time. My new breast looks fine. The surgeon did a marvellous job with the reconstruction. I still have a cleavage and I guess those looking at me outwardly won't see any difference as it looks normal. The new one is much perter! I do have pain in my new breast much more acute now. It's on the underside and into the armpit. I just know something is not quite right. I don't know if its linked to the seroma in my armpit but it's not great. I probably need to see the surgeon again to discuss. I am dealing with this as well as dealing with post effects of chemo.

I've no hair on the VJJ! It's totally bald not a single hair and the dryness down there is incredible *(I know not a nice topic, but you need to know)*. I'm not sure why the dryness is so bad clearly hormonal. It may be chemo, off my HRT or my meds but something is causing it. It doesn't cause any day to day issues just when I dry myself it's so dry paper tissue sticks down there.

This is where I'll say my wonderful Nigel has been just amazing in the bedroom department! Well that department is *closed.* We haven't made love for a while since just before my chemo started. He never says a word, respects me so much. He knows I'm not well and to be honest the last thing on my mind is love making, but I am always very aware of his lack of intimacy with me, but he never makes any demands or complains.

The hospital advises at each cycle of chemo you're not to have *unprotected sex* for a few days after your treatment due to the drugs being present in the body. When that was said to Nigel and me at the hospital, we just looked at each other. Later we had a giggle and thought how bizarre! Anyway, we certainly have avoided it and the days following each chemo cycle it's the last thing on my mind. I was fit for nothing and Nigel is just so understanding and when I say to him about his sex life being non-existent, he just dismisses it saying rather have you here for next forty years *how sweet*.

I got to spend time with my friend Zelda today. She took me out for lunch to Mill Farm in Hillsborough. Lovely catching up with her. It's so nice having people who care about me and its great spending time with them. We can chat about normal stuff not *cancer* and *sickness*.

SATURDAY, 19 AUGUST

It was mummy's birthday today. We had arranged to go out for tea with her to celebrate. My sister, niece and I took her out and we had a wonderful girlie evening. It was so good spending time together. We went back to mums after, had a cuppa and a bit of craic.

Whilst in mummy's my sister pointed to my ankles saying there were so swollen. They were indeed ! You couldn't see my ankle bones. That's never happened before. That was a NEW development *(another one!)* No pain in them just very swollen. When I got home, Nigel too confirmed they were very swollen.

Flip I wonder what's going on there then must be chemo side effects. Will keep an eye on this. I'm assuming its cos the skin on soles of my feet are falling off like peeling maybe its connected.

SUNDAY, 20 AUGUST

I awoke today to see my ankles still swollen.

Just not as bad as yesterday but not normal. Alex looked at them. With him studying Podiatry learning about foot and lower limb he's always interested in all that stuff. He said the skin on my ankles and lower legs are very spongy. He advised me to put hospital stockings on and to lie down on the sofa with my legs raised *(legs higher than heart)* so that's what I did.

I slept most of the day and did what I was told.

The pains in my legs continue so I assume it's all connected. My cousin Diane has told me her feet are very swollen and she had to buy bigger size shoes. How bizarre that my ankles swelling too. Diane has finished her Chemo a few months now but still having these issues. So again, I'm assuming this is all normal post chemo cycles.

Look it's good to know that there are *'late effects'* of chemo. I appear to be getting some sooner than Diane did. It's been great having her to chat to. I love her so much a great girl, a brave lady with a lot of fight. I am lucky to have such a great cousin.

There's so much to keep an eye on. You need to be alert and know your body. I have always been aware of my body what's normal and what's not.

WEDNESDAY, 23 AUGUST

I started my *Hormone Therapy* drugs on Monday. Tamoxifen a tablet taken orally. I will be taking it at same time each day which I plan to do so at breakfast time.

I have woke this morning after a night of heavy *flushing*. Oh, my days, the new drug appears to have made them worse. I had noticed over the last few months they appeared to be easing slightly either that or I had just got used to them. I honestly think it's the former, the new drug, but I'm gonna *ride the storm* as I need to take this drug for my health and future health.

I'm going to the hospital later for re-scan of chest/lung area. How am I feeling? Not nervous about the procedure its straightforward. Your just told to lie down on a bed and then the bed goes into a large CT scanning machine. You are asked to place your arms above your head. You are in a hospital gown stripped to the waist for this one wearing a gown. The whole procedure takes about twenty minutes. I am a little anxious about why I'm having it.

It's a scan to check my right lung where three months ago a *nodule* was found on it. A nodule of five millimetres.

I have thought about it thinking what if it is cancer in my lung? Well I just need to wait and see what the results bring and then we will deal with it.

When we were first told, we were so unprepared for the results. We had no idea this was coming. The original scan was checking for *clots* and then we get told something else has been seen and needs to be *monitored*.

We headed off to hospital for my appointment. Traffic was ok. We checked in. I was in the Cancer Centre again! It always makes me feel aware of the reality of what I'm going through. I got taken early for my appointment. I left Nigel in the waiting area and off I went, a routine we are both now used to. I changed and was taken to the procedure room. The large circular device within the machine rotates. It moves back and forward, and a recorded voice tells you every now and again to hold your breath. The machine then takes pictures which forms your CT scan.

It's not a procedure to be afraid off not at all.

Once over I asked the girl if she would page my physio as I needed to see her again as my right arm is giving me such bother the *cording* issues continues. I got dressed. I went for a pee and whilst sitting on the toilet think I need to ask them when will I get my results? I need to know these results real soon! So, when I ask, I'm told ten to fourteen days the report will be sent to my Oncologist. I thanked the guy, walked off thinking that's a long time to wait on results.

Back in the waiting room and Nigel surprised I was back so soon.

My physio would see me at ten twenty so we made our way to Level 1 another familiar route.

I got to see Joanna my physio. She worked on my arm and very quickly got a *'pop'* always good when you get a pop gives some relief. This time the pop was up at the elbow level and then again in my armpit area. I discussed with her the pain running up the back of my hand to my wrist and half way up to elbow. With a little swelling just above wrist I was starting to wonder if it's the condition called *Lymphoedema* - localised fluid retention and tissue swelling caused by a compromised lymphatic system. I'm high risk as I've had lymph node removal surgery. It's really cos the lymphatic system is not working correctly.

Joanna was satisfied it wasn't the start of Lymphoedema, most likely coming from late effects of chemo as I've had issues with my fingers over recent weeks, skin peeling, rashes, nails sore, numbness on the tips of my fingers. That's a relief I don't want that awful condition.

I'm still holding my nails, but they are definitely gonna come off. I asked the physio if my cording pain and the severity would be linked to the seroma in my armpit.

I have pain in my new breast on the underside maybe it's a pain I will always have now.

Anyway, physio got two *pops* maybe will ease tonight. I keep doing stretches with my right arm to help recovery.

I do advise good exercise regime after surgery. The breast nurse provides you with leaflets, and the physio sees you on the hospital ward to go through exercises. You should do them without fail. No matter how crap you feel. I did as I so wanted to recover as quickly as I could. I'm still doing them.

Had a catch up today with a dear friend Toni. We went for breakfast. She had arranged for a couple of work colleagues John and Alistair to join us. What a lovely morning. As I've said before, truly humbled people care and want to see and spend time with me.

Nigel has now taken some time out of work. He applied to his company for three months off. He says he wants to be at home with me to nurse me back to health. It's wonderful we are gonna get to spend so much time together.

He needs to rest too as he kept everything going these last eight months as I couldn't do anything. It wasn't easy for him, but I was glad he had his job to go to daily. It kept some normality in his life when nothing was normal at home. Our lives changed totally. He continually says he wants to waste not a minute but to enjoy everything today and not put off until tomorrow – you know that old saying! That's how I feel too as *tomorrow may never come*. We don't hold the answers. The great man above does. So, we will spend each day together have much more family time.

I have said this before, we are a very tight unit of four. Nigel, Matthew, Alex and me. Wonderful relationships which we treasure, long may it continue.

I have my dear, loyal, attentive, caring, loving, sweet husband by my side. He'll look after me, allow me to recover, continue to take me to appointments, rub my feet, hug me, make me cups of tea and just be *Nigel*. How lucky am I.

FRIDA, 25 AUGUST

I started my day with two phones calls -

The Oncologists secretary - I needed to try and establish when she would be seeing me again as I have now had my CT scan and results are very important to me. I'm trying to organise things in my head if nothing else.

Breast Nurses - I want to discuss the pain in my new right breast something just not right!

I spoke with secretary. She confirmed I was booked in to see Dr McCarty on twenty-seventh September.

Oh, my that's a good four weeks away! I must be patient!

It's a review for my Hormone Therapy and I'll get CT results then too.

I'm praying hard that all will be ok. I have given it over to God and pray he will give me strength and courage to deal with this.

The breast nurse answer machine allowed me to leave a message. I know they will ring me back as it's such an efficient service. Satisfied I had made my calls. Doing actions like that gives me order in this chaotic world I am in right now. I'm so used to things being orderly. It takes away any stress, allows you to put things in place not dwell on the matter.

I must do that for your peace of mind.

Breast nurse Kathy rang me back. My little *ground angel*. They always settle you and make you feel more reassured. They give you so much information. I know some ladies don't want it, but I always do. I like to be informed, it *empowers* you so when dealing with the medical team you are comfortable and know what's going on.

Sometimes I wonder is it just a *Wendy* thing or is it the *cop* in me? Police officers' deals with facts, gathers information and processes what they are given. Maybe it's a bit of both!

Breast nurse and I discussed what I was presenting with. I explained how I was feeling recalling what had happened and what was going on now.

It's difficult as my memory has gone. I cannot remember anything. I blame the chemo surely have *chemo brain fog*. I hear ladies talk of chemo brain like baby brain. I so agree and I guess it's understandable. I don't give a toss what people should think it is the way it is.

So, Kathy told me to keep taking pain relief I'm on. She will refer me back to see my surgeon Mr Mallon for assessment.

I'm not anxious about it.

I don't think it's anything sinister. It is just a physical matter. There's pain in the new breast I don't think is normal. She has indicated I should see him within four weeks that's good.

SUNDAY, 27 AUGUST

Another night of hot flushes and nasty stuff going on in my legs.

Didn't get light out until four in the morning. I just lay in bed and watched some TV.

Nigel made me a lovely breakfast and we went for a walk.

I just needed to try to walk. Oh boy it was not easy and only was a short slow stroll and back. I've been unable to walk since cycle six cos I have this strange feeling in my legs. I'm also now feeling muscle fatigue in my arm muscles so weird!

I was totally breathless and paused several times. Nigel made sure I was ok.

I will keep trying as I know the benefits of walking and I want to be back to my old self. Listen to me saying that and I know I'll never be *my old self* again I can't be. I'm both physically and mentally changed.

Life is different, life will be different as I move forward. I have said since getting cancer I would be living my life differently, but I guess it's one thing planning to live life differently and another when your forced through a change of health that affects physical ability or indeed your mental attitude.

When I look in the mirror each day, I have the constant reminder of my cancer. I have a new breast. I have scarring. I have no *nipple*. I've pain in that area so yes, I have changed physically. I'm ok with it *(most days)* and as I've commented many times since my second surgery on twentieth February I'd rather have *no* breast and be here living life with all my beautiful boys and seeing my sons flourish.

NO CONTEST - Breast v Life.

MONDAY, 28 AUGUST

Spent the morning with mummy that was nice.

Spent afternoon with Jill. She took me to see her mum and her new house. Some nice normal stuff so pleased for her mum Eva.

Jill and I went shopping. It's all very exciting cos I'm off to the Royal Garden party on seventh September so I need to get on with finding this *frock*. I've been a bit worried about what I would wear. I did have a pretty dress in my wardrobe that I thought would be suitable showed it to Jill and she agreed so I brought it with me today to see if I could get accessories to match but not ruling out something new!

Last night I started wondering about what I would wear on my head and really would like a hat but not sure if it would work with me having no *hair*. We had a browse in some shops. Such fun with trying on hats. Jill is mad about hats. We had such a giggle.

I tried lots of dresses then I found this outfit not something I would have considered but so very impressed. I felt great in it, so a purchase made.

I haven't been totally looking forward to the event as I am feeling so unwell, don't feel like I look good. My body is *ugly*. I think I have so many *humps* and *bumps*, numbness, swellings, marks on my skin, finger and toe nails taking a hammering, skin falling off my feet. You don't want me to go on - oh no hair, no eyebrows ok I'll stop.

Anyway, I now have a new outfit and of course I ended up in a shoe shop and got the most perfect pair of shoes. Jill took me to *Personal Touch* a hat and flower shop in Banbridge tow. Appointment made for tomorrow to see what they have and what might work for me. You never know I might just find an amazing hat.

I'm so pleased for Nigel getting to go to Garden Party. It will be nice for him getting dressed up and us feeling important just for a little while!

TUESDAY, 29 AUGUST

I got a HAT!

Yes, I got a hat for my Garden party.

It's fabulous. It's perfect with my outfit.

Jill was wonderful helping me choose and the man who owns Personal Touch was so attentive, so sensible with his advice and had great flair.

I'm so pleased.

I can wear a hat with what he's doing with it. I thought with no hair I couldn't wear a hat it would look silly, but this is nice.

WEDNESDAY, 30 AUGUST

Nigel took me out today.

He was trying to buy a wee old car as a run around for doing rubbish recycling runs with his trailer. Sold his BMW a week ago and has ordered his new car which I am thrilled for him. A nice new car. A treat for him.

So old car bought and a wee trip into to M&S for a new suit.

I get so exhausted but if I can sit down lots, I'm ok.

We went to the café and while sitting enjoying the cuppa I told Nigel I had made decision about *work*.

My job, my career, my profession, my future.

I told him I was not well. I still had a lot of physical issues post chemo. I had matters still to deal with. The road ahead is so unknown. I feel there are matters that won't get any better. The last eight months has changed me, my life, my outlook on life and having thought about it long and hard and with my mind a little clearer and not wanting to stress me or cause any unnecessary anxiety as I continue to recover, I have decided to *bow out* from work. I'm gonna *leave*. I am gonna *hang up my boots* it's time to *walk away* and *retire*. My management team had spoken to me about *ill health retirement* due to my diagnosis of cancer previously and to be honest I didn't and still don't know what that entails and more importantly up to this point I did not want to even think like that.

I couldn't give work any thought or my time as I needed all my strength to fight the cancer.

I thought I would return to work with all being well.

Look I don't know how long I'll live for, but what I do know is, all that matters to me is the *boys* and *Nigel*. I don't want to do anything that would or could affect me being with them.

My current position at work requires full attention and can be stressful. Being a police officer requires commitment and effort.

I don't want any stress certainly something you don't need when you get cancer.

So, I think it's time.

When I told Nigel all of this, I wasn't sure how he would react as me working affects him too and the whole family.

Throughout my journey he never has spoken about my work, but today when I discussed this with him, he got so emotional. He told me he was so happy with my decision *(which I said wasn't 100% yet but nearly). He* appeared to be so pleased and glad. I was a bit shocked at his reaction *(which I told him)* and he told me he never would have made any comments about work. It needed to be my decision and he didn't want to influence me to leave.

Well I feel I'm pretty much decided. I feel I can be more rational right now. It's been thought out. Deep down inside me I'm getting the strong feeling it is so the correct decision for *me*!

As soon as I had said it all to Nigel and by the time, I had finished my cuppa I felt an inner peace within me. I felt happy and content.

What I don't want to develop is a pressure from work *(and they certainly have not done that up to now)*.

I know my own body.

I'm a genuine person so nothing is made up or no pretending. I want to recover and do it at my own pace. I'll know when I'm there *(if ever)*.

I'm not going to discuss with anyone else right now.

These are my thoughts and I need to digest what I've just said out loud.

I have Nigel's blessing for sure.

I will pray to God to guide me and help with this *huge* decision. I know he will walk with me, be beside me, and I take comfort from that. I hear the words from scripture;

"Be still and know that I am God".

Inspector Gillian is coming down next week to see me.

Such a kind, supportive girl. Very blessed I have her.

By then I'm confident I will have made my final decision.

I will discuss with her fully.

When I joined the police service my plan was to complete thirty years' service so having reached twenty-seven years, I'm so close to achieving that goal, but how I'm feeling right now, the physical issues I'm dealing with and with the future unknown, that goal is *not* so important anymore!

SUNDAY, 3 SEPTEMBER

Matthew has confirmed he will be back home from England next weekend. Fabulous I'll get to see him. I know it's just for a few days but that's ok. Our wee unit of 4 will be back together again.

I decided I wanted to go to church this morning. Something I needed to do but wasn't sure if I could manage it.

Nigel by my side we went. It was so tough on so many levels!

Mentally it was very spiritual and what I needed – tough though as so many people hugged me, spoke to me, squeezed my hand and told me they were thrilled to see me out.

Such kind people told me I looked well - NO I DON'T. I found it very difficult.

The pains in my legs were so bad. To sit in the church was very difficult and getting up and down as the service required was too much. I just remained seated when I couldn't do it anymore. It was a large ask to do it, but I did. When the service ended, I just stayed in the seat and let everyone leave the church. Again, a lot of people came over to me, to hug and kiss me and say such nice things.

It was good to go to church today, although it meant I spent the rest of the afternoon in bed totally exhausted and needed to sleep a little more today!

TUESDAY, 5 SEPTEMBER

Today marks six weeks out from my last chemo cycle.

I write this because what's going on in my body where recovery is concerned its clear the body is reacting to what it has been enduring since March.

Nigel says we are entering *new* territory. The new symptoms appearing, side effects of chemo and how my body is.

I'm experiencing lots of pain. The pains are affecting my walking.

When I stand up it takes a while to get going. I have weird pains in my arms resulting in no strength.

The pains continue in my hands the numbness in the fingertips continue. I've started to experience joint pain in my elbows. I believe that's coming from my new drug Tamoxifen, a common side effect I've read along with the horrendous hot flushes. I don't care about them. I'll cope if my drug works and keeps cancer away I'll battle through.

I got some sad news today about my sister in-law sister in England. Debbie is a breast cancer survivor. Cancer within the last five years, and it looks like it has come back. Reared its *ugly* head again! She's not well and undergoing tests. It's not looking good. She's only fifty-three and a beautiful girl.

I'm praying for her and for the whole family.

I know it's very tough on my sister in-law Mandy. It breaks her heart. She also is a breast cancer survivor who is now diagnosed as terminally ill as her breast cancer has travelled to her bones. She's doing so well fighting hard such an inspiration! Its nearly five years since the breast cancer was confirmed in her bones. I love her dearly.

Cancer is tough and rough no point pretending anything different.

I had my lovely manager Gillian here this morning. She's a great girl. She brought some lovely scones ginger & treacle. They were different, but I love Ginger and been taking a lot of it since my diagnosis.

We had a great chat.

I was very emotional.

First time I discussed what I've been thinking about my future. I told her I am now seriously considering *pushing the button* and *bowing out* gonna *retire*.

I just blubbered.

I'd said the words out loud which up to now with my cancer I had refused to believe anything else other than I would get better and return to work. Those around me have said "you'll not return to work" "life has changed for you surely you'll retire" but I wouldn't listen to them.

It's my life, my body, my journey, my career that I've given twenty-seven years on a full-time basis. It's not for others to decide. It's my decision - but since Chemo has finished and what I'm experiencing now I'm becoming more realistic and things are clearer. I honestly do not believe I could ever return to my work and give it what I have done before. Gillian was great and told me to take my time and when told me when I could speak to her about it without crying or being so emotional we would have a further conversation.

Gosh what a surprise I got when Gillian was still with me at the house. The postman arrived and delivered an envelope addressed to *Mr & Mrs Walker*. I opened it and found a gift inside from my colleagues from Newry, Banbridge & Armagh. They had bought me a *weekend break* at the Slieve Donard Hotel in Newcastle, County Down with all the trimmings!

Well I couldn't speak.

I just cried.

Even Gillian got emotional and Nigel was overwhelmed.

How kind, how considerate. Totally unexpected.

I'm thrilled and truly humbled. Everyone has been so kind and now this. I will write an email and thank all the very kind people who was part of this.

THURSDAY, 7 SEPTEMBER

Special day today – Royal Garden Party at Hillsborough Castle. Very exciting.

I'm gonna get all dressed up in my new outfit. This is first time I've dressed up since my cancer diagnosis.

I'm a little nervous.

I hope I can manage the day cos I don't feel great and my pains are so bad. This is special and I'm gonna try very hard to get there. I have Nigel for support. I've never been a guest at such an event before.

I have worked at events as part of police close protection security team. I did so many years ago as a young constable getting seconded to be with the team when the Queen came to visit Northern Ireland and stayed at the Royal apartments within the Castle. I provided security outside her chambers. I also did duty when Charles & Diana visited Hillsborough. It was such a privilege to do so, but today is different.

I'm gonna get all dressed up and go off to the garden party with my beautiful husband.

Wait out for the update.

Wow what a day!

I got all dressed up. My mum and sister Shirley came to see me before I left. I think they were pleasantly surprised. They told me I looked well. I loved my outfit and felt *pretty* in it. Everything matched I had made sure of that. Nigel looked so smart in his suit. He told me I looked stunning awh sweet bless him. We got lots of photos before we left. My beautiful boy Matthew was home, got to see me and he took some pics.

We made a stop off in Hillsborough to let Nigel's mum and Auntie Pat see us. I think they were impressed too! We made our way to the parking area and were taken by bus to the castle. The weather was awful but didn't dampen our spirits. I managed to get a seat in one of the marquees, so I got to people watch throughout the day. A cup of tea and some delightful posh sandwiches of smoked salmon, egg and watercress with little victoria sponge pastries so good, so nice.

The rain came down but heh it didn't matter.

We met a delightful lady of ninety-two years young and her daughter. The lady was a special guest too as a result of her charity work. She was a wonderful lady as was her daughter, a retired GP. The lady said I looked well how kind of her.

Well the best part of the day was the *Royal Guest of Honour*. Wow wow wow, guess who? Oh, my days *Prince Harry*. His first ever visit to Northern Ireland. Sadly, I didn't get to speak with him but got *close* to him and we got some fab photos. Gosh the Prince is beautiful. Such a lovely young man, he's much more attractive in real life for sure.

I'm thrilled to have been nominated by my senior commander. Thank you, Mr B.

So special and I'm sure it will never happen again.

Nigel was so attentive. I think he worried how I'd manage the whole day. I was cold. I had pains. I'm glad I had a seat. I loved the whole experience. Felt safe with Nigel by my side. I got very tired but had a great day.

We were taken back in the disabled bus that had brought me to the castle. Yes, I was on a disabled bus and I so needed to be! I think I did look well all things considered. I destroyed my new shoes in the wet grass but again small price to pay! I can replace them.

I'm absolutely shattered tonight but happy. What a wonderful opportunity and delightful day I had. It was fabulous. Memories made for sure.

FRIDAY, 8 SEPTEMBER

Oh, my goodness yesterday has taken it out of me.

I'm shattered and exhausted.

I couldn't get out of bed until two in the afternoon. So tired but worth it.

It's the first time since my surgery and treatment that I have been so active in a day. It shows how weak I am and not fit for anything right now.

Patience is the name of the game.

SUNDAY, 17 SEPTEMBER

It's been a few days since I picked up my journal.

I guess it's been a period of *just the same*. Just the same side effects, pain, tiredness, same feelings in my body so nothing new to report on.

I have a new development on my right hand. Back of hand is swollen and painful a *big fat* hand. The pain is running in around thumb joint up the back of my hand to half way up my forearm and then stops. It's like it following the nerves perhaps it is. My first and second fingers on the hand at the joints are also painful. I believe its chemo side effects or late effects another one! I say this cos from cycle four my fingers on both hands have suffered with rashes, pain, skin peeling off, fingernails sore couldn't even touch them off anything and right now they are *falling off.*

Yes, you read right they are falling off. The old nails are dying and underneath a new nail bed now. That's excruciating pain. It's impossible to complete a task. I keep hitting the old nails off everything and they are so loose. Numbness continues. Again, all to do with chemo. It strips you right back, but again if this is what it takes to fight this disease then bring it on! I find cold water pleasant on the hands and warm water irritates them so using my *marigolds* at the sink.

This week was busy with appointments. I must pace myself, so I can cope with what the day brings. I know if I need to go to an appointment in the afternoon I need to sleep before I go out and I need to sleep when I get back.

I saw my physio Joanna on Wednesday. She had really helped me. Since the last visit the cording has been difficult.

There's so much going on that my breast gets forgotten about *(how could it!)* When you are on the *chemo train* you are concentrating hard on what it throws up. I started chemo five weeks after surgery number two. As you move so quickly to the next phase of the journey you don't get time to recovery post-surgery. Then chemo strips you back making recovery slower.

I also saw my breast surgeon this week. I had spoken to my breast nurse about the pain in my breast and she referred me back to Mr Mallon for review. Nigel and I both went in to see him. He was as wonderful as ever, such a lovely man with great skills in dealing with people. He examined my breast extensively and his views are *that the breast is still healing post-surgery.* Chemo has affected the rate of healing. It has reduced the body's ability to heal particularly the deep surgery I have undergone.

He spoke about a UK survey that had been completed looking at women who had a *mastectomy* and *reconstruction* and the levels of pain associated. There results were that the pain was so severe, the findings needed to be published to make people *(women)* aware. Mr Mallon commented that then *add chemo to the mix* and it makes it more difficult and slows down the healing process. He told me my breast was soft not any hardening. He said my skin and scars were good. He could feel my seroma in the armpit, but he wasn't alarmed which reassured me. Look I wasn't anxious about going to see him. I didn't believe anything was serious certainly the pain is bad and the feelings in the right breast is not great. Mr Mallon says it will take time. Chemo needs to leave my body. My body needs to recover from chemo and allow breast to heal in its own time. He says he will see me again in two months to discuss it further and assess the pain and what options would be available.

He also said he will have a bone scan carried out and he also mentioned an MRI scan may be considered. Now when I hear these things being said I feel it's such a positive for me as they are being so thorough, but equally your heart skips a beat cos I'm thinking is he worried about me and my health and what he sees or feels that causes him concern with the need to complete scans.

I'm ok with all of it as it means they are looking after me. I would rather have the tests as not.

It was a good consultation and I couldn't have asked for anything more.

A nurse was in the room with us along with Nigel. You know you can have whoever you want at your consultations and it's always good to have someone with you in case you forget or don't hear what's being said.

So, when Mr Mallon said my breast was looking good. I said I was happy with it and thanked him for maintaining my *cleavage*. He said that was his job! Yeah right a job the man has created a masterpiece! I did say, pity he couldn't have given me a *nipple*. Yes, my nipple went in surgery one. That was because of the location of the first tumour way too close to *areola and nipple* so nipple had to go. The incision took care of that. We did have a chuckle when he told me I could have a nipple created. Oh, a new one! No, I don't want one! I wouldn't put myself through such a procedure and anyway when I look at my new breast see the scarring and the shape a nipple won't change things. I don't need it *(sorry Nig you've only got one to play with!)*

There is one sure thing, when I look at my naked body, I have the constant reminder of my cancer. When I look in the mirror, I see my new breast. I see the scars. It's very visual so I'll not be able to ever forget!

TUESDAY, 19 SEPTEMBER

Today is an Anniversary!

Yes, an anniversary. Today is the nineteenth of the month. It's nine months from my cancer diagnosis. Unbelievable! Some of it is a blur. Some days it has felt like an eternity and others just like yesterday.

So much has happened in these last nine months.

Found the lump, tests, confirmation of cancer, surgery, results, surgery, results, consultations, chemotherapy, hospital visits, chemotherapy, emergencies, more tests, and here I am today at nine months *hooray*.

I'm very grateful.

Chemo has certainly left its mark. Surgery has left its mark. I'm still recovering, and I know its gonna take time. I'm still waiting on results of tests. I have more tests to go, but I continue to be positive and fighting hard staying strong *(well as strong as I can be)*.

I'm accepting that work is over for me in its current format. Accepting that if I cannot perform my role like before then I don't want to be there *half baked*.

It's all or nothing for *Wendy*.

I need to press the button and bow out. I've cried so much about this, but at this juncture in my life its time and the correct thing to do for me. I'm going to retire. I need and want to get better. I need to give myself the best chance to do so. My focus has changed totally I've said many times before *life is different now.* It's changed for ever. I'm looking out of a new set of eyes. New vision new future.

I'm retiring I'm retiring its strangely a feeling of relief. You know so many people didn't have what I had - such a great career.

Maybe haven't mentioned this before or maybe I have. Just cannot remember anything anymore, another side effect of chemo, I guess. Anyway, today I was going out with Nigel and I put some makeup on with having no body hair including my eyebrows which are gone. I have resorted to drawing on my eyebrows. Mum's pencil being used and so each time I put makeup on I draw them on. I think they look ok cos Nigel never comments (and he would!) Today they were much better I think much thicker. I haven't gone to any beauty counter or to any of the facilities provided within Macmillan. I had planned to, but the dates just never worked with my chemo cycles. I just do the best I can and lots of people have commented when they see me how well I look. Again, I think they are just being kind! But, having *slap* on does hide lots of things beneath!

The no hair thing yes, I lost hair from everywhere including my nostrils! I guess I have saved a fortune on hair removal products and hairdressing appointments every cloud eh! I have built up my headgear pieces. I like them to coordinate with my outfits so have splashed out a bit. Well I'm not buying wigs so why not. I've just bought a few nice autumn pieces very autumnal colours cos I know I'll need to wear them for a while yet while my hair grows back. I now have a small amount of head hair well like not much but clear signs it starting to grow. I guess it will get unsightly as it grows but let's see.

That's ok I can do this.

Nigel throughout the last nine months had never once been negative about my appearance. He has been the most wonderful man. In fact, he pays me compliments quite often at times when I don't feel very attractive. A few times he has told me my eyes are very *blue* of a day. The other day he said the whites of my eyes were so white and clear, so kind bless him – I suppose when I hear that I'm thinking I'm getting healthy again then I move and feel all the pains and aches but suppose I should separate what's going on inside and outside.

Well Nigel is so good, and I am very lucky and am absolutely thrilled he got his new car on Monday. A nice new Mercedes E300 a new *toy* for him! So well deserved. Even mum said after how brilliant he's been these last nine months it's just great. I know he has been devastated at my diagnosis but remained calm, stood steadfast, supported and cared so much. I'm so happy for him and of course I got taken for a little drive in the new toy. Wow!

Over the last couple of weeks, I have thought lots about the future and the words *tomorrow might never come*. My whole view on life is taking on a new perspective. I'm not going to put off things like I used to. I am going to try and live life to the max although not fit right now to do all the things I want us to do.

I mean making plans and moving forward. Last weekend we did a very impulsive thing *(we are so not impulsive we consider everything)* a dear friend Gemma told us about a great Caribbean cruise offer for October next year *(that's like fourteen months away!)* We checked it out and within minutes had it booked. An eight night cruise booked for next year oh my days! Gosh something lovely to look forward to and Nigel said something positive to focus on. We were so excited about what we did *(I bit reckless for Nigel & Wendy!)*

The other big thing we are gonna go ahead with is some interior house building work we've talked and planned this for a long time but never got around to doing anything about it. It was always 'tomorrow'. Nigel says fresh start. A new beginning *out with the old in with the new.* Changes in the kitchen area. It's so exciting although I am not fit to be here while the work is taking place. I'm gonna plan *(if my oncologist permits)* to fly down to our home in Spain, and I'll stay there while the work is completed.

My sister in-law's sister Debbie got the awful news today. It's confirmed her breast cancer has travelled to other areas within her body. It's so sad worst news ever. Cancer is a cruel disease. Hearing Debbie's news stops me in my tracks. You can't help thinking about yourself and the *what ifs* but honestly, I don't dwell on it, cos you can't.

Here's a little prayer today from my daily reading

"Dear Lord, thank you for the encouragement of fellow believers to help me on my journey. Help me to look for ways to encourage others".

Be strong ... Be brave enough to hold onto the hope that life will be beautiful again"

FRIDAY, 22 SEPTEMBER

Today Gillian my manager called. So lovely to see her. She continues to be so kind, attentive and supportive. We had a cuppa. I gave her a sick certificate from my GP *(need to keep records right at work)*.

We had a good catch up and then I told her. What you are asking? I told my Inspector that I have decided to *press the button and bow out.*

I need to retire.

My health and recovery so important, and I am no way fit to return to work at this time. I did cry again! Just felt so emotional. It's huge for me, but it's now final. I'm going to proceed with retirement. Gillian was so understanding and said some lovely things to me. I think she's honestly relieved for me. I just thought I would be better quickly and return to work like nothing had happened to me, but that's not the case and I need to concentrate on me. This is about *ME* nobody else it's what I want.

Am I relieved? Yes, I suppose I am but little anxious about the process as I don't want it to be stressful or cause me any concerns, although Nigel and indeed Gillian reassured me it will be ok. Gillian will now move the process on. I'll have to go see my OHW department and that it will all happen quite quickly.

So, I guess I may not be a cop for much longer!

I'm ok. I've got other things in my life that requires my attention. Its time!

SATURDAY, 23 SEPTEMBER

Today I got to chat with my dear friend Judy. I had hoped I would see her last week as I wanted to tell her face to face about by decision to retire but it didn't happen so in our telephone chat this morning, I told her that I had made decision to retire. There was silence at the end of the phone, but when she spoke she was delighted at my decision. She feels so relieved and says it's the right thing to do. She told me she was so pleased to hear it and said if she had a *firework* she'd go outside and let it off lol. I did cry with her.

So glad she now knows. That's now three people. Nigel, Gillian & Judy. I haven't discussed with anyone else just yet just getting my head around it all and those three are those that need to know. Nigel of course, my manager Gillian and dear Judy who has been my shield for work things and assisting in updates being provided through to work. I want to get it underway before I say to others.

Judy asked if I was relieved just like Nigel did. I guess I am but have the process now to go through to exit the service.

My hormone therapy clearly making me more emotional. I'm more tearful, cry at the least little thing. I can't help it. The hot flushes are in abundance much worse compared to coming off my HRT. I need to just try and deal with them. Night time is rough in bed. They are horrible they wake me up. I'm so hot need to get bedclothes off and pyjamas of and changed.

MONDAY, 25 SEPTEMBER

Today was a bit crazy, mad, sad and exciting all in one!

Crazy cos the building work in the kitchen going ahead. I can't believe it's happening. I feel a wee bit overwhelmed with it all. There's a bit to organise in clearing everything out.

I don't do stress anymore. I feel very different since my diagnosis. I just cannot cope with any stress even *noise* affects me. It's strange.

Nigel booked the flights today to go down to our house in Spain. I can't believe it's also happening. I never got to go down in last nine months and truly I did wonder if I'd ever be there again! Would I ever see Casa Walker my beautiful sanctuary? So, its gonna happen - I'm going soon.

We have said no matter what my results are on Wednesday from the Oncologist we are gonna take the trip. Just to escape and for me to have some R&R. It's a one-way ticket, not sure when I'll be back?

Yes, sad today too as Alexander left to return to university. Year two starting for him. He's gone back to Southampton. Oh, I will miss him so very much. When we left him to the airport, I did have a cry. He makes me chuckle cos as I say goodbye, and he hugs me tightly he always says into my ear "now don't you be crying" and I always do. He's my baby always will be, and I love him so very much. I'm so happy for him. He's loving his degree course and what he's doing. He's got it so right.

In my daily reading today, it was very apt as the writer today described her sadness of saying goodbye to her niece who was off to Uni.

"Lord help us to trust that your watchful care extends over those we hold dear who are far away from us, though we're far away from those we love, they are never far from God"

I have some questions for the oncologist on Wednesday. The rescan of my lung – what's happening with nodule?

I have a small cough and pain in my back? Can I take anything to keep my bone density up? Bladder issues. Tamoxifen is giving me joint pain. Hot flushes awful. I'm very emotional. More permanent solution to seroma in armpit. Bone scan or MRI in future?

WEDNESDAY, 27 SEPTEMBER

Today has finally come!

It's been a long five weeks.

Five weeks since my repeat CT scan. I will be getting my results today when I see my Oncologist. I have thought about it and been wondering how it will go. I feel it has held me back slightly from moving forward, as I keep thinking what will the result be?

Having a pain in my back and a slight cough concerns me a little. Although I think the back pain is muscular, but it's on the same side that my breast cancer was on. I've had a wee cough now for several months, especially since I started my chemo, so I put the cough down to it. I have been praying that all will be okay, and the news will be good today, and that I can move forward and concentrate on my recovery, getting better and getting back to the new normal.

Nigel and I have spoken about the results that's imminent. He asked me if I was worried? I said, "a little yes". I asked him if he was worried? He said right back without hesitation "I'm shit scared" Oh dear! He has told me again he can't lose me and can't do life without me - bless him. Well we are gonna know late afternoon.

Family and friends all also waiting. The messages on my mobile are coming in this morning in copious amounts. How kind are these lovely people who care about me. I know lots of them are praying for me and I truly appreciate all the prayers.

Look I will deal with whatever comes my way today.

Well!

It was the best news I could have got today for sure.

Prayers answered.

Dr McCarty my Oncologist confirmed that the CT scan results in relation to the nodule on my right lung is the same. *No change -* still five point eight millimetres. She said that if it had got bigger or smaller or was gone, she would have been worried but happy with the result.

It's just something that's present on my lung and nothing sinister.

Oh boy!

We were so relieved.

Nigel and I squeezed each other's hands so tight in that consulting room. We smiled at each other and were so overjoyed.

I cried. I was so emotional.

Dr McCarty was just so great and supportive and explained everything clearly. She spoke about the results. The CT scan even showed up my previous spinal surgery and it picked up seroma in the armpit. The report writer queried if it was a seroma or a lymph node? Bottomline nothing sinister *phew!* So relieved.

Fantastic.

We talked about how I was feeling post chemo. The pains, nails, hot flushes, tiredness, exhaustion. Dr McCarty says chemo is causing this. The pains are fibro pains and not arthritic pain. This will take time.

She spoke about my referral to Mr Mallon my breast surgeon and that both will continue to look after me. So, reassuring.

I give thanks to God and I thank all those people who have prayed. Prayers certainly answered.

Today the oncologist said she would be looking after me for next *ten* years. When I started this journey getting me to *five* years was mentioned so I remain very positive. When I mentioned my hot flushes I asked if the tamoxifen working well because they are so bad? Unfortunately, she told me there is no correlation between severity of flushes and how well my drugs are working! That's a pity cos my *twelve* flushes a day would surely be on the right side.

She spoke about percentage survival and it was positive - I'll hold onto that.

Nigel spoke to her about wanting to take me down to our home in Spain. She was pleased about that saying it was perfectly fine to travel now. We spoke about me wearing those delightful *sexy stockings* NOT! whilst flying *(may help where DVT concerned)* The flight to Spain ok.

Nigel also spoke to her about me retiring from work on ill health and that my authorities would be writing to her for an update. She said she hoped I hadn't made the decision based on waiting for today's results. I said No. I had taken a long time thinking about it before coming to this decision. I'm a police officer and if I'm not fully fit to be operational then I need to bow out. I want to recover get well and get on with my life which is unknown for how long. She wants me to be positive *(I am)* and not base my life on how I am feeling right now. I told her as I cried again, I am so very emotional and blaming the tamoxifen, but she told me it's more likely the chemo and common after it ends to *experience 'low ebb and feel down'* - I certainly do! So, its normal well that's something.

We had a conversation about her prescribing me with *Pregabalin* for pain and it can double up to help reduce *hot flushes*, but its early days on the meds so the hot flushes may ease up, So I'm to ask GP for it if needed.

Well that was best news ever today.

I'm totally exhausted such a wait and anxious time. We are both exhausted.

Phoned my beautiful boys to tell them the great news, clearly both very relieved and happy. Made my usual call to mummy she cried, my sister she was so happy, Jill & Judy everyone emotional. Everyone was waiting on the news!

Today I had so many messages. Thank you everyone. Too many to mention you are just wonderful and you know who you are.

Talking of kind words and sentiments - Alex said to me last weekend that he had Granny Walker (Nigel's mummy) out shopping, and she had said to him that his mummy *(me)* just didn't realise how much she was thought of by others. So many people care and that she has been getting stopped in the street by people who are asking after me. She told Alex that *his mummy* is so well thought of. Granny Walker got emotional with Alex saying how she loved me. Awh bless her. I love her very much. How sweet to say that and Alex said to me "its true mummy you don't realise". Well I do feel loved. I have had such support been inundated with visits, calls, messages, cards, gifts, flowers, teas and so much more. I am truly grateful and very humbled. I couldn't have got this far without so many kind people by my side.

THURSDAY, 28 SEPTEMBER

My BIRTHDAY!

Yes, it's my birthday. I'm 51 today.

This time last year I was celebrating the *big* milestone birthday and cruising around the Mediterranean with my darling husband and here I am on my fifty first having had the most awful last nine months.

I realise now that while enjoying that cruise I probably had cancer growing inside me, yet I felt so well and was so happy. It's funny how a few months can make such a change in your life. I didn't get to enjoy the fiftieth year. I had to focus on my breast cancer and push forward with it.

Anyway, today is my birthday. The best present I got was yesterday.

My cancer had not spread. It's not in my right lung all is well.

I have an appointment later with my Police Occupational Health & Wellbeing department. I'm seeing the same girl as last time. She was so lovely. Joanna was her name. I find it difficult to go see her. It's tough to recall and relive the journey thus far, but it's important to share so they can support me.

Jill took me to my appointment earlier. It went well. I went through everything with Joanna where I was in my recovery and how things were going. I cried a few times just so emotional. The biggest thing in the consultation was me telling her I was going to *retire*. That was huge for me to say out loud to a stranger, but I did it and confirmed it was the right thing for me.

I have so many health issues and I need to concentrate on getting better, getting to a place that's normal now for me! I'm still not well. I have a road still to travel and most importantly I need to do this for me.

I signed the medical release document and that was it. The process would now start. All a bit surreal and a bit of relief. Let's see how it all goes.

For now, I am going to forget about it leave to others to push it forward, and I will concentrate on me.

I had a little bit of lunch after with Jill and a bit of craic.

When I arrived back home my kitchen had been totally removed. The work is starting. Nigel calls it our *new fresh beginnings*. All very exciting but gonna be mad so that why I'm off down to Spain to escape from the chaos at Shanroe.

I'm excited about going to Casa Walker *(that's what we call our other home)*. It's been fifteen months since I was last there, and over the last nine months I have wanted and wished to be there so very much and now its gonna happen now.

I hope to fly on Monday.

My today's reading from 'Our Daily Bread' was something that resonates with me.

Very powerful words that I can relate to and have felt over these last few months particularly the first eleven days or so after each chemo cycle when I felt so poorly and just couldn't *pray* or *read* my Bible.

'The Day I couldn't Pray'

My body was so weary and my mind so fatigued that even the simplest of tasks seemed beyond my strength' When I tried to pray my thoughts would drift to discomfort, the inability to pray troubled me most. What a comfort it was to know that the Holy Spirit was even then raising my concerns before the father. What a gift also to hear from friends and family as they prayed for me. What a gift it is in a time of uncertainty to be reminded that God hears our heart even when we think we can't call out to him. God never leaves the voices of his children unheard!

FRIDAY, 29 SEPTEMBER

Nigel dropped me off in Belfast City Centre this evening as I was meeting Judy. She treated me to dinner and then a visit to the Ulster Hall to enjoy a performance by the Ulster Orchestra. A lovely birthday treat. What a great evening. She is a wonderful friend. I'm very lucky.

SUNDAY, 1 OCTOBER

It's been a crazy weekend.

I'm so tired continue to have lots of pains and a variety of emotions.

I went to see my doctor on Friday morning, a good consultation which involved a lot of tears *(from me of course)*.

I'm so emotional apparently its normal!

Talked about lots of things including the latest ailments. I now have bladder issues. I currently no longer can hold on, the need to go to the toilet comes on so fast and if I don't get there's an accident. Gosh that's not good. Never was like this before chemo started! It's so not nice. It must be a late effects of chemo. I forgot to ask my oncologist and doctor not sure. She did say she sees lots of women my age who have bladder issues and theirs are not linked to chemotherapy. She asked if she could examine me *(oh no I had to expose the bottom end!)* I've been through so much in last nine months I really don't care about doing this. Only thing I could think of was she's gonna see my VJJ with no hair on it! I'm sure she's seen worse!

I am going to be referred to Gynae physio and I was proscribed with a tablet to try to see if it will help.

Another matter I've developed since January but more prevalent since beginning of chemo *vaginal dryness* and no *libido*. Crazy stuff. GP has given me some vaginal moisturiser *(with no oestrogen in it – cannot use this with my type of breast cancer).*

I didn't chat to the doctor about my libido as it's the last thing on my mind with my current health but it's just something I am aware of. My dear husband makes no demands and hasn't done. He's so supportive. I have no desire for any real intimacy of course I get hugs and kisses but that's it. I'm not well enough to think of anything else. Hopefully in time things will improve for both of us and I can enjoy the closeness we have always had, honestly last nine months has rocked my world. I'm both mentally and physically changed.

The house continued to be cleared, everything upside down. With not feeling great and so very fatigued I'm no help. Nigel has it all under control taking charge and dealing with everything. I'm glad I'm relocating to Spain on Monday.

Saturday night we spent with our dear friends Jill and Alan. We had a lovely dinner with them and great craic. It's the first time we did this since my diagnosis, and it was just so lovely. Something normal. I'm lucky to have such wonderful people in my life.

MONDAY, 2 OCTOBER

Yesterday was Nigel's birthday. A quiet day as we made last preparations for leaving and getting ready for building work - we are knocking our dining room wall down making the two rooms into one as the new kitchen, with new kitchen furniture added including extending the island, a wood burner added to sunroom, new ceiling and I guess total make over *fresh start our new beginnings*. It's exciting and something positive to focus on.

We, are leaving *Shanroe* later, off down to *Casa Walker*.

I have been at home since nineteenth December. It has been my *cocoon* - my safe place. I've spent so much time inside the house. I've had low days where I have felt so ill, nights I lay awake, and now I'm leaving the confines of my *comfort blanket* so to speak. I am so excited though as I am now going to my other home. Not sure how I will cope with the travel little nervous about the flight. Nervous in case it triggers any ailments or affects my body in anyway. I am aware of deep vein thrombosis as my drug Tamoxifen can increase the risk. Nigel has arranged assistance at the airport for me as I cannot walk any distance. This will involve a *wheelchair*. I never ever imagined I would go through an airport in a wheelchair.

Another first eh!

My legs too painful. I have no energy.

Honestly, I'm very low and totally fatigued it's not good. Grateful I'm going. Let's see how it goes.

I'm leaving behind Matthew which gives me a heavy heart, but he's happy to be at home. He has some plans and has indicated he will try to come to Spain to visit.

So, I'm signing off now and God willing we'll chat when I get to Spain and settle in.

WEDNESDAY, 11 OCTOBER

Well I thought I would catch up. I know it has been ten days. What a first week I've had at Casa Walker.

We arrived late Monday night *(I did have assistance at the airport, my mode of transport was a wheelchair!)*

My initial view was I didn't want it and then if I agreed to take it I wanted Nigel to push me. I didn't want a stranger doing it. You know what, it was perfect, and I don't believe I could have done all the walking that was required. We were departing from gate twenty-five I think nearly the farthest gate away. It was great thanks to Nigel. It meant even carrying my bag was made easy.

I felt ok in the wheelchair. There was no real staring at me, well from what I could see. When I got to Alicante airport, I again had assistance. This time I got pushed by a kind Spanish man as its procedure there, the staff must do it. All was good.

We arrived at the house and I was exhausted mentally and physically.

The day had been *huge* in so many ways.

I was quite emotional several times throughout the day. When I got to the airport, when I got on the plane, when we left Alicante airport, when I arrived at my beautiful home in La Marina, so yeah lots of *tears*.

We made up our bed and went to sleep almost immediately. Both of us exhausted.

When I awoke on Tuesday morning, I couldn't believe I was here. Not sure if I said before but for all the months that passed there were times, I'd have given anything to be here in Spain at our wee piece of *paradise*.

I remember my dear friend *'Scottish Fiona'* messaging me back in June. Mark her husband and she were here staying across in their home opposite ours. Just hearing her chat about what they were up to, spending time on the beach *(we always did that often together)*. I wanted to be with them again. I remember that day lying on the sofa crying. I felt so sad. There were times I wondered if I would ever be back here again. If I'd ever be able to make the trip spend time at my wonderful *casa*.

Well I'm here.

We, have had a great first week. It has been fifteen months since last here, so a bit of cleaning required.

It's been ok. Nigel has been wonderful getting everything in ship shape and I've helped where I can and to my current ability. The pace is slow so that works ok. I've been having lots and lots of rest and availing of *siestas*. We have even managed a walk on the beach *barefooted* - something I've wanted to do for a long time. It was just wonderful. I took in the air, smelt the sea, breathed slowly and gave thanks to God for allowing me to come back to La Marina.

Apart from a bit of tidying we haven't done much. Had a couple of meals out.

We have slowly de-cluttered the house. Again, it feels like a fresh start, a new beginning and when you have battled with cancer you look at everything with a fresh set of eyes!

We went to Murcia yesterday and visited Ikea. It was just lovely making the trip and a little bit of retail therapy also helped. It took a while for us to get around the store. A few stops along the way, but with lots of time on our hands it went ok.

I guess it's a good time to talk about where I am now. I mean mentally and physically.

This is the perfect place to escape to and evaluate everything. I have time, it's quiet and no distractions well apart from Nigel.! He's been such a wonderful man, a wonderful husband, a patient lover, a great best friend and has supported me totally throughout the last almost ten months *(yes ten months oh my goodness)*. I'm glad he's here too, time for him to relax - catch his breath. He loves being in Spain and it always agrees with him so well.

I've touched on the lack of intimacy the no libido, the lack of desire for any shenanigans. Well since I've got to Spain all I'll say we've had a little bit of getting closer! It was lovely, all ok in that department - for all my worries and concerns it's been all ok - right you're not getting any more details!

On the subject of, dry VJJ, doctor gave me a moisturiser, but I haven't used it yet. Good to know you can have it and its *non-oestrogen*(need that cause my cancer driven by Oestrogen). I read the instructions within the product and says you put it in your vagina or on the man's *penis* Oh my! I am telling you this so you know if going through a similar situation that its normal, it happens, that everything dries up. So don't panic. You have so much to deal with.

WEDNESDAY, 18 OCTOBER

It's been another ok week.

I still have pain in my breast, my back, my armpit, my arm and my right hand is still swollen particularly first two fingers. Pains in the joints. I don't have much power in my right hand. Tomorrow is ten months from diagnosis. Ten months, can you believe it!

It's still a work in progress.

I'm far from back to my normal self, but I'm thinking I'm maybe not gonna ever be back to normal. My medication is going ok. Managing it just fine although, its causing such horrible hot flushes they are not easing up. My nights are the worst. I'm saturated. It wakens me and I'm soaking. The flushes last about five minutes then they go. Then they come back, then they go. I'm still getting about twelve a day. I must cope with them nothing I can do. My cording is difficult in the right arm last few days very painful. I can't get any release. It's so bad below the elbow to the wrist.

With all that said I think I'm doing ok pushing forward enjoying my time here at Casa Walker. It's great to escape. I'm loving the quietness and escapism away from everything back in NI. I have some thinking to do about my future.

My sister Shirley arrived yesterday to spend a few days with us. So lovely having her here and to get to spend some quality time.

I speak each day to my beautiful boys. It's good to hear from them.

Yesterday I had along chat with Alex. He wanted to talk to me *girl trouble*, we had a good long chat. I'm always there for him but he is so mature with his thinking and what he had to say he was working it all out himself, but I supported him gave him my views and measured opinion. I was relieved at the end of the chat about what decision he had come to. I hope he remains strong and I know he will get through this little difficult patch.

Tonight, I found out my neighbour across the street here in Spain had just undergone chemo for Leukaemia. Jean has cancer and is fighting hard. They arrived at their house today for a few months. Her husband John arrived at our door to ask a question and I went outside to greet him. I think I shocked him when he saw me standing with basically no hair. I thought he had known I had been sick, but he didn't - oh dear - I felt a little awkward, but we had a good chat. All four of us with something in common. John also has been ill. Just so many people being affected by this disease. Jean came over and asked lots of questions. You find yourself having to go over your story again and again. When you say it out loud what has happened it's all sounds a bit surreal.

SUNDAY, 22 OCTOBER

Well, I'm now all alone at Casa Walker.

Everyone has gone home to Northern Ireland. Nigel left Friday night to go to back to Shanroe as some work needed to be completed with the house renovations. Nigel is doing the electrical work so needs to be there to arrange stuff. I'm quite excited about it all, but glad I'm here while it is all going on and I don't want to see the changes until I get back. No photos no updates.

Shirley left yesterday afternoon. So nice having her here. We had a great time together.

So now I'm on my own for a few days - I wasn't sure how I would feel being alone cos I haven't been not for one day since nineth December. Nigel has said it will be good for me, give me time to gather my thoughts. He's right it's nice. It's quiet. I only have my own thoughts time to reflect, time to think about my future my health.

I think mummy a bit concerned I'm here on my own but I'm fine. Just a pity she didn't come down to stay with me. She continually saying she's missing me!

Oh, my hair is growing. Such a change since I got here. The heat and sun obviously making everything grow. I've got some hair now appearing on my legs, my armpits. My eyelashes have grown a little but not a lot. My breast is still giving me jip along with armpit. I feel the seroma in my armpit it's so annoying. Still no feeling in my upper outer arm don't think it's coming back. A few pains in my hips but a little better.

Being here in Spain where its much warmer and I have so much time to rest and relax. It certainly takes time to recover and you just need to go with it. It's clearly not something you can get over quickly and in a short time. You need to be patient and I continue my mantra *one day at a time.*

To be told so close to Christmas *(although I'm sure no date on the calendar is a good time)* that you have cancer is the most difficult thing I've ever had to deal with in my whole life. Honestly, I felt that the world had stopped turning. I still see Nigel's face in the consultation room that awful evening. My boys were devastated. My family in total shock. My friends flabbergasted.

We knew we had a long tough road ahead and I never for one-minute thought it would take ten months to get this far, and yet I still have a bit to go.

I can't wait to see where I will be in twelve months. How I will be feeling?

I hear other ladies speak about recovery and how it takes a long time. So patience is what is required. I've got plenty of it – *time.*

I came across a fantastic piece my dear friend Valerie sent me.

I want to share it with you …

'Life should not be a journey to the grave with the intention of arriving safely in an attractive and well-preserved body, but rather to skid in sideways, chocolate in one hand, wine in the other, totally worn out and screaming … Woo Hooooo what a ride! I wanna go around again! Anon.

Absolutely brilliant.

I've noticed since arriving in Spain my bladder is slightly improved. I'm nothing having the accidents I was having back in Northern Ireland. My need to go to the toilet is more controlled. I'm not sure why that is - just recovering or the heat here. Just don't know but I'm very happy there is an improvement. I honestly believe chemo did affect my bladder. It has weakened the walls. The tablets the doctor gave me I didn't take. I wanted to see if it would improve itself rather than pop another pill. Let's hope it continues to improve. I think it's important to share this just in case you experience something similar or someone you know undergoing cancer and treatment are struggling.

TUESDAY, 24 OCTOBER

My mother in-law Myrtle arrived today to spend a week with us. We have a couple of days on our own. She's good company.

We went to the Mercadillo *(market)* today. I had to take it very slowly but managed just fine. My hips just not as painful in the last few days, maybe just maybe its easing. My right arm and breast area giving me bother remains very painful and numb and weak. I'm not obsessing over it. It is what it is. I'm ok give it time and further healing will take place I'm sure. If not, I will have to accept it, because of my cancer, my surgery and the great bonus of still being alive and here.

Oh, my eyelashes are growing - brilliant.

I want you to know that there are many issues you'll have to deal with. So much thrown at you. You might experience all the stuff I've talked about, just some or maybe none! Remember every one of us are different - no two women the same. We are all beautiful and unique and isn't that just great. Remember you will get through the horrible stuff. No point saying its easy, or painless or not difficult, but as I have said so many times just take one day at a time. Once you get that awful diagnosis and get over the shock there is so much to contend with, you must deal with everything that comes your way. Surgery in my case, *two* major surgeries within four weeks of each other so little recovery time before into chemotherapy for six months. So yes, it's a rollercoaster. Throw in a million emotions and it makes for a *bumpy ride*.

I know some cancer patients hate that word *journey*, but I don't mind it at all cos that's what you certainly are on. It's a good word. A road I've never walked before, never ever and had no idea what was involved.

Nigel coming back down to Spain tonight, can't wait for him to return. We have not been apart until this week since I got told I had cancer. He's my *rock* who has kept me going, loved me, looked after me, been there through good and bad, supported, held my hand and so much more. I've really missed him this last week.

He'll be here soon.

THURSDAY, 2 NOVEMBER

Well another week has gone by.

We are now alone just the two of us.

All visitors gone home.

We've had a lovely day.

How have I been? I think I'm doing well. Continue to have issues with my right arm, but I'm getting so used to it now. So just try to push it out of my mind take some pain relief and carry on.

Oh, my hair is growing such a change in four weeks. It *must* be the sun and heat. It's great having sun on my skin, although I need to be very careful as I feel quite sensitive to the sun, but it makes me feel different.

Nice seeing my neighbours in the street everyone so kind and supportive. Our neighbours Johann and Jeannette *(Dutch couple)* have been so kind.

My neighbour Jean notices my hair growing, how cool is that! We live in a street with lots of different nationalities. It's great our Belgium friends Jan & Viviene are very kind. Viviene came to see me to have a chat and catch up.

Today I got to see Judy my neighbour here in Spain. She is from Ballymena in Northern Ireland. So good to chat to her. She had heard I was ill from her cousin back home. We had a great catch up. She told me I suited having no hair, lots of people have told me that. We plan to catch up when I am back in Northern Ireland.

Bernadette another old neighbour stopped by for a chat. Everyone so genuine and kind and wishing me well.

My trip to my lovely home here is *just what the doctor ordered* great to escape, plenty of time to rest and relax, and time to think about where I have been, where I've come from, how I'm doing and to think about future. I really feel the heat is helping. The weather has been so good so much warmer than Northern Ireland.

I miss my boys but got to speak with Matthew yesterday and to Alex today. I love to hear their voices and it makes me feel complete.

My breast still giving me jip. Some days worse than others but I do feel it's still healing. I'm still wearing my bra in bed each night. I hate that really do, but I need the support of the bra. Just so you know, it's needed to give support. Going to bed with your *new* boobie is different. Lying on it is *not* easy, can't lie on my front. That's different too and takes a bit of getting used to.

I'm very grateful for what I have, where I am, how I'm feeling and coping right now - I think I'm doing ok.

MONDAY, 6 NOVEMBER

Oh, I've had a tough few days.

Yes, I have.

You're asking why and I am sure thinking physically what's wrong Wendy?

Whilst I have physical stuff going on its not that. I've hit a wall with emotions. It's been awful these last few days. I've felt very low, very tearful and my mind is in turmoil.

Dr McCarty when I last seen her and told her I was very emotional told me this was common after chemotherapy finishes. Well I am certainly much more tearful, emotional, sensitive and feel a bit overwhelmed. These last few days I have felt a bit of *personal mental pressure* and not sure how to express it.

It's very personal.

It's about my relationship with Nigel since coming down to Spain. We have had some lovely intimate moments. Something I really worried about - getting intimate with my *changed body*. My new breast and how I feel about myself. How I look. Although Nigel never batters an eyelid. He loves me that I'm sure of. He's been so attentive and in the last few weeks he's touching me more, being affectionate, being sexual towards me and whilst that's flattering,

I've really struggled with it. I think its cos of a couple of reasons. I'm still recovering so my desire to be intimate is not there and yet I don't want to knock Nigel back or hurt him by shunning his advances. Also, my libido is almost gone so much has happened to me and continues to with the drugs I'm taking. So over last few days I have felt so low about it. I feel a little pressure *(my own pressure)* that things should be back to normal. They are far from normal! I don't think I will ever be there again. So, all this has made me anxious and it's making me cry. I feel I have gone back a bit in my recovery. When I got to Casa Walker five weeks ago, I was so glad to be removed from everything back at home in NI. This is just about me down here. I've certainly dipped in my mood.

However, this morning after a good cry and a long chat with my beautiful man, I got to share what I feel was the *elephant in the room.* All my feelings poured out about my body, my libido, my desires and I was able to hear Nigel's views, opinions and how he feels. He told me he loves me so much - I am his life, and if has me with him all the other stuff is insignificant. He made me promise I would in future discuss any worries I have and not bottle them up or hide them from him. I PROMISE - we made love and it was wonderful. I felt so ok and loved so very much.

I've had a much better day mentally, a bit stronger and no other silly thoughts pushing through my mind. It was about me again. I could focus on recovery and I have been able to not let any negative thoughts push through. I always feel better when I talk to Nigel. I think it is important you know this just in case you face such struggles. Dryness in the vagina a nightmare, lack of oestrogen, medication, trauma to the body. Whatever the reason it happens. You need to know its normal and it slowly improves so remember *don't* despair, it does take time.

My right hand has no power in it. The first and second fingers are still swollen, and I have joint pain like no other including my thumbs.

My sister in law Mandy *(the beautiful girl who is terminally ill with bone cancer and fighting hard)* told me a couple of weeks ago about the positive effects of using frankincense oil mixed with coconut oil on the soles of your feet *(rubbed into them)* So, Nigel brought me some back out to Spain and yesterday he gave me a foot massage using the products - it was so good. I so love my feet being worked on. I'm not sure of its true benefits but the smells of the mixture and foot massage was divine. I might push for another foot massage tomorrow in fact every day would be nice! The thing is when someone tells you that something might work to fight this cancer then you sit up and listen. I'm prepared to try anything.

There have been media coverage about *Cannabis Oil.* There have been people who has asked me if I would consider it. In fact, my sister in-law Wendy send me a pic of a CBD product asking if I would consider it? There are those who rave about its benefits and see it as a cure! I am aware of someone taking it having not been given a positive diagnosis and five years later they are still here. So, who knows! There are so many articles on things you should and shouldn't do - food to eat, drinks to drink or not to drink, supplements to take, stop eating some foods, and eat other foods. I'm not sure about any of it? What I do say is, you do what works for you. What makes you feel good, feel better, feel healthier, whatever. It's about survival.

For me, I must look at my own personal situation, and, be positive in the belief I no longer have cancer and therefore I won't consider cannabis oil.

Having walked the path for almost eleven months what I will say is *positivity* is vital. Being strong, facing each day with strength *and there have been many where I've had little strength,* but I always stayed positive. "I'll deal with this cancer and it won't deal with me" - Be strong - talk lots.

Keep those who are special really close. They do help immensely.

TUESDAY, 11 NOVEMBER

Ok a wee update.

My toenails are a mess. They are a dreadful colour, yellow yukky colour and nails are loose particularly the big toe nails not painful now just disgusting to look at. They are surely going to fall off.

I'm not sure if I mentioned this back when it was happening, but I just thought of this this morning when I looked in the mirror. Whilst I was undergoing chemo my eyes leaked! *(they were also very dry)*. I have had a *creamy colour* appear in the corners - must be effects of chemo. Again, just so you know so don't panic it happens and its ok.

My hand nails are also still in bad shape. They like my toenails have got worse since chemo ended. I've lost my nails, but new ones are trying to push through.

I am experiencing in my toes, the fourth and fifth ones a strange feeling. It's like *numbness* mixed with a *cramp* feeling. I'm hoping this improves. What I have noticed is your *extremities* gets affected. Tips of my fingers - my toes -bizarre.

I got a little update from my boss yesterday. She informed me that all my medical reports are now with my OHW department. What does that mean then? Well the next step will be seeing the police doctor in relation to me retiring. Oh, it's scary writing the word *retiring.* Its progressing along. It really is happening. I'm preparing for retirement from the police service something I only have known for the last twenty-seven years. That's emotional but equally I know how I am physically and mentally. I couldn't return to work at this time.

My trip down to Spain has been wonderful. It's given me time to think and consider my future. I now believe I have made the right decision. I want to recover and get back to the *new normal.* I want to spend my time with Nigel and the boys. I want to do all the things I have on my *bucket list* which has now come to the fore.

Nigel and I have always made travel plans and we've had a great life thus far with our holidays and travelling. We have decided we are now *not* going to put travels off anymore - gonna just go for it. We've always been *thinkers*, carefully considering everything, not impulsive at all, taking great care of everything and that's how we have moved through life - that's why we are very comfortable and have achieved a lot. We've worked hard and enjoy the benefits but since my diagnosis and honestly more so in last three months probably since chemo finished, we're a little more *impulsive.* Not putting things off - living life, doing what we can and want *right* now. Hence, the changes that are being made at home - the renovations we were gonna do eventually are *now* happening.

We have made other plans - things like a weekend to London, we've ordered a new car for Spain, off again to the Christmas pantomime at the Grand Opera House with my boys *(we always went when the boys were growing up so that must continue)* The night of the panto will be exactly one year from diagnosis so a very special evening to be had!

Nigel knows I love *Smokie* the band, takes this *girl* back a few years! They are coming to Belfast in February. Tickets bought as a treat for me. Can't wait. Then the biggest treat of all for next year, a Caribbean cruise. We will be flying to Miami for a few days then sheer luxury awaits us wow!

How special. I can't wait.

You see, we are certainly are not now holding back and putting things off.

An illness like mine really does make you sit up and act *'Tomorrow may never come'.*

Through all this my *faith* has been so important to me. God has carried me on days when I just couldn't function. His word has given me strength. Prayer has been vital, and I have had so many wonderful people praying for me. I will be eternally grateful. I couldn't have got through it without faith and being close to God. There were days I couldn't pick up his word - I couldn't even pray - I felt so unwell, but I didn't need to as others were doing it for me. I was hearing the words over and over *'Be still and know that I am God.'*

Thank you Lord I give it up to you - and it's only you that knows my future.

In the last five weeks I cannot control my *body temperature*. Not sure if it's the hot flushes or lack of hair on my body (although its growing back in places, crazy hair on my arms, back of my hands, legs, nose hair - yes nose hair. I had lost it all! Now it's coming back might have to *plait* it if it continues to keep growing.

One minute I am cold then hot then cold again. Hat on hat off cardigan on cardigan off. Anyway, it's all a bit crazy and a new development.

I really do feel the cold much more.

SUNDAY, 12 NOVEMBER

This morning I took the cases out to prepare for going back to Northern Ireland.

Very mixed feelings today.

I have got to escape, and it's been so good. I've never ever been able to travel down here on a one-way ticket and never stayed so long *six weeks*, but as I have told so many whilst here *"it's just what the doctor ordered"*. I've gone through so many emotions and had the odd wobble, been very emotional and it has rocked me. I tried hard to bring myself back from that. I'm feeling so much better mentally.

I am happy I am going home to see Matthew. I've missed him so much and he didn't get to come down to Spain and spend time with us - so excited to see him. I am also very excited about seeing the renovation work.

I'm also looking forward to preparing for Christmas this year. It will be different to last year which was *awful* not just for me but for all my family.

I'm a little nervous again about the further tests and scans that will be taking place. The actual tests and procedures are painless, but the results leave you anxious. It's because there have been so many over last eleven months and each time more *sad* and *bad* news came our way. Game changers that altered the path I was walking. Although, I am glad they are still completing tests as this gives reassurance.

I see Mr Mallon my breast surgeon next week. I'll get to discuss my issues with him in relation to my breast and armpit pain. I'm really hoping something can be done with the seroma in my armpit. I continually feel it and it's so close to my implant.

Talking of implants, it's been very difficult to lie on a sun lounger front down! It involves a lot of strategic placing of cushions and towels, but I managed *just!* It takes a lot of getting used to having this new breast, and I honestly still have healing ongoing inside.

It was strange looking at myself in a bikini top - stepping out in a bikini top exposing my body, my new breast - Mr Mallon did a fantastic job. I honestly believe anyone looking at me would not know I had had a Mastectomy and reconstruction in my battle with breast cancer.

I got another lovely message today from a work colleague Olive. So, kind of her to message. It was tinged with sadness as her brother is battling cancer. It's so sad to hear another young person and another family having to deal with cancer. It rocks their worlds - I had a cry. It makes me sad and makes me think how real this all is and how very fragile you really are.

My big toenail is hanging off - so sore now. It's just hanging on by a small corner. Its bloody sore. I'm catching it on everything, the duvet, my sock, hitting it off furniture, it needs to come off soon!

I've noticed new small growth on my fingernails - that's good.

WEDNESDAY, 15 NOVEMBER

Today I am flying back to Northern Ireland.

Felt a bit emotional last night, had a few tears. The end of six weeks where I have escaped to have peace and quiet and to recover.

It certainly was lovely, and I dealt with a lot of stuff. Emotionally I struggled, took a dip in mood but being alone allowed me to reflect and I certainly did that. I'm very grateful and it really has helped. I've also been able to deal with physical matters.

My hair is growing. Such a change in six weeks - that lovely sunshine helped.

THURSDAY, 16 NOVEMBER

When I got home last night I got the surprise of my life when I saw the renovations. Oh my days - what a pleasant surprise. It's wonderful - shaping up to be amazing. Matthew provided the lighting for us when we walked in and when I saw the transformation of course I cried. It's been a tough eleven months, and this is such a lovely treat something new and fresh, getting rid of the old bringing in the new. Although it's not finished a bit of chaos still, but I know it will be worth it.

Another reason for returning from Spain is that I must see my breast surgeon today. I've got mixed feelings about this appointment. Glad I'm seeing him to discuss my physical health in relation to my breast and the ongoing issues. I'm apprehensive cos I'm going back to the city hospital. It takes me back each time bringing all my emotions to the fore again, and you re-live everything. While your away from the hospital it allows you to forget about what you've gone through. So many memories that makes it all so real.

My appointment was at three forty-five back in Wing A in the tower block of the hospital. Nigel by my side. I go in to see Mr Mallon. He's such a nice guy and has always been very attentive and treats me like a *person* not just a *patient*. We had a good discussion about how I was feeling. I told him how my breast was, the current pain level. We spoke about my seroma, my concerns of my progress. He examined me, could feel the seroma. He thought my breast was visually good. He told me not to expect to be free from pain at this stage. Its normal to have the pain. I told him the underside was not as consistently painful, but I was getting stabbing type pains. It comes and goes. I think its healing pain. He agreed.

So, all in all good consultation. No need to be anxious or worry.

He confirmed I would have a bone scan just for reassurance. I told him about my back pain, so this scan will check if anything going on with the bones.

I'm also going to have a Mammogram on the fourth December. A letter has already arrived in the post confirming this test. It says *both* breasts! I didn't know I could have a mammogram on new one! I'm not sure. Although I have not great confidence in a mammogram cos it didn't pick up my tumours, it gives me reassurance and a feeling of not being left or forgotten about, although, you always have that awful feeling about getting the results and you think about *the 'what ifs'*. I've never been a person who gets all worked up unnecessarily. I do take it all in my stride. I guess I'd just like to be in a position where I don't need any more tests.

Mr Mallon acknowledged that I'd still be feeling pain and dealing with the late effects of chemo.

Oh, that's for sure!

I brought him a little bottle of fine wine back from Spain cos he's been so good to me - it's my way of saying thank you.

FRIDAY 24 NOVEMBER

I got the saddest news today.

Just when you think it can't get any worse - my brother Eddie telephoned from England to tell me that my beautiful sister in-law Mandy, his wife got told last evening that her cancer has *spread* again. This time to her *liver*. Oh no, it's so awful. Mandy was thirty-five when first diagnosed with breast cancer. Got ten years clear then it turned up in her bones. She has controlled and managed it for five years and now it's into her liver. She's only fifty-one - for goodness sake. She has fought so hard, stayed so healthy and did everything she could to stay alive. Her bone cancer was terminal and now crap it's into her liver - multiple tumours and may be aggressive.

Such sad news I don't want to hear it - I can't deal with this. I love her so very much - it's awful. To make it even more tragic her only sister has also got cancer in her liver, her breast cancer has travelled. When you hear this it frightens you, as it's so real and the *bugger* can return, but I can't dwell or think about this. I must move forward. Let's pray Mandy and Debbie can deal with this - a tough fight on their hands and one heck of a difficult journey.

Now I've returned to Northern Ireland I really feel my pains so much more pains in my legs, my right hand - joint pain. I have no strength in the right arm probably all normal as a result of surgery. Numbness in my armpit, cording, numbness in upper outer arm could be contributing to it.

WEDNESDAY, 29 NOVEMBER

Today I had an appointment to see the Doctor at OHW.

I made my journey to Belfast to the location advised. Huge thing for me to prepare myself for. I was so anxious, nervous, sad and emotional as this was so real in relation to retiring from work. The end of my police career, no longer going to be a cop.

When I arrived, I discovered the doctor was not there. He was in another location. I said I had it confirmed that I had to be at the location I reported to. They checked the computer and then confirmed administration team got it wrong - crap crap crap. Therefore, I missed my allocated time at the other location as I couldn't get to it. I just burst into tears went into total meltdown, sobbing. It took a while to compose myself. I left the building, got into the car and cried some more. How can people make such stupid silly mistakes. I phoned Nigel cried a little more to him, phoned my friend Judy and I was so upset blurting to her. She was *mad*, furious with what had happened to me. Told me to stay put and she would be ringing department to give off buckets. She's so protective of me. Anyway, as a result of the phone call a new appointment set up for Friday morning - proper location confirmed! So, I must wait and build myself up again for Friday.

Kitchen renovations are nearly finished, thank goodness. It's been manic since I got back, chaos everywhere, but it's all shaping up nicely very exciting.

I hit the eleven month mark on nineteenth November - unbelievable!

That feels just like yesterday and other times an eternity.

2017 has gone so fast some of it a blur. It will soon be one year.

That'll be a time for reflection for sure.

THURSDAY, 30 NOVEMBER

It's the last day of November and I'm now back at the cancer centre.

The journey back to here brings everything to the fore in my mind.

Today I'm having a bone scan organised by Mr Mallon.

He did say it's for *reassurance* which I'm relieved about.

The pain in my back is still there so it will be good to rule out anything sinister. They are so good to me, being very attentive. I can't ask for anything more. Having the bone scan will confirm all in the bones *ok* or *not*!

Never had a bone scan before so this will be a benchmark and good to hold on my records in the event of future comparisons required.

I reported to the *nuclear medicine department*. Yes, back here again.

Attended in January before first surgery where they put dye into my body.

I always laugh to myself when I get to this dept - *'Nuclear Medicine'* oh my days conjures up all kinds of thoughts.

Checked in. I had to wait a little.

I was taken to have the injection. The injection is a *radioactive substance* that goes into the blood stream and then will travel into the bones in prep for the scan. Nothing goes easy with me! The lady administering thought she had found a vein in my left arm, needle in *nothing*. Had to be taken out and needle re-inserted into the back of my hand.

The procedure got underway - substance administered, and just as last bit went in and they were flushing it through my vein broke down wasn't working anymore. Had to remove needle and it did bleed a lot.

I now must wait two hours before they start the scan.

I'm having a cuppa. Nigel downloaded a few episodes from Netflix for me to watch while I wait.

All is well, with my boys, their lives are busy. They have lots of plans.

Matthew said this morning he wants to get an Australian Visa sorted. He is planning to go at end of January. This is something he wants and needs to do. I'm excited about the adventure he's planning, but boy oh boy I will miss him for sure.

Alex got notification today of his placement locations in relation to his podiatry degree. A bit stressed about it, but I told him all will be ok. He's in Berkshire for first one and then Sheffield. He is working on getting his exams over first. He'll be home in two weeks for Christmas.

The scan was very straightforward.

You get to keep your clothes on. You lie on a bed and then go into big machine and it takes the images. You lie on your back. They strap your arms by your side. There's no pain involved. You just lie there. They bring the machine down really close to your face, you could experience a bit of *claustrophobia* if that way inclined.

I'm much more anxious and worry about stuff more now than I used to *(before I got cancer)*. So here I am lying in the machine and thinking what if this device doesn't stop where it should and crushes me *(how stupid am I - silly girl!)* There were no issues, no pain, stress free *(after crushing crisis)* pray all will be good.

Results takes 10-14 days.

MONDAY, 4 DECEMBER

Today I had a mammogram.

The one-year mark well almost.

I wasn't sure if I would be getting both breasts tested as the letter said both.

A pleasant lady looked after me and advised when I got to procedure room that they would be taking one image of my implant breast and the machine would *not* be compressing breast *(thank goodness for that!)* and two images of my left breast.

To let you know there was no pain involved with new breast and only took a couple of minutes. So, no need to stress if you find yourself with a new breast and need to have a mammogram. I suppose for me it's one of the tests I don't have any confidence in anymore (I don't want to put you off and you must always have your mammograms) as they didn't pick up my cancer tumours. I had had a routine mammogram (February 2016 ten months before I got told I had cancer) which was normal (perhaps my cancer wasn't there then!) Also, it didn't pick up the tumour on nineteenth December and subsequent mammograms didn't detect first or second tumour. Okay they say I have dense breast tissue, the tumours were clearly hidden, but I would have thought it could have seen through the dense tissue detecting the tumours. I suppose what I am saying is it's not the best test for me to be reassured that all is ok.

I would say to you if undergoing tests for any concern you must ensure you have a ultra-scan, much more accurate.

I'm still waiting on my bone scan result and praying all will be ok.

FRIDAY, 8 DECEMBER

I went this morning to see the doctor at work which I was not looking forward to.

This appointment is one that's gonna change my future. I've thought about it very seriously.

It's not about financially cos we are ok that way and will be ok.

This is about my ability to continue working and the answer is no in my current profession. No at being a fully abled operational police officer and if not able to do that then I've come to correct decision. My health doesn't permit it and being honest I need to concentrate on getting better. I want to spend my life with my husband and my boys.

I saw a doctor Humphries. He apologised for the mix up the other day. His consultation was so straightforward not what I was expecting. A few questions not difficult. I think he had clearly read my file and made up his mind that this was correct decision for me to retire on ill health. I had to sign a form. It's official now, the process is underway.

I have some procedures to go through in next few months before I know outcome. I'm relieved that's over. I did get a bit emotional in front of the doctor. It's a bit overwhelming and a big thing for me!

SUNDAY, 10 DECEMBER

I'm currently sitting in Gatwick Airport.

Nigel and I have just spent the most wonderful weekend in London. What a lovely treat. Nigel booked it six months ago as something to focus on, and to look forward to. He said, *'let's live Wendy'*. It was wonderful we packed a lot in. I'm totally exhausted and shattered. I'm going home now to prepare for Christmas 2017 and oh to await a couple of results!

Kind of a crazy week when I got back from London with Christmas approaching. I'm not sure how I feel about it this year, I do know I don't have the energy to decorate as I normally do around the house. I've decided I'm not going to, just gonna put couple of trees up. Last Christmas still very much on my mind. I think we just went through the motions. I couldn't wait for it to be over. I didn't want it happening. I knew I had way too much to deal with and didn't know what lay ahead.

I'm hoping this year will be better. I can't wait to have my boys' home and back in the house. The *nest* will soon be full again.

Hopefully results I'm waiting on will come through soon. The pain in my back is sore. It's a constant pain not easing up. I guess that concerns me a little.

Received a letter from hospital today results from Mammogram *NORMAL*.

Well that's good news. I must remain positive and push forward believing all is good all is well nothing going on in my breasts. I'll keep checking my left breast best I can. The new right breast more difficult to check with the implant in place.

I continue to take my Tamoxifen. It's easy to take, there is nothing to be frightened off. Some side effects but I manage them, joint pains in my hips and my feet particularly when I get out of bed in the mornings.

My fingertips still have the strange sensation like pins and needles and numbness like my toes.

I guess it's all related to chemo as both areas have had nails falling off

MONDAY, 18 DECEMBER

I got the best news today a call from my breast surgeons secretary saying that Mr Mallon had viewed my report *(bone scan)* and there is *no* evidence of any cancer in my bones.

Hooray - hallelujah that is so wonderful. I was anxious about it if I'm honest and I knew Nigel was too.

So, on this one-year anniversary yes, one year tonight from that fateful Monday night when I got told I had breast cancer I've got some positive news. *NO CANCER* in my bones. That gives me a little longer on this earth. No, secondary cancer or metastases (spreading to the bones).

Thank you, Lord, for being with me for these results. I give thanks.

Well I was certainly emotional getting it. There's a funny story to that one. My boss Gillian was visiting when I got the call. I took it said that's fantastic news, hung up and carried on chatting to her not saying a word until about a minute or so after when I turned to her and said I've just got the best news ever - no cancer in my bones. Well she was thrilled for me (albeit thought I was on a different planet not saying a word to her after the call). I honestly was in shock. I couldn't believe what I was being told and it was such a positive good phone call cos a year ago it was so awful.

Anyway, everyone as pleased as me. Lots of tears. Nigel very emotional when he got in and I told him.

My phones calls to the usual first people; mum, sister, Judy, Jill all filled with happiness and tears.

Well as I am now at the one-year mark I just want to say with total honesty it's been a very difficult year. It's gone by so quickly. Yet at other times it felt like an eternity. I could only take a day at a time.

There's so much I've forgotten, but my journal is a clear reminder of the journey.

When someone is diagnosed with breast cancer please remember it's a huge fight. It's a toughie, so many things to deal with. I was faced with so many side effects, so many issues that I had no idea I would need to deal with, but hopefully me telling you about them will help whether that's you who may be facing such challenges, a family member, a friend, loved one, whoever. Some lady whom you treasure may have been given such difficult news.

You can do it, you can fight it. Positivity required all the way. It's the only way you can get through it. Well think on - what's the alternative!

I am not going anywhere. I've too much to live for, my dear husband Nigel and my beautiful boys Matthew & Alexander. You don't come through it without it having an impact on your family but with the love of a good family along with amazing friends I'm now about to celebrate Christmas one year later.

I know I have still a bit of recovery and you need to understand this. It's not a quick fix. It takes time and if you know that and are prepared for this then that will help. Listen to your body, rest, relax, sleep, eat, do whatever it takes.

I'm very blessed to have had God in my life. He walked with me and on days along the way he carried me, when I just couldn't function as the person I was before. Prayers have been answered.

You'll know by now having come this far with me that I like to read and be informed, but I also know that doesn't suit everyone. It worked for me. I was empowered, and it allowed me to be strong going in to see the professionals and be treated as *Wendy* not a *patient* or just a *number* – but Wendy.

In relation to my care over the last year it was *amazing* such professional attentive people. Through from my diagnosis, my two surgeries, my time in the cancer centre, the Bridgewater suite, follow up emergencies (and there were a few!) my oncologist, her team, those who scanned me, x-rayed me, prescribed meds, took bloods everyone was just amazing. What you need at a time in your life when everything is falling around you, and it's scary, and you have these calm caring professionals with you. Belfast City hospital was first class. They are a *centre of excellence* and I certainly saw that - thank you.

I have been called back by the breast nurse team first week in January for a chat, check-up, review. They have given me a questionnaire to complete and take with me. It's such a great service giving reassurance and they make you feel that you really are important to them and you matter. They keep everything very real don't hold back but deliver it as they should.

As 2017 is coming to an end I am thinking about my future plans.

Well if my retirement is finalised, I'm going to be a retired lady in 2018. If that's the case I'm gonna rest and recover, build my strength, see how my physical issues develop.

Will they improve or is this the best it will be? I'm gonna try and exercise, stay as healthy as I can. I want to live life to the full. Do some things that I haven't done before, travel a bit more, hobbies, spend time in my garden and be here to support my boys.

I decided some months ago whilst walking this journey that if I could recover enough, I wanna give something back. So, I'm gonna do a *fundraiser* of some kind. I wanna raise some money for a *cancer charity.* That will help those coming after me, and those that need help and support just like I did.

I really want other ladies to know that getting breast cancer at fifty is okay, getting breast cancer at any age is okay. Please don't *DESPAIR* you can do this - you really can.

Just remember "One day at a time."

TUESDAY, 2 JANUARY 2018

A new year.

2017 is behind me - Christmas and new year was a lovely family time.

We all enjoyed our time together. Different to last year, and quiet and peaceful just how I wanted it.

I'm off for another appointment today. I'm going to see breast nurse.

These appointments always unsettles me.

I went to my appointment. I saw Patricia the lovely breast nurse who did my pre-op assessment last year. She was lovely.

I had tried hard to stay strong and hold it together as I'm feeling very emotional right now, but I just couldn't. I just started crying she said, "what's wrong Wendy?" I don't know was my response. Just emotional and get overwhelmed when I must speak or think about last year. I can't help it and I keep thinking I've always been such a strong person, and now I'm a mess. It's the tears, anxiety, panic, worry more than the norm. The appt went ok. Lots discussed and the nurse touched on PTSD yes PTSD!(Post Traumatic Stress Disorder) Imagine that, I have symptoms of the disorder. Just a build-up of all that's gone on in the last year. It would explain my emotions I guess, and yet I feel I'm am coping ok. She has given me some suggestions and things that can be done, so I'll think about those. We discussed my HOT flushes cos they are so bad. It's funny she spoke about buying a magnet from the chemist that you put in your knickers. How funny, when I think of that it makes me laugh out loud could be interesting! I also came home today with a set of nipples! Yes nipples. They are sticky on ones. Nurse and I had a conversation about me having NO nipple, which doesn't bother me. Our conversation was the around the everyday reminder of breast cancer when you look in the mirror and your naked. You are reminded of what has happened to you, the physical side of breast cancer. Don't think I'll be using my new nipple! You can have a nipple tattooed on if you want, but it's not important to me nor does it appear to annoy Nigel who is the only other person who will see my breast. In fact, he's quite attentive to the new one it does get kissed! I have another appointment to see my Oncologist at the end of January, so appointments keep coming.

TUESDAY, 9 JANUARY

I bought new bras today. That's the first since surgery on the twenty-third January last year. Back then I purchased M&S non-wired post-surgery ones. They do have such great post-surgery bras available.

Mine needed replacing not just cos of wear and tear but for the *mind too*, so I can remove the words *post-surgery* from my head and the constant reminders of the bras I've had to wear every day.

I think I'm getting used to my new boob.

You are so anxious about lying on it, damaging it, squashing it or bursting it!

It does take a bit of getting used to but slowly I'm getting there. I look forward to wearing new bras still *non-wired* at this stage for comfort. You never know maybe one day I'll get back into wired ones or maybe not.

I continue to be very emotional, cry at the least wee thing, and I can't explain it, quite overwhelmed and not coping like before.

Thank goodness I'm not at work I really couldn't do it. Home is safe, cosy and the right place to be.

10 - 17 JANUARY 2018

I spent a week down at Casa Walker in Spain with Nigel and Matthew. A lovely week away some special family time. Did ok.

WEDNESDAY, 24 JANUARY

Today I saw my Oncologist Dr McCarty.

Before I left home, I wrote down all my issues. Why I hear you ask, well I cannot no longer remember anything. I'm struggling with memory and if I go in to see her, I won't remember what I want to ask, and I might miss something important. My advice to you for any of these important appointments you write it down, take it with you, bring it out of your pocket and read from it. They don't mind and its good for you that's what matters. Don't be frightened or embarrassed.

Consultation went well. She reminded me it's still early days in my recovery six months since chemo finished. The *late-effects* of chemo still emerging. We discussed my fingers and toes. It's called *Peripheral Neuropathy* wow! more big words. PN is where it affects my fingers and toes giving nerve pain, numbness with pins and needles. Doctor did say it might never return to normal. It's the weirdest feeling in those areas. I really notice my feet in the mornings when I get out of bed. I struggle to walk to the ensuite everything so stiff and movement slow. The numbness, pins and needles don't go away just the stiffness.

The Doctor discussed my bone scan and we discussed my right lung. Another scan will take place end of February. That will be six months since last one. For reassurance she says which I'm extremely happy about. She's gonna see me again in four months cos she says there are still things going on with me and she would like to see how I am then.

She will speak to me after I get lung scan with the results most likely by a telephone call.

My hot flushes continue, so *bad*! She was so good about them saying need to try something to help. She brought up an article on her computer about drugs being trialled that can help the effects of flushes one such drug is *pregabalin*, now I cringe at the thought of that drug. It's awful to take so many side effects. I have been on it before for neck pain. However, hot flushes so bad I will try anything. Dr McCarty mentioned the fact that I'm on Tamoxifen for long term she said this drug might help. I'm gonna get to take seventy-five micrograms twice a day.

Today, she said when she sees me again in four months' time hopefully, she will be saying, I'll see you in two years' time for review *Wow!* How good would that be. No more appointments and surviving another *two* years. Getting to that mark would be just wonderful.

When you must keep going to hospital for appointments it's just not finished and, in your mind, it brings everything back to the fore.

THURSDAY, 25 JANUARY

I went out this evening for tea with all my work colleagues from my department. I was nervous about going to see them, but it went well. I had a lovely time catching up. I do see most of the girl's constant contact. They have been so good to me, so attentive and caring. I think they were shocked when I got my cancer.

My appointments continue to come in. It's still not over.

Got my CT rescan date. When the brown envelope appears in the post box I know (have had so many) that's it's an appointment at the hospital.

I've also today received an invitation to a Breast Health & Wellbeing event. Nigel says I should go. I think I will. It's a half day and the itinerary does looks interesting.

WEDNESDAY, 7 FEBRUARY

I haven't felt so well in the last four weeks.

When I went down to Spain, I had issues with my *water works* department which developed into a pain in my left side. It just hasn't cleared up and I'm feeling the effects of it. I believe it's an infection like a kidney or urinary tract infection.

As I went to bed I felt really faint and had to lie down on the bed. Nigel barged me saying "look you need to see the doctor I don't want to lose you to a silly infection after you battling cancer" that's me told!

I'd better go see the doc.

THURSDAY, 8 FEBRUARY

Today I saw the GP.

Got an appointment so quickly it surprised me.

Saw a new GP. My old doctor Victoria McCandless *wonderful* lady has left the practice. It saddens me that she's gone. You get to know your doctor and they you and she had been so supportive.

The new doctor was lovely, Dr. McAuley. (a very young and attractive young lady). She was very attentive when I went in. I found myself having to tell my story to her, going over the history and what was going on currently.

I had to go *pee* in a container, provide a sample (gosh you really need to be good at aiming don't you!) She tested it and confirmed there was *blood* and *protein* levels showing. I knew there was something not just right!

Sample will be sent away for further testing. *Antibiotic* prescription and a further prescription for *Pregabalin* (the drug for the hot flushes)in hand I left the surgery.

She wants me to come back and get some bloods taken just to check things.

There's a definite weakness to my *right side*, if I try to do anything physical my right-hand swells. I thought it would be a good idea to wash the car. I had been told by Nigel *not* to do it, but I wanted to try. It's all about the *normality* thing. I was pleased with myself I could do such an activity but boy oh boy what a mistake! I've annoyed the cording in my arm. It's become so very painful again, it had settled down and I was coping with it, but it is excruciating right now between elbow and shoulder bugger! I might need to go see Joanna the Physio at the Cancer Centre.

I keep thinking where I would be in respect of recovery if I didn't have all these issues like cording, seroma, numbness, peripheral neuropathy.

These are longer lasting issues that are nasty little buggers!

FRIDAY, 9 FEBRUARY

This is such a huge day for me.

Today I'm off to the policing board for my medical consultation. This will decide my fitness levels and current capabilities, and if my employer the Police Service of Northern Ireland will retire me from the service on current ill health grounds.

This was *so not* in my plan. I had no intention of giving up work. I had a few years left (there was mileage in the old girl yet!) but no *cancer* decided to make an appearance and change my path.

I'm anxious about today cos I don't know what to expect. I'm glad Nigel is going with me. I'm hoping he can come into the examination room with me. I need him there. I know it might sound corny but *'he's been my rock'* and is always there.

"I will call on you, my God, for you will answer me; turn your ear to me and hear my prayer" Psalm 17 v 6

We arrived early at the appointment location. It wasn't so easy to find, and I was anxious we would be late. We signed in (all very official). I felt so cold. Nigel could see I was, not sure why? Was it *nerves* or my continued *thermostat malfunction?* which I continue struggle with - hot and cold all the time and then throw in the hot flushes, cracker! We sat in silence in the waiting room. I had never been to policing board before. I had just seen it on the television or heard about it on the news or within my workplace. I needed to pee (always needing to pee now), can't wait, can't hold it, must go. I found a toilet and when I get back a guy was standing waiting on me. He takes us to Level one. We were told to take a seat. It was very quiet. No one else there. I could feel myself getting overwhelmed in anticipation of the medical consultation.

Just then a tall man appeared and said *Sergeant Walker*. I stood up and asked him if my husband could come in with me, the answer was yes.

It was a difficult fifty minutes. He was a lovely doctor never seen the man before. His job was to decide if I was *medically fit* to continue as an operational police officer. They have their criteria I understand that. He showed me to a seat and gave Nigel a seat across the room from me. I only had sat down in the seat and I could feel myself welling up (this is not gonna be good I'm not gonna hold this together) I just heard him say the first sentence and then I was gone. I started crying uncontrollably. Poor man! He just looked at me. He had a very kind and compassionate approach. He explained he had read my file and said, "its breast cancer you've had."

Oh yes, its breast cancer I've had.

He said he needed to ask me some questions and there would be an examination, but he quickly said he wouldn't be examining my breast!

It's the most emotional thing I've had to do. I had to relive the last year from finding the lump right up to present day. I snattered my way through it. He was very understanding.

Then a physical examination. I had to go behind the screen take my top off. He examined my seroma saying he could clearly see the swelling without even touching it. Yip it's a bugger He carried out a few further tests on me. All very straightforward with no pain.

Nigel sat across the room looking so sorry for me. He reassured me several times and spoke to the doctor when I couldn't speak.

Then it was over. Not as stressful as I had thought it would be.

The doctor advised he would submit a report to the *board* upstairs. I would hear in due course and we left.

Today, would decide what happens next with my career, my almost twenty-eight years policing career. I loved my job had such a great time. Ups and downs, but it was wonderful.

I await the outcome.

When I got home I was exhausted, totally shattered and rest of day was spent sleeping.

'MY HOT FLUSHES'

Well I'm now on my drug Pregabalin (75mg) prescribed by my oncologist Dr. McCarty.

When I saw my GP yesterday, she confirmed I needed to be taking *two* a day. Oh right two! Oh my days this should be interesting as I was only taking *one*. I'm gonna start taking one during the day and one at night.

Is it helping?

Well I'm now on it ten days or so, can't really tell for sure but I'm thinking there is possibly a change. They are still happening of course, but I have discovered they are not *peaking*. I am not as soaking wet, my body not as hot and not the normal full on flush, so maybe just maybe this will work!

Of course, side effects with this drug. You don't feel so fresh on Pregabalin. A bit groggy and it bloody constipates me. I'm onto *D*ulcolax again. I always keep it in the medicine cupboard as constipation is just not nice.

Let's see what *two* Pregabalin does.

I'm sleeping a little better not sure if it's cos the drug is helping with the flushes and not waking me up. I'm currently getting 4-5 flushes each night.

I don't like taking unnecessary drugs, but I need a little help right now with the flushes.

I'll keep a check on it.

THURSDAY, 15 FEBRUARY

My mobile rang today, and it was the lovely Gillian, my manager.

She's been amazing, honestly such a good girl this whole time. She has supported me throughout, taken charge over me, been exposed to a lot of my emotions in fact she jokes that *it's her duty to make me cry* and she has *100%* record at doing so! We, do laugh about it, but yes, I end up crying with her. I think she has found it tough seeing me in my raw state. (she didn't know me before I got sick).

The first day she met me was a few days after one of my cycles of chemo. She came to meet me as she was now my *new* manager. Judy came with her as they had gotten to know each other through looking after me.

Well on the day she arrived it was a *bad day*! I wasn't in a good place, not at all basically on my knees. Was so unwell post chemo (it was day four after treatment) and I was so fatigued. I just wanted to lie down on the floor.

I'm sorry I scared her. I know I scared my dearest friend Judy, as she contacted Nigel the next day saying she didn't realise the process was being so tough on me, bless her I love her dearly.

Anyway, back to my call from Gillian - she told me she had some news for me. She told me that I had got my *ill health retirement* and my last day of service in the police would be *twenty-seventh*

March 2018. Oh, my goodness. I could feel myself welling up. I had been driving the car at the time as I was coming back from having breakfast with Jill and Katie.

I started crying (she managed it again, making me cry) I told her I couldn't speak I was so upset. She said it's the fastest result she's ever known.

Oh, my goodness (I had a thought, they must think I'm gonna die quickly, oh stop it Wendy!) Gillian told me she would see me the next day with some paperwork.

I still couldn't speak said I see her tomorrow and hung up with tears running down my cheeks.

I dialled Nigel's number. He was at work, but I needed to tell him.

I'm retiring on the twenty-seventh March 2018, I'm retiring on the twenty-seventh March 2018. It just doesn't feel real.

FRIDAY, 16 FEBRUARY

Yesterday afternoon Nigel arrived home from work early cos he was so worried about me being alone after getting the retirement news.

It was a pleasant surprise, nice having him with me as I absorbed the news.

My hair is growing back quite quickly it's a NEW shade of Grey. My hairdresser Jill said it's like a *slate grey* colour. I'm getting loads of kind comments from lots of people about it. Friend Jill says it's very Jamie Lee Curtis! It's a trendy pixie style. Some think it's growing back curly not sure if it is or maybe just cos, I am now putting some styling gel into it, well, you must keep on trend eh!

The other amazing change is my fingernails. They've started growing back too and looking healthy. I'm so glad as I always had good strong nails which I loved. I always had bottles and bottles of polish. I'm not painting them at present want them to grow back and get healthy, but I really look forward to the day I can paint them again it's a girly thing to do.

Not sure what I will do with my hair when it needs trimming. My hairdresser (who has been amazing over this last year and been coming to check on me at home) has broken her shoulder. Oh, my days she fell out of the roof space. I do want her to do the first cut of my new hair as she has walked the path with me.

I attended the wellbeing morning I had been invited to arranged by the breast care nurses. A room full of ladies all on different journeys, all ages, all looking different. Lots of short cropped hairstyles and most a new shade of *grey*! Definitely fifty shades going on! It was an informative morning lots of different speakers talking about health, diet, help and assistance and my lovely oncologist

Dr McCarty was one of the key speakers this morning. She talked about real facts, about breast cancer numbers in Northern Ireland (quite scary!) lots of graphs showing survival rates. It's all very real when you see it and hear it.

Not everyone can be lucky if you want to call it luck, but you know what the figures of survival are positive and that's what you need to be positive. I only knew one girl at the event who had gone through her surgery when I was having my second operation. She was looking well. Her hair had grown back not grey like mine same colour as it was before her chemo which clearly pleased her. She had so many issues about her hair. For me who had amazing hair (if I do say so myself) it didn't matter. It was all necessary in order to give me best chance of survival.

A good morning, but I think the timing of the event needs changing. I think it would have been much better earlier in the journey, better for lady's post-surgery and before treatment, though I am grateful I got the opportunity to attend.

TUESDAY, 27 FEBRUARY

I'm back at the Cancer centre again.

It doesn't get any easier walking through the doors. Its eight twenty in the morning. I am having a repeat CT (computerised Topography scan) on my chest area. This is to have a look at my right lung again. It is now scan number three in this area. This morning is to check six months later if any change.

So, let's see what this wee bugger is doing.

CT was painless so don't fret if you must have one.

Lovely staff completed the procedure. Its quick and easy.

So that's me now waiting on another result.

Prayers that all will be ok and that I can finally park this one!

Hopefully will know in next two weeks. Dr McCarty said she would ring me or ask me to come in.

I so want tests to be all over its been a long road. I'm now experiencing silly little health issues.

My bladder patterns have changed annoying, and in my private area its sore. I have a strange sensation down there along with a pain in my left side. This problem continues.

I must have full bloods done and they want to do an ultra-scan on my abdomen and urinary tract area. Another scan but I understand the doctor is wanting to check if maybe a kidney stone cos of severe pain (it's awful!)

I was back seeing my physio Joanna (great surprise - she is having another baby).

My cording has been playing up again along with upper arm and neck pain clearly linked. She discussed my posture and the fact I have been compensating on the right side, cos so much has been done through surgery. I've been given some new exercises to try.

So that's me, no longer gonna be with cancer physio. Felt a bit strange when I left. The thought of not being able to get help with my arm but Joanna says I have done well with movement and dealing with it. She now will refer me to a physio from local hospital to where I live. It makes sense.

I don't want to keep walking into Cancer Centre I need to move on.

I went today to the Macmillan support centre. I'm registering to have some *complimentary therapy.* I have got a consultation next week. I think I now need to have some treatments that will help me relax and open the flow through my body.

I'm looking forward to what they will offer. There's such a variety of services. It's a wonderful facility. This might be good for me.

"and the God of all grace who called you to his eternal glory in Christ, after you have suffered a little while will himself restore you and make you strong, firm and steadfast" 1 Peter 5 v 10

FRIDAY, 9 MARCH

Today I saw Mr Mallon.

This appointment was a review of my breast reconstruction. This is normal and will take place annually. It's for the surgeon to check the new breast.

I went alone today. A rarity in this last year.

There was no need for anyone to accompany me. It was purely a check-up.

Mr Mallon is one of the nicest guys I've come across. There's like a shyness to him, but in the last year I've got to know him so it's all very comfortable. He has such a kind way, his delivery and approach warm and he clearly cares. Very talented man. (imagine working with boobs all day every day!) He came in and we shook hands. He said I was looking well (very kind) and asked how I've been. He also reminded me that he had viewed my notes and it's a year now since second surgery.

Oh yes, it's a year!

I discussed with him a new pain that has developed in my breast since Wednesday. Central pain that affects me lifting my arm. Its new and a little concerning as I think it is a bit swollen under my armpit. I still have the seroma in my armpit which is a bugger, as

I can feel it every day, and it presses against my implant or it feels like it does. I keep wondering what it would be like if I didn't have the seroma.

Mr Mallon asked if he could examine my breast (always so courteous) of course he could. He was very satisfied with my new breast, happy with warmth, shape, firmness. All good. He felt my seroma and understands it is annoying me. He explained it takes a long time for everything to settle explaining my muscles takes time to settle around my implant. I understand that, but I guess you feel it's now a year and surely this should be all ok, but he said it takes a long time, so patience still required. Healing process is still ongoing.

However, Mr Mallon always thorough and wants to have it rescanned to check all is ok and he will have the seroma drained.

That's was all very reassuring.

I did tell Mr Mallon today when he asked how I was, that one thing I understand is that you don't get diagnosed with breast cancer, have two surgeries to remove the cancer, six sessions of chemotherapy, and medication for foreseeable future and come out if it *unscathed*! All of this leaves something behind, and you must deal with it, get on with it and understand where you have come from.

Be proud of yourself, your strength, determination and ability to push through. I am proud of myself. I believe I've done very well. I've dealt with everything thrown at me this last year. I'm still here. *It's not the end*! I'm looking forward to my new life after cancer.

Just need these final checks and results then I will get on with life, the *new normal.*

I had a consultation at the Macmillan centre with a lovely complimentary therapist. I'm being offered six sessions, (how wonderful funded by Friends of the Cancer Centre) what a fabulous charity it supports so many people affected by cancer. My therapist was called Jacqueline a lovely lady and I immediately felt so comfortable with her. After some paperwork completed, I got treated to Reflexology oh my days! It was so good one of my favourite therapies. They work on your feet bliss. The six sessions are coming at a great time for me allowing me to relax, forget about all the medical and surgical stuff and focus on just me. A feeling of well-being. Oh, I'm looking forward to this so much.

I have had so many acts of kindness these last twelve months. I have been given so many gifts - massages, afternoon tea, reflexology, hotel breaks, meals out. They have been backing up, so I'm gonna start enjoying these treats and hopefully they will aid my recovery.

MONDAY, 12 MARCH

Oh! I had a very tough day.

A mixture of sadness and elation.

My dear friend Judy and I made a visit to the Marie Curie Hospice in Belfast.

Why?

Well one of our dearest old bosses Alasdair is sadly currently there for pain management. Alasdair was diagnosed with cancer over five years ago and has fought hard to beat the bugger, but it's been a tough road and struggle.

It would be impossible to tell you the whole story how Alasdair, Judy & I came together, but we know him a long time and it's fair to say Judy & I adore him, always have and always will. A great guy, a great boss. Through our policing years we have the fondest memories of him, and he holds a special place in both our hearts.

We had arranged to take him out for a coffee, but circumstances changed, our meet up was cancelled. He went into the hospice. I contacted him to check if he was up for us visiting him at Marie Curie. What an amazing guy! His concern was about me attending the hospice in case it upset me cos of what I have been going through.

It wasn't about me - it was about him. I so wanted to see him, we both did.

His one condition was for us to bring him an americano coffee which he loves.

I was nervous about going into the hospice and seeing Alasdair.

Well, what a lovely visit we had. We had not planned to stay so long, but we were there well over two hours. We laughed and cried - *lots*! We remembered old times. We talked about our policing paths and how they crossed. He's such a brave man only fifty-five years old and he knows his fate. He told Judy and I some very heart wrenching stuff, that involved more tears.

The hospice is the most wonderful, peaceful and sad place you can visit as those within are very ill. At that moment I was so very grateful and felt blessed.

While I was visiting my phone rang. I stepped out to take the call, as it was showing *private number*. It was my oncologist. My heart almost stopped beating. Results about the nodule on my right lung. Fantastic news - no change. All good. Happy days - I was so thankful.

I immediately felt a little guilty that I had got such great news whilst Alasdair is in such pain and his condition very critical compared to me.

Now it's time to park the *nodule*. I must be positive that it's a *nothing* on my lung, and not linked to my breast cancer.

Slowly my results are coming to a very good conclusion!

I have mentioned before that during my journey I told my family and friends if I could get strong enough, I wanted to give something back.

I knew the charity I would choose, 'Friends of the Cancer Centre' and what better way than a coffee morning. A coffee morning that would be very special to me, as it would be an opportunity to bring together *all* the very special people in my life who have supported me with love and kindness this last year.

So, I've started to plan - what I wanted, how I wanted it to be. I knew I wouldn't be able to do it on my own, as I wouldn't be strong enough or well enough so that was a concern!

I needn't have worried! What a great bunch I have around me.

They helped pull everything together and rallied around me. Shirley and Jill became my *committee*. I created a WhatsApp group called *coffeemorninggirlies*.

I booked the venue and planning commenced. I wanted it to be special, so careful planning required. I arranged a lunch at my house to pull the organising together. Everything went smoothly with my girlies who knew there's no such thing as a free lunch! A little panic over crockery that I wouldn't have enough with the numbers I had hoped would attend. My wonderful sister sorted that securing all the crockery needed. I circulated details through all my contacts. My sister put it on her Facebook page and on *Mothering Sunday* my beautiful boy Alex posted the most amazing message about me (which I didn't know about until I was told!) on his page. The response was tremendous.

However, I doubted anyone would turn up and said so to my nearest and dearest - what if no-one comes?

Donations started coming in and items for the raffle.

The offers of baking from lots and lots of women confirmed. So, all food would be provided for.

Just wonderful and fantastic.

Mum and I went shopping. She bought all the teabags, coffee, sugar and jams. So kind and wonderful.

On the eve of the coffee morning the food started arriving. *"Operation Traybake"* truly underway.

SATURDAY, 24 MARCH - THE COFFEE MORNING

This is it - a massively important day for me on so many levels!

I just got a text message from a dear friend Shauna saying

"My wish for you - For every storm a rainbow, for every tear a smile, for every care a promise, and a blessing in each trial." AN IRISH BLESSING

All the planning is now completed.

I'm having my coffee morning. A day I wanted to have for many months. An important day for me, as I'm hoping I'll have in the room very special people who over the last fifteen months have supported me in so many ways. I can't even start to express how I feel about those that were there for me.

I will have them all together in the room with me (that's if anyone turns up!)

I am also at a big juncture today. It's now fifteen months since my diagnosis. It's about drawing the line under me being that *girl with cancer.*

I'm retiring on Tuesday so it's all very poignant like *final closure* for me.

I've got this far.

It's not the end.

It's time to start the rest of my life.

WOW! What a coffee morning.

I truly wasn't expecting that.

What do you mean I hear you ask?

Well my wonderful team pulled it all together on the morning.

It was hectic from we arrived getting set up at the Bowling Club I had hired. Such effort by the troops. The coffee morning was to run from ten to twelve.

At nine fifty-five the first person arrived. It was an amazing morning. We were packed out with wonderful people. All the important special people who crossed my path had come out to support me. The hall was so full. We didn't have enough seats for everyone and I had *one hundred* set out.

I cried a lot!

I got hugged and kissed and squeezed from ten o'clock to one.

Everyone talked to me, everyone held me.

I had created a slideshow of my cancer journey which I had projected onto a wall. Now that caused a few tears in the room! Again, for me it was important to do this. It showed how I walked the path and showed where I was, where I went and where I am now.

I'm totally overwhelmed and truly humbled by the support. A fantastic morning. Very special indeed and for my chosen charity

I raised £3683.00. How amazing and unbelievable!

Thank you to everyone - you know who you are.

I've been back at the hospital to see Mr Mallon. Had my new breast scanned to check the dimpling. All ok. It's just the muscle tight.

I had the seroma drained again. It's a little painful no its very painful.

The lady that removed it called it an *oily cyst* today. I got to see the fluid that had been removed. Immediately I got some relief. Hopefully now will be much better.

I've noticed that my cording has eased too. Mr Mallon happy with everything currently. I told him much and all as I like him I hope not to see him anytime soon.

The complimentary therapy is continuing and it's a wonderful treat.

TUESDAY, 27 MARCH - RETIREMENT

Today I retired from the Police Service of Northern Ireland.

Another closure.

Not sure how I felt today, mixed emotions, but it was made very special by some lovely ladies. The girls from my department arrived on the doorstep with an array of gifts - balloons, cake, treats and a very special *retirement tree*, which I plan to plant in my garden to mark this occasion.

We all had a bit of craic.

I handed over my *warrant card* to Gillian. She presented me with my *Certificates of Service* that displayed the words *Sergeant Wendy Walker - Exemplary Conduct*. I did it.

I always tried my best - worked very hard.

I loved my career, but that chapter is now finally *closed*.

It's now been fifteen months since my cancer journey began. I can't believe I've come this far. I'm not there yet with recovery - a bit to go, but I've done so well (well I think so!)

I'm so proud of myself. A quiet pleasing feeling of making it this far.

It's been tough - good days and bad and some low awful days, where I didn't feel very well, the worst was always post chemo cycles, but I always picked up.

I really listened to my body. I looked after myself. I went with what the journey threw at me.

Yes, I was very unlucky with side effects, but as I said before, God gives the heaviest burdens to those who can carry them.

Life is now changed forever - yes forever!

I'm off down a different pathway. The *new normal.*

Retirement has come sooner than I planned, but I'm now ok with that too. I understand that due to the kind of career and demanding job I've done for last twenty-eight years it's the most sensible decision.

I'm excited about my future, whatever that may be!

I will continue to listen to my body. I will continue to be aware and check my body the best I can and particularly my breasts.

For all you *ladies* out there, please promise to be self-aware.

Don't ignore anything you believe is just not right!

You know your body and if you don't start getting to know it *NOW!* Early diagnosis has positive outcomes.

I pray I have put cancer behind me and that it's gone forever.

Now I'm going to hit the *start* button on the rest of my life. X

ACKNOWLEDGEMENTS

Thank you to the National Health Service in Northern Ireland. From my GP at Moira surgery to Belfast City Hospital. The doctors, nurses and everybody else in between - you were amazing. I was provided with the best service I could have asked for.

A special big thank you goes to my breast surgeon Mr Mallon. What a great guy who gave me the best attention. My oncologist Dr McCarty a fabulous lady who always treated me as Wendy. Dr Ronan McLaughlin who was always there when I arrived with an emergency. Each one cared for me guiding me along the way and making the right decisions. You gave me the best chance for survival, and I will be forever grateful.

Thank you to my mum, my sister, my brothers, my family. I know you were broken at my diagnosis and it was painful, but you stayed the course and were there for me.

Thank you to my other mummy Myrtle - thank you for your continued love, support and prayers.

Thank you to Nigel's family.

Thank you to my best friends Jill and Judy, you certainly walked the path with me.

Thank you to all my lovely friends. I am lucky to have so many faithful, kind, caring individuals in my life and too many to mention but you know who you are! I have been truly humbled by the support. You all were amazing and very special people in my life.

Thank you to my bosses at work. You treated me so well with utmost compassion. It was such a pleasure to be a member of the Royal Ulster Constabulary GC and Police Service of Northern Ireland.

Thank you to Nigel, you were amazing. You looked after me, loved me, cared for me and kept everything going, kept normality when there was nothing normal in our world!

Thank you, Matthew and Alexander you are such good boys, fine young men who were so very sensitive, caring, loving, supportive and everything I could ask for in two sons.

And finally, to Spit our cat who was around to provide lots of cuddles when needed.

Me enjoying summer 2016

Cruising on the island of Santorini

Fiftieth celebrations continue - Nigel and me all dressed up

I've had my beautiful hair cut

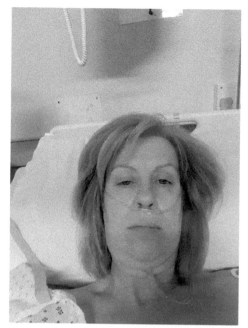

Back onto hospital ward post-surgery number two

My three drains – taking fluid from the breast area post surgery

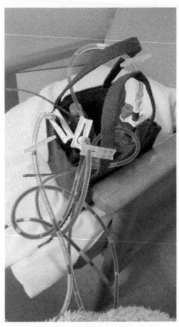

Carried my drains around the hospital ward in a little bag

Some of my many cards and flowers

Afternoon tea treat with Judy

Spit our cat who provided lots of cuddles

In the big pink chair getting my first cycle of chemo

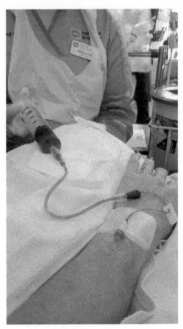

Chemo being administered through my arm

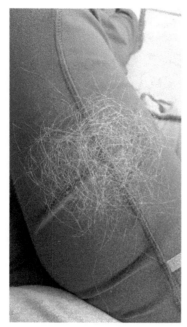

First signs of hair falling out

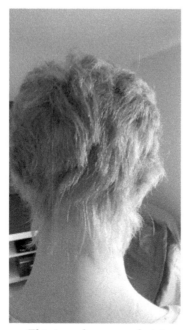

This is no longer my hair!

Nigel shaved my hair off

Job done hair gone

My two gorgeous boys Matthew & Alexander

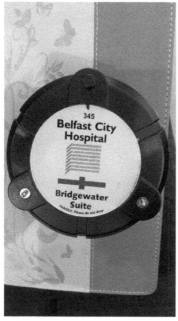

Bridgewater suite – pager and journal ever present

Chemo number two

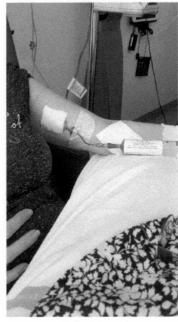

Chemo going through my new friend - 'Pippa' the PICC line

Me and Nigel enjoying a special day in Donegal, Ireland

On the steroids

My lovely treat from work colleagues

Delivery of beautiful tulips

Chemo number three

Doreen, Jill, Valerie and me in Carlingford

Chemo number four

Planted my special chemo tree in the garden

The flowers keep arriving

Me with my mummy, sister and niece Zoe at Castle Leslie having a treat

Teas and potions just for me

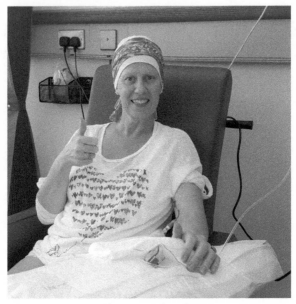

Chemo number five

Casa Walker

Getting a little foot massage from my man

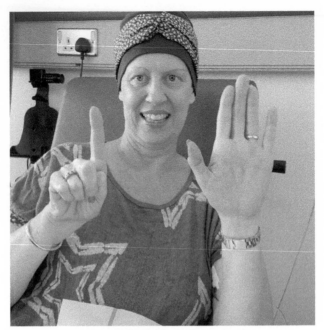

Chemo number six, last one - hooray

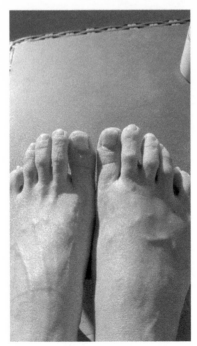

Toenails dying

Skin falling of my feet

Having breakfast with Jill and Katie

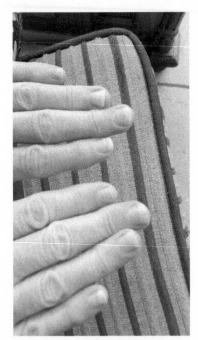

Fingernails almost ready to come off

Me and my crazy boss Gillian

Retirement day - balloons from the girls from work

Off to the Royal Garden Party

My transport at the airport – off down to Casa Walker

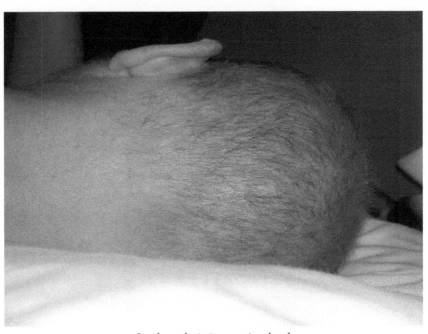

Look my hair is growing back

Enjoying London

Me and my fabulous hairdresser Jill

My coffee morning – my wonderful team

Sergeant Wendy Walker – Royal Ulster Constabulary
GC & Police Service of Northern Ireland
This is me receiving my police long service medal in 2011 – a proud day!

Lightning Source UK Ltd.
Milton Keynes UK
UKHW010917310120
357938UK00002B/36